The Vertical Ghetto

 CONSULTING EDITOR: Peter I. Rose, *Smith College*

The Vertical Ghetto

EVERYDAY LIFE IN AN URBAN PROJECT

William Moore, Jr.

FOREST PARK COMMUNITY COLLEGE

RANDOM HOUSE   NEW YORK

To

Rosetta, Sharon, and Dana,
who make it all worthwhile

*The Three Hundred Rules of Ceremony could not control
men's natures. Three Thousand Rules of Punishment were
not sufficient to put a stop to their treacherous villainies.
But he who knows how to cleanse the current of a stream
begins by clearing out its source. And he who would
straighten the end of a process must commence with
making its beginning correct.* —Taoist inscription

Acknowledgments

Like many other books of its kind *The Vertical Ghetto: Everyday Life in an Urban Project* was born with a liability. It is indebted to the 2,100 families who were residents of Blackmoor. It is specifically indebted to 100 of those families whom the author accompanied as they engaged in their daily activities: trips to the employment office, welfare office, grocery store, laundromat, church, tavern, or playground.

A writer is always deeply indebted to his spouse, who tolerates and submits to his wrath, negligence, and withdrawal. More specifically, he must be grateful for a wife who is willing to forgo those family pleasures that she has a legitimate right to expect. Finally, the author must acknowledge the help and assistance he obtained from Mrs. Betty Lou Pollard, who proofread the manuscript and who probed, argued, and intimidated him until he organized his thoughts and recorded them here.

Contents

Introduction   xiii

I—Matrix of the Tragedy   3

II—Soliloquy of a Tenant   9

III—No Place Like Home   14

IV—Not by Bread Alone   38

V—Who Am I?   56

VI—Masculinity Without Status   70

VII—Room at the Top   111

VIII—Say, "Ahhh"   134

IX—Cross My Heart   152

X—Idle Hands   170

XI—The Home and the School   177

XII—The Road Ahead   214

References   251

Index   255

Introduction

This volume is the anatomy of a tragedy. It is a book of social description—composed in the kitchens and stairwells and on the rooftops of a public housing project; consummated in the marketplace, welfare office, public health clinic, and police precinct; and finally written on the kitchen tables of a ghetto, utilizing the consultation and insights of the residents of a low-income, high-rise federal housing project that we shall call Blackmoor, located in "Midwest City," U.S.A. More specifically, this narrative describes the pathology of a low-income, high-rise public housing project and its deleterious effects on the residents, especially the children.

The purpose of this involvement was to take an intimate look into the apartments, halls, and elevators of an inner-city public housing project and its environmental corollary facets—the neighborhood schools, taverns, store-front churches, police precincts, and gutters. This commitment provided an opportunity for a first-hand appraisal of the conditions, attitudes, and patterns of behavior of a group of people who have been labeled culturally disadvantaged, as well as a chance to determine, to some degree, the pervasiveness of project living on the lives of the residents.

A further rationale for this endeavor is to make the knowledge and understanding gained from this experience available to lay and professional people who deal with the culturally disadvantaged. Armed with this information, they may ultimately be able to support those agencies and institutions that effect change.

Any serious attempt to get to know people's habits, values, attitudes, behavior, and language is a monumental undertaking—one that requires a one-to-one relationship with the individuals involved. It was precisely this kind of relationship that proved fruitful in writing this volume; the author went to live among the people.

But the writer who goes to live among his subjects can, in the final analysis, only empathize with them. No matter how hard he tries to walk in the shoes of a disadvantaged child, he is not a child. When he knows what the child eats, where he sleeps, what he wears, and what makes him laugh and cry, he still cannot feel what the child feels. Regardless of how much he learns about the mothers, fathers, and neighborhood, if the situation becomes intolerable he can always leave. Nevertheless, the author wanted to eat, sleep, and live in a public housing project. He did.

He took a tape recorder with him to Blackmoor, and for nine months he listened to the tenants and recorded their conversations. He observed the socioeconomic conditions, behavior patterns, and idiosyncrasies of the project residents as he accompanied them through activities of their daily lives.

Almost immediately, he discovered that the traditional social-science techniques of collecting data would not fulfill the objectives of this study. Although questionnaires, check lists, and other such sociological methods were used, it became apparent that the use of these procedures alone to gather information from the tenants of Blackmoor would elicit the all-too-commonplace pattern of responses and deceptions found with the use of such instruments. Furthermore, these methods could not reveal the apathy, conflict, paradox, and dilemma that is Blackmoor.

On the other hand, surveys compiled by official agencies were valuable in gathering the basic demographic data that will be included here. These data provide some of the obvious background and perspective necessary to understand the degree to which the conditions in Blackmoor affect the lives of the residents. Tables 1–4, based on figures compiled by the "Midwest City" Housing and Land Clearance Authority in April 1967, present the demographic factors basic to an examination of 2,100 families making up 1,700 households of Blackmoor.

It would be a formidable task to present an intimate look at all of Blackmoor's families, however, so only 100 of those families were chosen as the major source of this book. Some basic demographic data for these families are given in Table 5.

Table 1. Population by Age and Sex

Age Groups	Male	Female
0–2	486	487
3–4	414	376
5	225	226
6–9	985	931
10–12	723	626
13–16	721	744
17–20	326	376
21–30	195	610
31–40	216	675
41–50	140	350
51–60	82	205
61–62	143	284

TOTAL POPULATION   10,546

Table 2. Make-up of 1,700 Households

Average number of adults per household	1.5
Average number of minors per household	4.3
Average number of persons per household	5.6

Table 3. Income of 1,700 Households*

Income	Number	Percentage
Under $1,000	54	3
$1,000–$1,999	376	22
$2,000–$2,999	541	32
$3,000–$3,999	379	22
$4,000–$4,999	206	12
$5,000–$5,999	99	6
$6,000–$6,999	34	2
$7,000 and over	12	1

MEDIAN INCOME $2,780

* Excluding those over sixty and minors.

Table 4. Economic Characteristics of 1,700 Households

Characteristic	Number	Percentage
Households having no worker	647	38
Households having one worker	985	58
Households having two workers	66	4
Households without a male head	1071	63
Households of mother and children only	629	37
Household heads with ADC* as principal income	476	28
Households partly dependent on ADC*	595	35
Households receiving some other form of assistance	85	5
Families on public assistance †	1,166	68

* Aid to dependent children.
† Some 2,100 families make up 1,700 households.

Table 5. Selected Statistics for 100 Families

Age*	Male	Female
0–2	22	44
3–4	32	50
5	29	24
6–9	47	49
10–12	15	25
13–16	18	39
17–20	19	47
21–30	8	18
31–40	5	11
41–50	11	28
51–60	7	23
61–62	9	23
TOTAL NUMBER	605	

* Ages 0–20 are considered minor children in this study.

No sophisticated experimental design or formula was used in the selection of the participating families. Only two criteria were used: (1) the family selected would have minor children and (2) each building in the housing project complex would be represented in the sample. The sources for locating families with these criteria were the census files of three elementary schools serving Blackmoor and the local office of Midwest City's housing authority. The school census files were used because Blackmoor comprises thirty-three buildings with children attending the three schools mentioned. The housing authority records were used as a source to validate the names, addresses, and family size and composition obtained from the school census files.

Having obtained the names and locations of families that satisfied the above criteria, the author sent a letter with the appropriate return form and envelope to the family head in each of 500 households, requesting their participation in the study. A total of 314 returned the forms, agreeing to become participants. Follow-up on the family heads that did not reply revealed that 39 of them felt that such a study was an invasion of their privacy. Some 68 reported that they were not interested and had exercised their prerogative of ignoring the letter and form without explanation. In the two-month interim between the time their names and addresses were obtained and the time the letters were sent, 23 had moved out of the housing project. An additional 2 were deceased and the surviving family planned to move before the interviews were scheduled, and 1 was blind and was afraid to "get involved." Some 14 family heads reported that they were tired of being researched by people from the colleges and universities in the area as well as researchers from the local welfare agency, poverty agency, and housing authority. Of the family heads, 13 were never found at home although a minimum of four attempts to contact them were made in each case. Another 17 did not understand what the study was about and questioned its subsequent use; explanation to this 17 did not alter their decision. And 9 shut the door in the face of the investigator.

The total of 314 families was a larger sampling than was needed. It was decided that approximately a third of that number was an adequate sampling. Consequently, 100 of the 314 families were chosen by random selection. The writer informed 3 family heads in each of 32 buildings and 4 family heads in 1 building that they had been chosen for the study and that further contact would be made to set up appointments for interviews and visits with the family.

The author knew hundreds of the families in Blackmoor, had been closely involved with two of the three schools from which he obtained data described, knew many of the families prior to their residency in Blackmoor, and knew the idiomatic expressions, colloquialisms, slang and dialect peculiarities of the area and ethnic group involved. He knew on a social and professional basis six of Blackmoor's former managers and could enjoy the freedom of movement and communication in the project community that another researcher who knew neither the area nor the people might not enjoy.

Although in some cases a specific family member (not a family head) refused to engage in dialogue with the author, most members of each family (adults and children) talked freely with the author and permitted him to tape-record the conversation. These families represented households receiving welfare and those that were self-sustaining, broken homes where the mother was family head and households where the family was intact, households that had both preschool and school-age children, and households where there were aged tenants as well as minors. This sampling is representative of the families who live in Blackmoor.

Many of the statements that appear here are in the plain unvarnished words of the people. They are the statements as given, usually without intellectual sophistication; however, they span the gamut from erudition to illiteracy, and the messages are frequently universally applicable. Moreover, they encompass the complete emotional and intellectual range; they are candid, sometimes proud and witty, frequently cynical or risqué, but almost always informative and profound with a sensitivity to reality that cannot be overlooked. There has been an attempt to record them with a minimum of alteration. The wide variation in speech chronicled here is commensurate with the wide educational range of the people. This range extends from no to fifteen years of schooling.

Although *The Vertical Ghetto: Everyday Life in an Urban Project* embraces all the distortions, exaggerations, and subjectivity found in any description, it is written with the primary purpose of capturing and conveying the pulse of the public housing community and people it describes.

It is not a prescription for change. Rather, it is a specific attempt to sensitize the reader to the poverty, conflict, dilemma, alienation, and other social discrepancies between the needs of housing project residents and their present conditions. If this volume can successfully project these insights to the reader, the book may then become one of the sources of information which may affect change.

The people of Blackmoor are corrupted by need, confused by bureaucracy, exploited by merchants, and eroded by despair. Their conditions, struggles, and quest for survival obligate the writer to tell their story.

The Vertical Ghetto

1 - Matrix of the Tragedy

Several years ago the term "culturally disadvantaged" emerged as a new name for an old tragedy. Other phrases and labels began to creep into the American vocabulary to describe the poor and where they lived. Such words as "dropout," "undercultured," "deprived," "inner city," and "high rise" were among them. Poverty became the nation's point of reference. In the midst of this cultural syndrome was a new symptom and edifice of poverty, the high-rise public housing project.

Housing projects are different things to different people:

*A housing project is low-cost housing we put up for
the poor colored people down
in the city.*—Suburbanite, age thirty-nine

*It's a misplaced piece of hell where the rent
comes due on the first of the
month.* —Poverty worker, age twenty-seven

*Well, I know a lot of people talk about how bad the
project is but I came from Alabama and anything is
better than what we had in Alabama. We think the project
is a fine place to live. The people—well, that's
something else.* —Rural immigrant, age forty-one

*A project ain't nothing but a slum with the
kitchen furnished and an absentee landlord; except,
we know who the landlord is—it's the city and
government.* —Project resident, age thirty-one

*Whether it is a pig pen or not isn't important. When
people have done nothing to contribute to the society
but make an application for welfare, a housing project
is more than they deserve.* —Lawyer, age forty-three

*Baby, they ain't wrote the script that can tell you what
this place is like.* —Dropout male, age eighteen

By the housing act of 1937, the United States Congress created
housing projects to provide adequate shelter for low-income
citizens. Federal tax dollars purchased the land and financed
the design and construction. Local housing authorities were responsible, for the most part, for the management and maintenance. Originally, housing projects were constructed in urban
areas in which there were large concentrations of low-income
families. In Harlem, for example, one-fifth of the population lives
in public housing. Cities like Chicago, Detroit, St. Louis, and
New York were among the first to construct high-rise housing
projects. Now projects are constructed in smaller urban areas.
When thousands of people moved into these buildings, which in
most cases comprised only a few square blocks, the public soon
discovered that high-rise housing projects developed characteristics distinctly different from those of other types of housing. These
projects evolved into multistoried reservations with all the ethnic
insularity and symptoms of an inner-city ghetto. Yet part of this
phenomenon was a paradox: while certain elements of the slum
image were present, certain others were missing. Here were slums
without rats, filth without alleys, and halls and stairways soiled
by human waste where there was adequate plumbing. Still the
symptoms prevailed: poverty, frustration, broken homes, crime,
and deficit of dignity.

In housing projects one found a high percentage of rapes, assaults, and other crimes of violence, illegitimacy, and a reputation
for concealing narcotics pushers. Because the projects developed
these ominous qualities of a slum, the proponents of business,
industry, education, and religion did not venture within their
towering walls. Only a few outsiders would nibble at their boundaries. Finally, housing projects fell into disrepute and in some
communities have come to be considered a civic disaster. In

spite of their notoriety, this new phenomenon had to be dealt
with by the community.

The first institution to be affected was the school. School personnel had some knowledge and experience in dealing with children who had come from the traditional slum tenements of the
inner city, but they had had no experience with the children who
came from high-rise housing projects. As thousands of these
children enrolled in the neighborhood schools, school officials discovered that the pupils brought with them a new jargon and
related new experiences. The children were heard using such
terms as "resident adviser" and "project commission"; they gig-
gled as they talked about the activities that took place in the
project elevators, stairwells, and laundry rooms; they expressed
the cunning they used to outwit the project management; they
talked about the rules that governed the way they lived.

Although the lease granted for most apartments carries with
it certain stipulations for the lessee, the rules and regulations
imposed on project residents were more than stipulations—they
dictated a life style. Teachers began to hear the parents of their
charges voice resentment as they talked about their forced style
of living. Every aspect of living—from the notification that residents' apartments would be periodically inspected to instructions
on how to care for the refrigerator—was covered within the
guides issued to the project residents.

Perhaps, as to be expected, the school and its agents were not
prepared for the changes that were taking place because of the
construction of high-rise projects in communities. The population
density of school-age children was a case in point. The enrollment of many schools quadrupled, but at the same time, there
was a compactness of the area from which the children were
drawn. Never before had an entire school district's population
come from the families that could be housed within one square
block. In some cases, the neighborhood school drew its complete
enrollment from three buildings. Entire schools were designated
for the primary grades. In numerous cases, one could find more
children attending a single elementary school located near an
inner-city housing project than comprising the combined enrollment in three elementary school districts located in suburban

communities. Patchworks of new schools were constructed around the housing projects, but the busing of schoolchildren was frequently necessary to alleviate the overcrowded conditions.

Due to the abrupt increase in school-age population densities, new methods had to be developed to handle perennial school problems. For example, school attendance officers knew the traditional patterns of truant pupils. They knew most of the corners, poolrooms, and movie houses where these children took refuge; they knew exactly in what dime stores and toy departments truants were likely to be found. However, the children from the projects did not repeat the traditional patterns of truancy. As an attendance officer walked through a high-rise public housing area during school hours, he would see few, if any, children; yet hundreds of children from this area would be absent from school. Because of the immense size of each building, a child could play hooky for weeks and never leave the structure. Moreover, he could play several stories up in a building and see a school attendance officer coming long before that officer reached his destination.

As teachers continued to pick up more and more fragments of information about how people in a public housing project live, they began to note that living in these structures seemed to affect the behavior of the children when they came to school. This, of course, affected their teaching. Obviously, many teachers were confused and ill equipped to cope with the situation. Consequently, they and their principals, along with other auxiliary school personnel, such as the school social worker, went to the colleges and universities to learn about this cultural phenomenon. They found, in many cases, that their own information was more recent and relevant than their professors'.

Traditionally the urban school in American culture had been oriented toward a middle-class ideal but operated in a multi-class society. The problems inherent in such a cultural plurality were many and complicated. One such problem of major magnitude was the education of the poor. This problem, however, did not become one of major concern until the late 1950s and early 1960s. The public was indifferent to the problem. To some extent, there was educational apathy on the part of the school and its agents, which resulted in a failure to evolve an educational program especially designed to meet the needs of the disadvantaged group.

In philosophy, the school had long since removed the shackles of its class-structured origin; in practice, however, it was still class structured. It was restricted by a cultural paralysis or a middle-class fixation that prevented the necessary academic flexibility and social orientation to meet the needs of all cultural groups.

The mass exodus of middle-class families (usually white) from the inner city to the suburbs created a population vacuum that was quickly filled by the poor (usually black). In many cities a part of the slums was torn down. As urban renewal plans were carried out, much of the slum housing was replaced by housing projects. The education of project children became a paramount problem. As a consequence, the school's orientation needed some modification. The traditional inner-city school found its middle-class bias out of step with the behavior, habits, and values of the project child. Some type of educational metamorphosis was apparent. The school located within or near boundaries of a housing project began to reexamine its role, reevaluate its responsibility, and reappraise its curriculum in order to deal with what was now called the disadvantaged child.

The child of poverty, in what was beginning to be called a _depressed area,_ became the focus of attention for educators. James B. Conant was one of the first to write a book with some emphasis on the education of slum children. His _Slums and Suburbs_ (1961) gained wide attention, but it appeared to be a superficial commentary on the children from the slums, embracing many of the traditional biased methods of education of the poor.

Other educators spoke out:

> . . . [_The_] _school should assume responsibility for a systematic plan for the child . . . by the time the child reaches kindergarten or first grade._ —Martin P. Deutsch (1962)

> _The job of obtaining excellent education for the children of deprived urban areas is now a national problem._ —Kenneth B. Clark (1965)

8 **The Vertical Ghetto**

*During the past few years, both laymen and professional
educators have become increasingly aware that chronic
school failure begins early, and that there are numbers
of children to whom school life offers nothing but defeat
almost from its beginning.* —Edmund W. Gordon and
Doxey A. Wilkerson (1966)

*The plight of disadvantaged children, as they slide
through the school, must, of course, be due in part to the
failure of the schools to provide more effective education
for them.* —Carl Bereiter and Siegfried Engelmann (1966)

Although some of these authors disagreed with each other, they all
shared a concern for the disadvantaged child.

There were other unique discoveries related to public housing
projects. Although social workers found more broken homes in
the twenty-square-block area where the projects are located than
there were in whole suburban communities of comparable population, the legal divorce rate was almost zero. Divorce was an
alternative only of the affluent.

The records of public housing authorities contained some star-
tling revelations. They showed that 49 percent of all federally
assisted public housing units were occupied by nonwhites. Half
a million families lived in 3,500 public housing units in 1964.
This represents 2,200,000 individuals, and half of them were
children, according to Robert C. Weaver (1964). Housing projects were discovered to be "islands of poverty" or to represent
what John Kenneth Galbraith in *The Affluent Society* (1958)
called "insular poverty."

Outsiders began to respect some of the power of the tenants.
The politicians learned that complete precincts could be housed
in two buildings and a few square blocks could constitute a
whole political ward. Public school systems discovered that they
could pass school-tax and bond-issue proposals with the required
two-thirds majority vote only if they had the affirmative support
of the tenants in public housing. Nevertheless, in the tradition
and vernacular of the American class structure, living in a public
housing project meant living on the wrong side of the tracks.

Such were the matrixes that gave rise to our tragedy—the
disadvantaged child and his new edifice of poverty, the public
housing project.

11 - Soliloquy of a Tenant

What is it like living in a housing project? Mister, you ain't got that much time. Besides, I got to go to the store, but if you want to walk along, I'll talk with you. Wait a minute while I lock my door. We have to go over to the stairwell and walk down a flight to the elevator—it don't stop on this floor.

I hate to bring you in this stairwell with all that bad language written on the walls and all that trash and stuff piled all around, but this is the only way to get to the elevator. I know you can't see where you're going too well 'cause the light's not too good but you better be careful where you step; you'd be surprised what's on these stairs sometime. Watch out for that wine bottle! Look how we have to live. That ought to tell you something. Excuse me, gentlemen, we're sorry to interrupt your game, but can we get by?

That's a laundry room there next to the elevator. The windowpanes are out in it and the sinks are stopped up, so they just put a padlock on it and don't even bother to fix it. This elevator must be out of fix again. I guess we'll have to walk down six more flights of stairs. I'm getting a little old for all of these steps, but it's the going *up* that really takes a lot out of me.

They call this place the problem child of public housing. Like it or not, it's where I have to live. I'm a tenant. Ask anybody in town and they got a theory about us. And so many nuns run around down here on Sunday that the tenants call it Penguin Row. As a matter of fact, you can always find volunteers and other tourists down here mingling with the natives. When I first moved down here you didn't never see a white face. Now them women from the suburbs are falling all over each other volunteering. They say they want to help us, but that's pretty hard to swallow. They tell us things to do and everything will be all right. It's like telling us to go to the Grand Canyon and spit, then watch it fill up. More than that, they think because people down here can't talk proper, they can't think.

One of them women will grin and smile when she's down here volunteering, but see her downtown and she acts like she'd sooner be in hell than to speak. This is the type who tells you to use the toilet in the basement when you work in her home or to raise the seat if you use the one upstairs. Frankly, I can appreciate the one who won't speak to you and won't try to hide it. At least she's honest. I don't want you to get me wrong. I know that there are many people who come down here who really want to understand and help us. It's not hard to pick them out. They're the ones who don't tell you how much they love you; they don't apologize for everything and they don't act like missionaries. The nuns are a good example. I kid about them but they're for real. Still, if you never got a letter that wasn't a bill and never been invited to nothing but to get out, it makes you wonder—are people drinking to our health or to their own? Funny—I didn't even know I was *deprived* until they told me.

Let's take a shortcut through the rent office—it's air-conditioned. People that live down here got feelings like other people, but most folks talk about us like we're *things*—not *people*. We're not really considered—we're just an afterthought. Everybody feels he is nobody here, so we just numb our feelings in whiskey, and not listening, just trying to forget we're nobody. Our children are some of the most experienced in the world, but it's the wrong kind. How can you make them feel important when you don't feel important yourself? I'm just the tenant in apartment number 812, a number on a door and a name on a mailbox. Speaking of mailboxes, do you know when I want to send off a letter myself, I have to take it clear out of this place? The post office didn't even put one single mailbox in this whole project and 11,000 people live here. As my neighbor next door says, "Honey, you're just a number and—even in prison there's

111 - No Place Like Home

In Midwest City, where a high-rise luxury apartment goes unnoticed, where a taxi driver won't know the location of a new school, where a motorist takes only a glance at a monument, Blackmoor stops traffic. Most people don't just look; they stare. Blackmoor is one of the city's high-rise housing projects. Perhaps no other housing project is more of a caricature of adequate living facilities than Blackmoor. It was built in the middle of one of the city's worst slums and is centrally located: ten minutes from downtown, ten miles from the suburbs, and ten decades from the mainstream. More than thirty buildings occupy thirty square blocks in a strip of the city once called "crime village." Included in the area where Blackmoor is located are the sections of the city with the highest crime rate, the largest proportion of uneducated and undereducated, the largest proportion of unemployed, the largest concentration of nonwhite residents, a predominance of absentee-owned rental units; in short, it epitomizes an inner-city ghetto with all its problems.

Blackmoor has many derogatory appellations. One writer calls it "the ville of human stagnation." A prominent sociologist calls it the worst in the nation. Some call it the bowels of the city. Almost 11,000 people call it home. Whether Blackmoor was a great accomplishment or a greater sin is subject to speculation; nevertheless, the man who lives there is forced to accept what many others cannot. Out of what appears to be inextricable chaos, 2,000 families fashion their lives.

Blackmoor has few rivals in public housing projects for no-

a picture that goes with the number." She don't know how right she is. The public comes down here and look at this monument to human despair and try to feel better because they helped build it. They even say we don't appreciate what they have done for us. You tell me, who could appreciate isolation? I don't have to tell you how we're cut off from everything.

What really gripes me, though, is how a lot of the so-called middle-class Negroes that's just a white shirt and credit card away from here come back and act the same way. Most of them don't come back. Them that do are like "wetbacks," except they live in the city. They teach down at the school, do social work. And the doctors will treat some of us, but at five o'clock this place is off limits. Naw, they got another word for it—taboo. They ain't never here for the swing shift—that's when things are really happening.

I really get filled up when I think of some of the girls I went to school with who used flour to starch their clothes; now they turn up their noses at me because I live down here. I can remember when they ironed their dingy blouses with dusting powder to make them look white. Now that some of them are doing better, they don't remember that—but I do. The men are just as bad, but I guess we can excuse them more. Everybody treats *them* like dirt even when they're smart. If their wives didn't work too, they couldn't go around talking about they're middle class. If one of them got out of work for a month, he'd have to hang up his gloves.

I don't mean to ramble on. Let's see now, you were asking about living in public housing. Well—a house ought to be more than just a place to stay. You ought to get a special feeling when you talk about where you stay. Down here you don't. You almost apologize when you tell somebody where you live. Nothing is here that will help a person express himself, nothing you can get your teeth in. If the women just had a fence to gossip over. But this is just a stopping-off place for many people and quicksand for others.

The people who built this place certainly didn't know nothing about human beings, especially children. And it's what happens to the children that hurts most. When they drew the plans for this project, seems like they didn't expect no children to live in it. But it's 7,000 of them here, and one playground and two "tot lots." The only way I can keep my eye on my kids when they're playing is for them to play inside the building or close around it, because the playground is three buildings away and I live on the eighth floor. If the kids just had a place to go and dig a hole. But look at that tot lot over there with all of those broken bottles and other junk scattered about. A kid takes his life in his hands every time he goes over there to play. Them janitors don't ever clean up the trash. The kids can't even play in safety.

This place ain't even healthy. The bathroom don't have windows and them ventilators are always busted. When somebody uses the bathroom, the house stinks so bad the rest of us can't hardly stand it. If something happens to the plumbing or the heat, seems like it takes forever for the janitors to get around to fixing them. And another thing, there's too many people crowded up in these little spaces they call apartments. But all these conditions wouldn't be too bad if the children just had daddies at home with decent jobs so they could take care of their families.

We have to cross the street here. You're on your own, mister. I bet in your neighborhood if you had 7,000 children living this close together, you'd have stoplights and crossing guards on every corner, wouldn't you? You know, a group of us tenants got together and had a meeting. We did it all proper and everything. Anyway, we went to see the committeeman of this ward about getting some stop signs to make it safer for the children to cross the street. He said he didn't have time to talk to us because he was expecting some very influential people. I wonder what he thought we were. We put the son of a bitch in office. Excuse me, mister.

Getting back to the kids who live here, they don't have enough of anything. We hear all this stuff about school dropouts. Most of the kids barely drop in. They get to school all right but they don't take nothing with them to help them learn much while they're there. It's like walking barefooted on cinders. So a lot of them just stay in school until they're old enough to play hooky or frustrated enough to quit.

Another thing, everybody is trying to tell us how to raise our

children. They tell us not to whip them to make them mind we're supposed to use psychology. The mamas of the worse k I know use that. What they don't know is, one whipping is wc a thousand words—wasted.

Now when you go in this store don't expect it to be like one in your neighborhood. The floor ain't clean, the clerks a polite when they talk to you, the vegetables ain't fresh, and meat ain't even red. But when you get to the cash register, prices are higher. Mister, if I've got to tell you what it's like li down here, you're blind. And even if you're blind, you can s what it's like living here.

. . . so it is with the tenant from apartment 812.

toriety and adverse conditions. Its predicament has been repeatedly inked across the front pages locally and, on at least
one occasion, was discussed on television nationally. Blackmoor's
degradation has been recounted for city officials and described
in congressional hearings. Its reported depravity has attracted
graduate students by the score from nearby colleges and universities who have come to observe and probe the problems of
this housing project and its mass of possibilities for research
data. Private organizations and government agencies have financed studies of Midwest City's most notorious apartments.
Near Blackmoor, black power advocates, Black Muslim wor-
shipers, and black nationalist activists coexist in an atmosphere
of anger. They attempt to recruit black tenants from the projects
into their ranks. But the foregoing are only a few of the dis-
tinctions of this housing project; there are others.

VIOLENCE AND DEATH

People die violently in Blackmoor. A woman is cut; a man is
shot; a bill collector has his head bashed in and is robbed in
the elevator. A pedestrian is struck by an automobile and has
his pockets picked and his overcoat and shoes stolen before the
ambulance arrives. Occasionally, a child falls from an apartment
window. As he lies dead on the ground below, the project community gathers to watch. The play of children stops; a dice game
comes to a temporary cessation; a wino emerges from his hiding
place, looks, and reinforces himself; and the mother, who is
often the last to get the news, can be heard screaming as she
attempts to reach her lifeless child. The ear attempts to trace
her movements as her screams alternate in clarity. First they
are loud and piercing; then they sound muted. Anyone familiar
with the project knows that the screams are loudest when she
passes an exit from the stairwell at each floor and muted when
she is moving between floors. A woman several floors up bends
her own body in an arc of potential death, attempting to view
the body of another where death is already confirmed. Except
for the screams and sobs of the mother, the project is strangely
quiet. It is one of the few times when it is quiet. The crowd

that gathers does nothing and says nothing; it simply stands in quiet resignation to death and remains until the ambulance departs with the lifeless body. It disperses only after the flashing light and blaring siren are no longer seen or heard. Some children are herded home by their parents; others go back to their play. The dice games resume, and the wino returns to his exile. For a few days, other children will be careful when they play near windows. After a week, the dead child is a statistic and the other children have forgotten the danger.

Violence is as common as motherhood in Blackmoor. "M.," the shoeshine "boy" (who is sixty-three years old), has a shoeshine stand across the street from the housing project. He has seen the momentary rage and animal fury of people living in the ghetto cause the death of many other persons in Blackmoor during the almost one and a half decades of its existence and is accustomed to seeing violent death. He talked about it:

Between now [Friday afternoon] and Sunday morning, at least one person I know—maybe two—will be dead. We don't worry about that though—we just try to keep living. Somebody might kill you out here on the street—almost for nothing—and five minutes after they haul you away, some stray, mangy dog is licking up your blood. Who cares about the dead?

COMFORT AND CONVENIENCE

Little is done about the convenience and comfort of the tenant. Everything from the skip-stop elevator service to the lack of adequate toilet facilities at ground level indicates that those who conceived, designed, and built Blackmoor cannot be suspected of genius. The manager reports that the electrical wiring is inadequate. Fire hoses have been torn from the walls and have not been replaced. Much of the other equipment has not been replaced since the project was built. Sinks and bathtubs are rusty and stopped up. Some heat pipes are without insulation and children have been severely burned on them. There are no freight elevators in the buildings. Consequently, everything—animal, mineral, and vegetable, the quick and the dead—that must be carried to and from the apartments goes via the same passenger elevators. To compound this problem, the elevators are not well ventilated. Incinerators are not located on each floor in every building and elevators do not stop on each floor. When the elevator stops and the incinerator locations are on different floors —and this lack of structural coordination is common—the only route to the incinerator is the stairs. This creates a particular hardship for the aged, who must carry garbage and refuse to another floor to dispose of it. The elevator does not stop on the second floor; many children who live on the first floor and who are assigned the chore of emptying the trash leave a trail of debris when they go to the second-floor incinerator. There is a further accumulation of refuse around the trash chute because the doors are too small to consume the volume of debris that must be placed in them. Elevators are frequently stuck, and tenants have spent hours in them before they could be extricated. Sometimes elevators remain out of service for weeks. This situation is particularly crucial for older tenants who live on upper floors.

There are no toilet facilities at the ground level in Blackmoor. This arrangement constitutes both a health hazard and a physical inconvenience. A child playing on the ground level who has the need to eliminate must go back to his apartment, unless he happens to be on or near the one play area that has a toilet. Like most children, he waits until the last minute before attempting to reach his apartment. In his haste to reach his household, he must somehow gain access to the elevator, which may be held up by someone on an upper floor. It may also be necessary for him to use the stairs, since the elevator services only every third floor. So he dances and prances for some relief until the elevator arrives. This course of action is basically no different from that of a child living in an apartment anywhere. There is, however, one essential difference. The disadvantaged child has seen his peers, and perhaps his siblings, seek the privacy of the closed elevator for physical relief. This practice may even have parental support.

I know it's filthy—but I'd rather see him mess up the elevator than his pants. I'd be willing to bet that the elevators in them terrace apartments stop on every floor. I guess they're more important than we are.

Older boys carry this activity a step further, often making a clandestine game of it by becoming scribes in filth on the walls of the elevator. The secrecy with which this game, of necessity, must be played, adds to the appeal it holds for the players and its fascination for the spectators. Although boys everywhere have always done this sort of thing, the slum child seems so completely lacking in any feeling of loyalty to his structural home that he will urinate within the confines of its walls, on his own landing, and just outside his own family's apartment.

Blackmoor homes are tall, boxlike towers of concrete and steel that absorb this city's 85- to 100-degree heat in the summer. They become so hot that even the walls are warm to the touch inside and outside. By afternoon, the apartments are so unbearable that the residents are driven out into the comparative relief of the street below. Except under very unusual circumstances—when someone's health is in jeopardy—project regulations prohibit the operation of an air conditioner or a window fan even if the residents can afford them, because of inadequate wiring. Consequently, tenants congregate on the ground level during warm or hot weather. Nighttime's coolness rarely affects the inferno above and inside. So, far into the night, the dwellers, adult and child, roam the area seeking some respite. Toddlers in wet diapers get dirty while playing on the ground, but the diapers do not get changed until the family returns upstairs—usually in the wee hours.

The more daring residents from affluent areas of the city driving through the project area smirk and wonder about the slum dwellers' nocturnal roving and roaming. Many remark about it and about the penchant for "hanging out" of windows. Some tenants sit in chairs by the window and put pillows on their window sills so that they will be more comfortable. It is not unusual to drive through slum areas in early morning and see people at the windows asleep, their heads cushioned on their arms.

In winter there are different problems. Broken windowpanes

are not replaced, so tenants place cardboard, plastic, plywood, and anything else they can find in the spaces to keep out cold air. There have been heating failures during which the 11,000 tenants have been subjected to harsh winter temperatures for periods of two days and longer. Sometimes half of a radiator is operative while the other half fails or one room is cold and another is warm in the same apartment. Clothes often freeze on the clothesline in the laundry room. The heating plant breaks down and tenants are forced to turn on the surface burners and ovens of their kitchen ranges. Family members have to sit in the apartment with their coats on. At least one Blackmoor child is alleged to have died from overexposure to the cold within his apartment.

The tenant has few choices about the manner in which he may organize his home in Blackmoor. The local housing authority makes most decisions for him. He is told the length of time he may have a house guest, the kind of pets he may own (goldfish and birds only), the paint he can put on his walls, the kind of floor covering he may use, and the scheduled day he may sweep his steps and use the laundry room. This latter restriction becomes unrealistic for large families of poor people who have insufficient clothing, linen, and other items to last from one scheduled washday to the next.

The handbook issued to tenants contains statements that transcend the usual information, regulations, and agreement between the lessor and the lessee. It is written in a maternalistic style that implies irresponsibility on the part of the tenant. And the content is not only condescending and threatening but also insulting:

> . . . do not pour boiling water into the toilet stool. . . . We hope you will be careful in the treatment of your window shades. . . . It will help to make everyone's "blue washday" a little brighter if you take the time to clean up the room after you finish. . . . The only pets allowed are goldfish and canaries, or if you prefer a talker to a chirper, we'll say O.K. to a parakeet. Can you imagine life in a project if half the tenants had dogs and half had cats, or if we had a few fanciers of more exotic animals? . . . Your primary obligation to your family is to provide them with a place to live. Therefore your first financial obligation is to pay your rent on time. . . . Any-

one who has not paid his rent by the fifth day of the month may have a suit filed against him.

Everything costs something in Blackmoor. When a key is lost, the tenant is charged $3 to have the door to his apartment opened and the key replaced; a worn-out lock costs the resident $3; $1.25 is paid to have a fuse replaced; at one time a tenant was charged for a broken window in his apartment regardless of who broke the window—windows have been broken by bricks, bottles, and bullets coming from the outside, but the man who signs the lease pays the bills—a screen of inferior quality costs the tenants $6.50. Even light bulbs and bathtub stoppers cost the tenant. Everything that wears out, is stolen, or is broken is put on the tenant's bill. Those things that cannot be put on his bill are not replaced or, on few occasions, are replaced with poorer quality goods. Blackmoor's residents pay for services that other apartment dwellers take for granted, yet the tenants get less service. There is not even a United States mailbox within the boundaries of the housing project.

STAIRWELLS AND LANDINGS: CENTERS FOR VICE

Landings and stairwells, which are essential to the tenants, are also accessible to narcotics pushers, sexual perverts, gamblers, and other wrongdoers. These passages are completely enclosed and frequently are without any artificial illumination—day or night. They provide optim^l conditions for robbery, assault, and rape, and many such crimes have taken place there. During the nine months of investigation, in no single instance was an artificially illuminated landing in evidence. The light bulbs had been removed—perhaps by an enterprising tenant who needed them, by teen-agers who wanted darkness for their amorous pursuits. Often the bulbs were burned out or the whole lighting fixture had been damaged. Moreover, the landings present a danger to health by providing an unauthorized place for disposal of garbage and other debris. There is frequently the odor and vestige of human feces on them. The walls are covered with chalk-, crayola-, and lipstick-scribbled obscenities.

Landings and stairwells also hide floating dice games and provide community winos ideal concealment from the police. As one stated, "When it's cold outside what better place is there to meet 'Sweet Lucy?' " (drink wine).

When project residents were asked about dice games, their attitudes were, in essence, that such behavior was the participant's own affair. If the tenants complain, they run the risk of physical retaliation from the gamblers. Sometimes they can see the humor in the situation, as the following story might suggest.

On one occasion, a project resident left his sixth-floor apartment with thirty dollars, which he had saved for the purchase of a used television set. He waited briefly for the elevator, then impatiently headed for the stairs. He got as far as the fifth-floor stairwell. He was broke before he reached ground level. He later recalled, "Wouldn't have happened if that damn elevator had come."

It is as natural for young children to watch dice games in the landings and stairwells as it is for them to see games of checkers elsewhere. They interrupt gamblers long enough to obtain coins from an older sibling, a cousin, or some other male known to them. They learn the jargon of the game early and use such terms as "pass" and "fade" as children in the class hierarchies above them tell Mother Goose stories. They learn to play the game and to understand the triumphs and adversities of the participants.

Parents who try to prevent exposure of their children to this activity must keep them within their own apartments. One mother asks:

What can we do? We got to live here. The children can't help but see what goes on. When my child leaves the apartment and goes downstairs, we are as far apart as we'd be if he was two blocks up the street. He can hear me call him; but it would take me as long to get to him as it would take you to run two blocks—maybe longer if somebody's got the elevator tied up. I just forget about the dice games.

Although most parents attempt to shield their children from dice games and other gambling activities in stairwells, many children, in fact, act as lookouts for gamblers. From the corridor, they keep the streets below under constant surveillance for the approach of policemen, a project manager, and other persons in authority who may prohibit the gambling and cause the arrest of the participants.

A TOUR OF BLACKMOOR

From the same spot where a child stands and acts as a lookout for gamblers he may view the contours of the city that contradict what he sees around him. A mile away, the skyline shows society's sensitivity to accomplishment in architecture, its center of corporate finance, and a unique monument. Structures that make up that skyline not only are indistinct and remote in terms of distance but also are remote and unreal because they touch his life only indirectly. Two blocks away from the housing project, in any direction, evidence of society's apathy and failures is reflected in the dilapidated, twisted, and falling buildings, its pavilions of poverty. The project itself is a monument to the tragedies of urban renewal. Two blocks away the view is tangible and ugly: trash-littered rooftops, derelict automobiles, and factory smokestacks. There is an incredible amount of broken glass, paper, and litter on the ground; there are buildings in varying stages of demolition. A network of alleys and streets surrounds partly filled basements, piles of bricks, stacks of used lumber, and other debris that are the remnants of the headache ball. "Push cart peddlers" (junk men) poke in the trash for some item that is salable while authorized construction companies salvage most of the old bricks and construction scavengers steal the remainder of them.

Several blocks away are the financial centers of the slum— the pawnshops and loan companies. In the pawnshops, the most prized possessions of a ghetto are in hock at a quarter on the dollar, and at the loan company, according to "N.," a janitor who lives in Blackmoor, "Man, you use your soul for collateral."

Here the disadvantaged live, work, and play.

Most visitors to Blackmoor come expecting to see obvious structural decay and squalor: rundown buildings, battered garbage cans, rat-infested alleys, and junk-filled yards. In addition, they expect to encounter hostility from the tenants. However, even with the thousands of broken windows, Blackmoor has few of the trappings of the traditional urban slum. There are no rats or alleys, and though the buildings may not be well maintained, they are not dilapidated. However, take the elevator in any building and the senses revolt against depravity.

Blackmoor is a series of buildings eleven stories high. In each one the elevator door opens onto a long corridor, called a galley. Heavy mesh wire covers the windows of these galleys, which children use as makeshift play areas. There are a landing and stairwell at each end of the corridor. Three apartments are grouped around each landing. Children play on the stairs, which are the only direct route for the resident from the first floor to the eleventh. They play in and on top of the elevators. Most of them, however, play in the corridors, which the tenants call "streets within a building—upper floors with sidewalks." And the landings near the doors of the apartments have been appropriately described: "It's like livin' in an alley; you see and smell the same filth." Thus, the project child opens his door into the "alley," runs and plays in the "street,"—while he is still inside the building. Corridors bustle with activities that are found on city streets in every ghetto: children are throwing balls, riding bicycles, running, and playing. It is common to see persons using a large galvanized tub as a barbecue pit and cooking on the sidewalk on the average slum street, but it was indeed a surprise to see one mother prepare her holiday meal on a makeshift barbecue grill in the seventh-floor corridor in the midst of brisk activity, congestion, and noise. There is always noise. It is another distinct dimension of project living: "From morning till night, you can't hear your ears."

The Apartments

Everything about the apartments' structure except the door is made of poured concrete, steel, or concrete blocks. The door is constructed entirely of metal, so that on the inside one cannot see who is outside without opening the door. In the project apartment, the kitchen-living-dining area occupies a single room; the number of bedrooms is determined by the size of the family. There is only one bathroom in the apartment regardless of the family size.

Through the open door of a typical project apartment, the eye encounters disorder. The physical appearance of the furnishings, the inadequate space, and a lack of symmetry emphasize the disorder. Upholstered furniture usually needs repairing and cleaning. Springs in the sofa and stuffed chairs may have broken from the mountings and may be protruding, puncturing the fabric; padding scattered about is swept up and discarded, but this bit of fastidiousness soon makes the furniture uncomfortable. The couch is flanked by a television set and tables and sometimes a record player. The room is cluttered. Kitchen chairs are often found among the living room pieces. A discarded bed sheet is used to cover a worn sofa or chair and is tucked in around the cushions. Linoleum covers the floor.

Utility in such a home is the dominant motif. Regardless of the sparsity of the furnishings and the physical appearance of the home as a whole, however, there are always curtains at the windows. This last touch is ironic—it salvages a remnant of pride; it is a vestige of vanity and a badge of respect; it is a typical feminine embellishment that transcends class.

The furnishings of the kitchen-living-dining complex are usually discordant. On one side of the room, the living room furniture is usually modern. The middle of the room, which is the dining area, may be furnished with pieces from two different dinette sets. Sometimes, half of the chairs are metal and the other half wood. The tabletop may be Formica or wood; in either case, it may be covered with oilcloth. The other side of the room is the kitchen area. The stove, refrigerator, sink, and cabinets are provided, if desired, by the housing authority. These items are usually in good repair.

Most project apartments are furnished with odds and ends and castoffs. The "chifferobe" (chiffonier) is still common. Couches are still called "davenports," "day beds," and "divans."

Bedrooms look like barracks; in many of the apartments beds are arranged in rows with little or no space between them. When the child retires, he must climb across the foot of his bed or the one he shares. Similarly, if his bed is farthest from the door, he must crawl across the beds of others to reach his own. Older children who stay out late or children who must get up during the night usually occupy the bunks nearest the door. In other apartments beds have random arrangements; their juxtapositions are perpendicular or at right angles, creating a pattern that resembles a maze.

The living room couch doubles as a bed. Members of the family also sleep on roll-away beds, on pallets, and in sleeping bags, whichever is available in the household. Because family members sleep in the kitchen-living-dining complex, the project home can be called a house of bedrooms.

One sees in a bedroom the full range of bed styles and a mixture of periods—bunks, fourposters, cots, French provincial, and modern—chosen not for fashion but for utility and economy, and a full array of bedding. Most of the small children do not have pillows, and bedspreads are frequently made by sewing an inexpensive pair of draperies together. Many large families, however, do not own spreads. Sometimes, four heavy canvas clothing bags are sewn together to make a blanket. The bedrooms, nevertheless, *do* reveal variations of personal responsibility. One bed may be well kept with clean bedding while another has urine circles, concentric and blending with the previous day's, and still another, with the exception of something for cover, is completely without bedding.

The bathroom in the project apartment is never a salon for vanity. Too many people use it. It is not a place where a member of the family goes to read the evening newspaper or to soak in a hot tub of water. It is more than a place to rinse out stockings and other delicate underclothing. Because the family wash must be done on a scheduled laundry day and there is rarely sufficient clothing in any household to last the interim between scheduled washdays, the bathroom becomes a maze of hanging clothes. It is small, poorly ventilated, constantly dirty, and always in use. Every person in the family needs to use the bathroom, almost at the same time, because frequently they are all going to the same place and are all due at their destinations at the same time. The smallness of the bathroom and the number of people who use it—sometimes as many as twelve—emphasize the perpetual chaos around the most essential room in the home.

Many tenants in Blackmoor are accustomed to a lack of sufficient bathing facilities. Twenty-seven of the hundred family heads interviewed in the project had never resided in a home that had a bathroom before they moved into the housing project. Yet twenty-three of these twenty-seven family heads had lived within the boundaries of a metropolitan urban area since childhood, and nineteen of the twenty-seven had moved more than four times. As one said:

> Can't see what's so surprising 'bout living where there ain't no bathtub. Most of my life was spent where we didn't have no bathtub—no inside toilet either. Don't think it's just country folks that ain't never had these things—you can go all over this here town and still find outdoor toilets. I used to live over on H Street; that's one of them streets that they urban renewed. They had a bathroom all right, but they didn't never have no heat in it. It wasn't never no good in the winter except maybe to use to store things up.

Here we can see urban dwellers with a kind of rural hangover.

Overcrowded Conditions

Overcrowding is one of the conditions public housing is intended to cure. Nevertheless, a project is often overcrowded because frequently individual apartments house far more people than there is adequate space for. Everywhere in Blackmoor the symptoms of overcrowding are apparent. People live in such close proximity that the common cold is a family affair. There is little or no privacy. A child shares his bed with his siblings. It is usual for two or three children to sleep together. Only one child in five among preschoolers in the sample sleeps alone. Children of different sexes often sleep together and occasionally a child sleeps with a parent. Together, members of the family share rooms and every other available space and use couches, beds, and pallets on the floor. In addition to this overcrowded sleeping condition, more than a fourth of the children under age fifteen from the families considered were enuretic. And more than half of them have never owned pajamas.

Inside the apartments the rooms are cluttered. Refuse containers always seem filled to capacity because so many people use them. There is not enough closet space, and articles of clothing hang on doors, are piled on chairs, and are placed in cardboard containers and stored under beds. Members of the family, usually children, cannot find their belongings as they prepare for each new day. A project apartment does not have extra rooms or other spaces for storing the myriad items.

There is also the smell of overcrowdedness. While stale cooking odors seem to linger in the whole house because of poor ventilation, the bedroom, bathroom, and other rooms have their own distinct odor. And, of course, there is always the smell of people in Blackmoor.

In spite of Blackmoor's location, reputation, and condition, it nevertheless provides a home for many people. And the home has a definite effect on its inhabitants, especially on the child. It is the effect of the housing project on the child that will be the persistent and consistent focus in this volume. Almost everything will be related to him. For even before the child is consciously receptive, everything about the home environment is methodically hewing his life style and adjustment. This shaping of life style is particularly significant for the disadvantaged child in the housing project. He is completely submerged in the congestion, the noise, the mobility, and just the stigma of living in high-rise public housing. A new resident sums up his feeling about bringing his children to live in the housing project:

> If you put your head in a garbage can, you're going to smell garbage.
> You feel like you can't breathe. People are everywhere. Children are in the bathroom when you are using the toilet, somebody is sitting in every chair in the house, you've got to eat in shifts. . . . People on the landings, people in the stairwells, people in the elevators, people milling around downstairs . . . everywhere. Sometimes you feel like you're going to bust wide open if you don't get a chance to turn around and nobody be there. Often I just have to close my eyes and put my hands over my ears to be by myself.

Noise

There is never a complete cessation of noise in and around Blackmoor. Main traffic arteries surround the housing project on four sides and branch off a few blocks beyond it to serve a network of trucking terminals. Consequently, the movement of large interstate trucks continues twenty-four hours a day. From the apartments, one hears this movement: the screeching tires, air horns, diesel engines, and shifting cargoes. Taxi drivers, who infrequently answer calls in Blackmoor, drivers in car pools, and new boyfriends never leave their cars when they go to the housing project. They sit in their cars and blow the horn until the customer, the rider, and the girlfriend come down from the apartment. The sound of sirens is heard all through each day. It is one of those sounds indigenous to the city.

The child who lives in this environment must have a tolerance for noise. He learns quickly to adjust to the simultaneous operation of television, radio, and record player. He listens to babies crying, people arguing, other children running and playing inside and outside the building. In fact, 7,000 children yell, shout, and play within the boundaries of Blackmoor—in the breezeways under each building, on the playground, on the tot lots, on the stairs, on the landings, in the elevators, in the laundry rooms, and in the corridors. These conditions in the housing project provide continuous stimuli, which a child must be able to ignore or tune out for his own mental health. Consequently, a child in the projects frequently develops a "closed ear" to all but motivational stimuli—those sounds that, in psychological terms, have reinforcement value for him; for example, he hears the bell on the ice-cream truck no matter where he is and in spite of the noise.

Deutsch (1962), an authority on the disadvantaged young child, writes this about noise:

> . . . while the environment is a noisy one, the noise is not, for the most part, meaningful in relation to the child, and for him most of it is background . . . In actuality, the situation is ideal for the child to learn inattention.

For anyone who has spent many nights in the projects, even as a house guest, one of the most unusual phenomena encountered is the lack of quiet. On no occasion—day or night, including the early morning hours between one and four o'clock—does one experience silence. Noise and loud extraneous sounds reverberate through the buildings twenty-four hours a day. The time of day only increases or diminishes the volume. The people even use each other's noise.

To illustrate: Some teen-agers were observed dancing in an apartment where there was no visible source of music. Inquiry revealed that they were dancing to the music from the apartment next door. Most striking, however, was the experience of walking through the project area in the afternoon and listening to the simultaneous blaring of rhythms of the "new bop" and "soul" music from radios in numerous apartments. These radios were tuned to the same station and appeared to be amplified to one volume. This produced the effect of a single radio playing. The sound reverberated throughout the area. Here one observed variant behavior. Some children were clapping and patting their feet to the rhythm of the ' music; some were making sensuous gyrations, while still others went about their games, their play, their fantasies, seemingly completely oblivious to the sound of the music.

People in Blackmoor work widely varying shifts. Some people try to sleep while others carry on the current hour's activity without consideration of those who work at a different time. Many women who are employed as barmaids and cleaning women work until the wee hours of the morning. Most of the men in Blackmoor work as janitors. The men going to work start early so they will have enough time to ride the bus up to two and a half hours to their jobs in the suburbs or to walk to and from work, some as much as ten miles per day. For example, the man who must report to work at 6 A.M. must start by 4 or 4:30 A.M. He therefore may have to arise by 3 A.M. These early risers meet the women coming home, and sometimes warm friendships develop as they pass each other at the beginning and end of their respective work days.

Psychologically, every child needs some time to be quiet and alone and a place that offers some privacy so he can shut others out and listen to himself. Blackmoor has few places where a child can find quietness and solitude.

Quietness, then, is a state the project child must learn when he goes to school. He has spent his earlier years learning, through conditioning, to be inattentive and to speak loudly to be heard. Consequently, when he enters school, he has had five years to practice ignoring what is not of intrinsic value to him. When the teacher talks to him, he is aware of the sound of her voice but often pays little attention to what she is actually saying. When she verbalizes vowel sounds in reading lessons, her *oo*s and *ah*s do not break through the barrier of selective "tuning out" with which he protects himself mentally. This ability to ignore anything he does not consciously desire to attend is a response of five years' habituation to the chaotic myriad noises at home. This conditioned response must be, in psychological terms, extinguished. He must now be taught to listen.

The same conditions do not exist for the rural child. Though his deprivation may be to the same degree, it is usually different in kind. He can always find a quiet place.

THE STIGMA OF RESIDENCE

Overcrowding and noise are only two ways in which a housing project affects its occupants. In addition, they are affected by the stigma of living in Blackmoor, the mobility of the families, and the drabness of the housing project. Families, adults and children, are socially and psychologically victimized by their place of residence. Many parents living in other sections of the city do not want their children to associate with the "project children." They indiscriminately label all of them as immoral, as having poor background, and as having undesirable character traits. Project parents and children alike feel this, are hurt by it, resent it:

> All most people have to know is you live in the projects. Right away they think you're some kind of criminal or something. They don't know that most of the lawbreaking done down here is by somebody that don't live here. There is a lot of smart people down here that you don't ever hear about. You better believe it.

It appears that mere residence in Blackmoor makes the tenant suspect. Many people in Midwest City believe that all the tenants in Blackmoor receive welfare, that all the children are illegitimate, that all the homes are broken, and that most of the residents are criminals. Yet among the citizens (one talks to) who express these opinions, one rarely finds a person who has been there. A considerable number have never seen it. The vast majority who render these opinions do so on the basis of hearsay and newspaper reports. Not infrequently, the negative attitudes about Blackmoor are buttressed by community agents. A professor from one of the local universities supports this last statement with the following story:

> She explained that she was returning home to the suburbs from a downtown movie with a group of children from her neighborhood. The professor suggested to her riders that they should take a detour so they would have an opportunity to see Blackmoor. The children agreed and the housing project was added to the list of things to see. As the children were being chauffeured near the project area, the professor violated a stop signal. She was immediately stopped by two policemen in a squad car. When the police officers approached her car, they noted that she and her passengers were Caucasians. The officers asked her for identification. Having satisfied themselves that the professor was who she said she was, they then admonished and warned her about the neighborhood and the dangers of the housing project and departed. The professor recalls: "I was never so surprised in all my life. There I was . . . had violated the law . . . and had been stopped because of it, but once the police found out who I was they never mentioned it, they were more concerned with getting this white woman back to her suburb."

The people are stigmatized by the size, type, and location of their homes as well as the racial composition Blackmoor represents. Vulgarly called the "cliff dwellers," they are bound by their class, caste, color, and poverty, fostered in part, at least, by the place in which they live. If they are introverts, then the very propinquity of their existence keeps them in a threatened environment or, if they are afraid of high places (acrophobia),* then the height of their apart-

* In one case of acrophobia, a tenant and his family had been re-assigned an eleventh-floor apartment from one that they had been assigned on the second floor. Although the man was a good tenant and appeared to be a good family man, he suddenly began to stay away from home for long periods of

ments makes their existence a constant stress situation.

One way a child learns is by imitating the behavior of his peers. When the residential constellation of his peers, the economic imperatives, and the living conditions are substandard and not in keeping with the standards of the larger culture, the behavior that he mimics is conspicuously inadequate to enable him to function effectually in that larger culture.

Eight out of ten of the people the author talked to in Blackmoor are ashamed of where they live. Some teen-age girls meet their dates at the homes .of relatives in another part of the city; teachers and ministers are rarely invited into the apartments of the tenants; old friends nourish their friendships away from the housing project. Job applicants are reluctant to give their addresses to personnel managers because these managers always appear overscrutinous or even biased when they see that the addressee lives in Blackmoor. For these reasons and others, people are obsessed with trying to move away from the housing project. Transiency, however, is a part of project living.

It was originally intended that low-income housing would be transitory for its occupants. Public housing was to serve only as a way station for the poor and other aspirants who were en route to the mainstream. But what was intended as a way station has become a way of life for many high-rise public housing residents in Midwest City. Other residents, however, move away from Blackmoor frequently—but for reasons other than those originally intended by the public housing idea. Some people move away because they do not feel that it is a good place to raise children; others, because they are afraid; still others, because they are evicted. And of course there are people who are like gypsies. Their habits of residency are migratory. They move away from the housing project during summer months and reside in more dilapidated slum areas of the city where the rent is sometimes less. A young eighth-floor resident explains the rationale for his migratory behavior this way:

---

time, sometimes for days. Because his wife was concerned, she related the new behavior to a social worker, whom the husband agreed to see. After several discussions it was revealed that the tenant was deathly afraid of height. Moreover, he could never ride the elevator. He would walk eleven floors.

I ain't gung ho on taking baths, but when it's cold, I like to be where the bathroom's warm. And another thing—when I pay my rent, I don't have to worry about the electric man, gas man, and fuel, like I used to. But come summer—man, that's where it's at! You know, daddy—about rolling stones and all that jazz. Besides, ain't no big deal on moving, anyway. Me and my broad have shacked all over this town. One pad is just like another to me. It's the "bread" [money] that counts.

Tenants return to the projects with the onset of colder weather. Although the housing project is physically more functional in terms of furnished utilities, in summer the transient dweller in a project feels that he can get more for his dollar if he forgoes such "luxuries" as hot water and perhaps a bathroom. From the viewpoint of one project manager, "Cleanliness, after all, is a matter of degree with many of these people."

Tenants in Blackmoor invest little of themselves in the housing project:

There is little point to sinking roots here. Nobody cares about anything. If you sweep the steps, somebody else or their children just mess them up again. The only people who live here anyway is them that can't do no better.

In spite of this tenant's feeling of futility, apartments and people in public housing run the complete gamut. There are individual apartments that are fastidiously clean. Many are tastefully furnished and well maintained. The occupants of these apartments are not necessarily more affluent, nor do the families necessarily have both parents in the home; however, they function and behave according to more acceptable standards. Robert Weaver (1960) characterizes this observation this way:

Slums in American cities today house families which hold a wide range of values and evidence a variety of behavior patterns. Some are households with female heads and are stable nonetheless; others may be ungrammatical, but adhere to high moral standards; still others evidence all of the attributes of middle-class behavior and are dedicated to its values, if not recipients of its rewards. All these groups have ambition and talent, but fight an uphill battle in maintaining respectability and achievement for themselves and their children.

THE RESPECTABLES

Every community has its "respectables"—that group of people within an area who appear to be good citizens and outstanding examples of civic virtue both as parents and as community participants. A housing project is no exception. There are families in Blackmoor who were the original tenants; parents have since seen their children go on to become milkmen, mailmen, factory workers, and nurses and to matriculate in the local college. They have become productive and contributing members of society. There are mothers in Blackmoor who have watched their daughters marry, become good homemakers, and produce healthy, happy children who are in fact advantaged; and there are fathers who have seen their sons move well into the mainstream of society. It is not difficult to identify the respectables. They are the PTA regulars, they are registered voters, and they take part in voter-registration drives and other civic activities. Their children are well behaved when they are young and are never a problem for the juvenile authorities as they grow older. Among these people who rise above their surroundings, it is readily discernible that members in the family help and show mutual respect for each other. A sense of pride, a definite routine, and clearly defined adult roles are also discernible. The respectables set individual and family goals and objectives; their values, attitudes, and commitments would be labeled middle class. Yet the income of most of these individual families is no more than $5,000 per year, sometimes much less.

The respectables often represent that large group of people who have worked in the service occupations—doormen, janitors, clerks, and domestics—and who have been regularly employed. There are also some among them who have worked in such lower-paying local government jobs as operating elevators. These working respectables have taken advantage of the low rent in the housing project but have not compromised their values and goals or succumbed to the slum ethic. They have always lived in the project or near that area of the city that is dilapidated but have maintained their living quarters in good condition. Find any slum neighborhood in Midwest City and you will find respectables. These are the people who never move away; they love the neighborhood and the people but mind their own business. They are the models that project managers use to influence other tenants; they are unusual in a housing project.

AGAINST THE CURRENT

It is difficult to assess the full extent of the psychological impact of the home on the deprived child. To be sure, he must suffer psychologically from the many sociological, physiological, and emotional traumas associated with the cultural deprivation of his home. Family disorganization, transiency, and group status are but a few conditions that contribute to the instability of the home. Oscar Lewis (1961) describes the social and psychological characteristics to include

> living in crowded quarters, a lack of privacy, gregariousness, a high incidence of alcoholism, frequent resort to violence in the training of children, wife beating, early initiation into sex, free unions or consensual marriages, a relatively high incidence of the abandonment of mothers and children, a trend toward mother-centered families and a much greater knowledge of maternal relatives, the predominance of the nuclear family, a strong predisposition to authoritarianism, and a great emphasis upon family solidarity— an ideal rarely achieved.

The conditions that inundate the culturally disadvantaged home make adequate preparation for meeting the challenges in the mainstream of urban society at best a difficult, if not impossible, task. These conditions are not the exclusive predicament of housing projects alone. Any impoverished home, whether in the coal fields of Appalachia, in the deltas of Mississippi, in Watts, or in Harlem, is pitifully poor in the tangible and intangible resources necessary to a full life. However, housing projects, distinct from other types of impoverished homes, were built to eliminate many of the housing problems of the slums traditionally encountered by the poor. Nevertheless, too many housing projects show similarities to the slums they were supposed to have replaced. They are rundown, uncomfortable, inconvenient, in some ways unsafe, and in numerous ways unhealthy. One has but to walk along State Street in Chicago, Cass Avenue in St. Louis, and scores of other streets in other cities to be convinced.

There are other ways in which a public high-rise project parallels residence in a slum tenement: a lack of services and facilities, a lack of maintenance in many of them, quick evictions, and the ruthlessness of the bureaucracy. These conditions have made public housing tenants come to regard the office and agents of local housing authorities as oppressive landlords. Many tenants view these authorities as being worse than the absentee and slum landlords they have always known, because the local housing authorities are their legal representatives. Blackmoor exemplifies much that is bad in high-rise projects. What are conditions in public housing projects? Robert Weaver (1960), former Secretary of Housing and Urban Development, sees them this way:

> Housing projects pose a special problem . . . Families are admitted on the basis of financial need and removed whenever their resources advance beyond a given point. This tends to create a population without an adequate range of capacities, aspirations, educational backgrounds, etc., for good social organization. In addition, there is an air of impermanence about living in the projects. No one expects to stay long. This becomes the rationale for not investing much of one's self in anything that goes. And finally, thousands of families have been gathered together in vast dormitories with kitchen privileges. Absolutely no provision has been made for shopping, entertainment, commercial timefillers, churches, professional services. There are no pieces, no bones, no nothing around which or out of which a social structure can easily grow . . . This condition in the housing projects and their population is crucial.

The tenants of the housing project are becoming more militant and are making new demands: more police, more heat, more maintenance, more respect, while the housing authority is demanding more rent from people who cannot afford to pay the rent they are currently paying. Placards and other signs of the rising protest of the poor have begun to appear periodically around the housing authority to protest the increases in rent without the corresponding increase in service. The leader and spokesman of a rent-rise protest has her indistinct and almost ominous warning quoted by the local newspaper:

> We have tried picketing, talk-ins, pray-ins—the whole bag. And we've gotten nowhere. There's a lot of feeling among some of the young people down here. I see them every day. Some of them say they're just through marching and asking and begging. They have been through channels and they're angry. Something's got to be done.

Thus a project home is not one in which the individual tenants really make a choice to live. Rather, it is a place to live because they have no choice. It appears, then, that the deprived child and his family become little more than human driftwood in the urban stream of social turbulence—never fulfilling, never being fulfilled.

IV - Not by Bread Alone

Blackmoor was built more than a decade ago. In the interim, children have been born and children have been reared there; some have been corrupted; a few have been honored; the vast majority, however, have simply endured. From the very beginning the project was the embodiment of urban poverty. Tenants from the former slum dwellings that Blackmoor replaced, as well as other urban-renewal refugees, secured a lease in this cluster of high-rise homes but could not discard their poverty. All the tangled problems rooted in generations of destitution found in big-city slums everywhere abound in Blackmoor. The men who live there calculate job tenure in days, rarely in weeks. To consider job duration for six months is unimaginable; for a year, an absurdity. Relief is an assumption; crime, unemployment, and delinquency are routine; broken windows, broken bottles, and broken spirits are commonplace. The sum of these constraints is the potpourri of human problems found in Blackmoor.

Since they moved into the project, the homes of many former slum dwellers for the first time met the requirements of the city's building code. The tenants no longer maintain night vigils to keep the rats from biting their children; no longer is raw sewage a foot deep in the basement; little children no longer are put to bed in the early evening in winter to keep warm, nor do they get sick from eating spoiled food because there is inadequate refrigeration. There is hot water and a bathtub. Still the people are not satisfied. The housing project eliminated many of the problems of inadequate housing facing the people, but this was only a part of their difficulty. They need more. The economic pressures have not changed; the families still face the depressing future of most slum dwellers. The frustrations brought about by too many people living in too little space remain the same as they were before. The disillusionment and patterns of defeat that characterize the poor have mounted and have continued to be a persistent challenge to the people. More than 65 percent of the tenants have had to succumb to the mercy of the welfare department as they have learned that they have no alternative but to exist in this self-perpetuating and desperate existence of the new-style ghetto. Fathers, as their fathers before them, desert their families in order to ensure the continuation of welfare payments. The people have learned that dependence on the public dole gives them little to be thankful for and nothing to make them feel proud.

Through its social welfare organization, society attempts to provide some of the basic physical needs of poor people; however, many people with a long tenure of welfare assistance know that their important psychological and human needs have often been ignored.

Mrs. W., welfare recipient, mother of six, states it succinctly: "I appreciate the help I get; it takes care of a few of the things I need, but it don't never help how I feel."

The individual is unlikely to be inclined toward desirable social goals unless many of his physical and psychological goals are met. Poverty can affect both goals. In the physical sense, poverty limits the home and community where one can live, his educational opportunities, the medical attention he can provide for his family, the transportation available to him, the job that he can expect to obtain, the way he handles his leisure, the kind and quality of his purchases. More precisely, poverty determines his physical life style, providing him with few alternatives. Correspondingly, in the psychological sense, poverty affects the attitudes, values, commitments, aspirations, and self-image of the individual, and this is reflected in his behavior. Yet despite the delineation made between physical and psychological needs, both needs are inextricably bound to each other. When the economic strivings of the individual are not successful enough to produce the basic necessities, he tends to lose esteem, become fearful, develop anxieties, and become hostile. In a word, when the physical needs are not met, this deficit state exposes the individual to a poor psychological climate. Paradoxically, under conditions where the satisfaction of physical needs is gratis, as in the case of many disadvantaged people on welfare and other public assistance, the attitude of the benefactors can affect the attitude of the recipients. Thus, we have the same poor psychological climate. Poverty, as we have seen, affects the mental and physical well-being of the disadvantaged family. This is especially crucial for the children.

The needs among disadvantaged children transcend simple physical fulfillment. A deficit in the "other" needs of these children can have a disastrous effect upon their mental health. Being respected, being understood, living in a warm and friendly environment, and having desirable models to emulate are but a few of the experiences to which a child should be exposed if he is to grow into a wholesome individual. Without these experiences, he grows up with an emotional disadvantage.

Every child looks at himself favorably relative to the acceptance of himself that he senses in others. The attitude of society toward him is frequently indicative of the behavior in which he will engage. He acts the way he is treated. For example, merchants just beyond the boundaries of Blackmoor treat all the children who come into their establishments as potential thieves. The children are followed and watched. Huge mirrors hang throughout these establishments, and gates and cages of mesh wire limit movement and inspection of merchandise. Everywhere in the store the customer is under constant overt surveillance; many small children are searched before they are permitted to leave the store. It is not surprising that the prevailing attitude and behavior of these deprived children and their parents is to beat the system. They do beat it.

> *He ain't got no business searching me—didn't do no good though. Want some bubble gum?* —First grade boy, age nine

> *Everybody don't steal; if they did—you couldn't stop it. Locks just stop honest people. Thieves don't pay no attention to no locks. Besides, they*

[merchants in the area] steal more from us poor
folks than we could ever steal back. The last time they
broke into that store, everybody knew
who did it. —Unemployed male, age thirty-four

>*You've got to pay higher prices here than you pay*
>*everywhere else and get less for it. Some of that stuff*
>*they sell to people ain't fit for animals—no wonder*
>*somebody is always breakin' in. They're just gettin'*
>*what they deserve.* —Mother of six, welfare recipient

A child from Blackmoor is sent to the store frequently, perhaps three or four times daily. Still, he remains anonymous to
the proprietor, who never bothers to put a face on him and who
neither knows him nor trusts him. And a child cannot learn the
value of honesty unless he has the opportunity to experience
its worth and rewards. If he is never treated with. trust, he learns
to be neither trusting nor trustworthy.

The disadvantaged child who lives in Blackmoor rarely hears
the names of either of his parents prefaced by "Mr." or "Mrs."
People who serve the project community withhold these amenities. Many policemen, public clinic personnel, social workers,
and teachers treat the residents of Blackmoor with a lack of
courtesy. Respect is not withheld from every person every day,
but every day some person is not respected by community serv-
ants. Sometimes several. Those tenants who do demand respect
become the victims of professional aloofness, antagonism, and
oversolicitous scrutiny when they have legitimate complaints or
requests.

Although the child in Blackmoor never hears the names of
his parents prefaced by a title, he constantly hears himself labeled and described; many people call him many things. The
storekeeper calls him a thief; the welfare worker explains that
he is illegitimate; the policeman calls him a delinquent; the
psychologist labels him aggressive or even disturbed; and the
teacher says that he is a slow learner. The sociologist calls the
community where he lives a ghetto. He hears his home described
as broken and his family referred to as indigent. He listens as
he is called poor, black, Negro, colored, nigger, slum child, and
deprived; the labels continue to mount. When a twelve-year-old

boy heard a volunteer worker in his neighborhood call him disadvantaged, he responded abruptly, "Lady, I know I'm everything else—you mean I'm *that* too?" As the child in Blackmoor searches for identity, he soon learns that few of the words others use to describe him convey a positive image of him. He becomes affected with what Charles Silberman, in his book *Crisis in Black and White* (1964), calls "the crushing sense of nobodiness." And he knows that if he is a "nobody," there isn't anybody who will respect him; and it is hard to respect himself.

In addition to the labels assigned the poor, many better-off residents of Midwest City's suburbs hold attitudes and assumptions about Blackmoor's tenants that are unwarranted. A considerable number of the majority who live in plenty insist that, with a little gumption, the poor people who live in the housing project can help themselves. Some of the affluent are convinced that people are impoverished simply because they are shiftless and lazy and would rather be on relief than work and provide for themselves. Still others of that majority believe that poverty is the lot of poor people as their penalty for failure. This latter belief is one that Wilbur J. Cohen (1964), former Secretary of Health, Education and Welfare, points out as being based on the wrong economic considerations to be appropriate today: "The notion that . . . poverty is a penalty for laziness, error or failure persists as an almost unconscious hangover of attitudes conditioned by a wholly different set of economic facts." In addition to Cohen's comment, the records of employment agencies in every major city show that literally thousands of poor people have, in fact, attempted to find employment. In Midwest City, hundreds of unemployed workers report to the state employment office each day. At 6 A.M. they can be found lined up tò secure the few jobs that are available on a first-come, first-serve basis and last only for a day or two, rarely a week. However, in view of the supposition held by many of those who are above the poverty level in society, it is not difficult to see why the welfare assistance offered to deprived families carries with it the resentment and contempt of those who pay for it. These attitudes have made many among Blackmoor's poor prefer the shocking and degrading realities of poverty to the equally shocking and degrading hypocrisy of welfare. Those who are recipients of welfare payments hate relief most of all. They recognize its insidious and degenerating subversion of the spirit. The tenants in Blackmoor speak for themselves:

> *Asking for welfare is begging and I don't know*
> *nobody who can hold his head up*
> *begging.* —Waitress, age thirty-one

Just to have to go ask for welfare is enough to make
you want to vomit. When those self-righteous
bitches sit there and ask you all about your
business—you want to spit in their faces but
you've got to sit there and grin and hope they got
some feelings for you. —Unidentified female tenant

> *Why would anybody want to be on relief if he had a*
> *choice? Relief break up more families down here than*
> *anything. There ain't no man can stick around very*
> *long if he can't feed his family. So he does what any*
> *self-respecting man does if he can't get a job, he leaves*
> *home so the state can feed his children or he goes out*
> *and steals to feed them. So I ask you, where is he going*
> *to get pride from? Nobody respects a deserter and nobody*
> *respects a thief—except those down here who know what*
> *it's like.* —Laundress, age forty-seven, former
> ADC recipient

Sure my husband drinks! The poor bastard ain't had
a job in two years. I remember when he went out to
look for work every day for nine months. Did anybody
ever say naw to you for nine months? Even iron
wears out. Me and my daughter work, which is the
only thing that keep us off relief. God knows we'd
rather have him here—I don't care how much
he drinks—than to have him leave and go on off
somewhere, so we can get on welfare. Maybe
he drinks so he can come in day after day and look
us in the face. —Domestic worker, PTA president

In spite of these cries and explanations from the ghetto, society has been slow to understand and appreciate the problems of the disadvantaged home and family. It has, in fact, rarely been concerned with why people were poor; it has always been more concerned with why people were rich—and how they got to be that way. However, as the number of people living in poverty in our big cities continues to increase, society is beginning to refocus a little of this concern and modify some of its behavior, if not change its attitude. The disadvantaged living in these cities are still not understood; they are still not respected; but in the wake of the riots of Watts, Newark, and Detroit, there is charred testimony that at least some of them refuse to be ignored.

The misinformation and lack of understanding of the poor community and family are particularly significant in relation to the disadvantaged child. Despite the millions of dollars spent to support the hundreds of programs that both local and federal agencies have developed for the benefit of the disadvantaged child, society shows an appalling ignorance about him. All the stereotyped assumptions and generalizations about the disadvantaged child persist: his deficiency in learning is interpreted as lack of ability; the tendency of the child to be loud and boisterous is believed to be due to his poor self-control; the profanity that he may use is considered to be indicative of the low moral fiber of his home; if he is illegitimate, some believe that his illegitimacy was desirable and even intended so that his mother could have her welfare payments increased; the child from the disadvantaged community is frequently assumed to be one who is dirty, lazy, mean, bad mannered, and aggressive. In addition, he is said to possess a poor attitude. Many people feel that he is not loved and has no values of his own that can be used in the mainstream of society. Persons who hold the ideas and assumptions described above—and far too many do—are misinformed in many cases and uninformed in others. Although one or more of the above situations, as well as many comparable situations, may apply to an individual child, there are many disadvantaged children to whom none of these things apply. In the chapters that follow, many of the conditions in the life of the child will be described. Perhaps this description may help clarify some of the misinformation and misinterpretation held about the disadvantaged child. For example, what is frequently considered uncooperativeness in the deprived child is often his assertion of his own early independence.

Precocious independence is a characteristic of the disadvantaged child. In effect, he defers his childhood while he learns to become an adult. By the age of four, a child living in Blackmoor can cross busy intersections alone going to and from the store. After the age of seven or eight, he never needs a baby-sitter while his mother works or shops or visits. Frequently, he is a baby-sitter himself by that age. This child can get his own meals, care for his own clothing, and make many of his own decisions long before he would be expected to do so in a more privileged environment. Although the quality of his tasks and decisions may leave much to be desired, he performs the tasks and makes the decisions.

In the disadvantaged home, parents and others are frequently indifferent to some of the problems of the child. Therefore, the child learns to become resourceful and independent. After about age four and a half nobody laces his shoes. As a result, he must exercise alternatives: let his shoes stand open without laces, to trip over the shoe laces until he reaches the limits of his endurance and learns to tie them, or to knot the laces and not to bother to handle them at all as he slips his shoes on and off. He rarely receives an allowance; consequently, at a very early age he earns, begs, or steals such things as his movie fee. He stops asking parental permission to come and go much earlier than the child who is more advantaged. A parent in Blackmoor may not know where his eight- or ten-year-old child is at eleven o'clock at night and will simply go to bed seemingly unperturbed. At least one study has found, however, that poor parents do not willingly permit their children to "run the streets" and try to prevent it but are ineffective in coping with the competing environmental influences. Yet in Blackmoor almost no parent knows who his child's playmates are. Unlike the child in a social class above him who complains that he has nothing to do and nobody to play with, the disadvantaged child is more concerned with his ability to "slip off" or simply walk away from home. He can always find something to do and someone with whom to do it.

The child in Blackmoor speaks the language of adults and the streets before he can, in fact, handle the intricacies of the ABCs. He can understand the intrigue, problems, and taboos of his community with more facility than he can handle the plot in his basal reader. Fighting his own battles and, in most cases, bearing his own misfortunes are expected of the disadvantaged child much earlier than of privileged children. When his mother punishes him for his misbehavior, he rarely interprets her actions to mean that she doesn't love him. He knows either by instinct or from his mother's subsequent behavior that a lack of affection for him is not a factor in her conduct. Consequently, this child takes what's coming to him and attempts to make sure that he is not caught the next time. He learns to keep "little things" little in his environment. Truancy, for example, may be a serious alternative for a child in a more highly structured community; the underprivileged child, however, does not consider playing hooky even a mild rebellion. In the ghetto where he lives, this behavior is a way of life, one that he learns almost before he goes to school. Very early, the ghetto pedagogy teaches the child the art of being independent and the technique of controlling his own survival. It also teaches him to "play the game and pay the toll." The reciprocal loyalties he holds with his peers teach him another ghetto dictum: when an outsider comes into his slum and tries to probe, the child is to see, hear, and speak no evil. Whether the child is in the Taylor projects in Chicago, the Jefferies project in Detroit, Pruitt-Igoe in St. Louis, or Blackmoor in Midwest City, the conditions of his life and the realities of his ghetto guide him to early independence.

Many times the early independence of the child creates later problems at home and school. For example, Judy lived with her mother, who was an excessive drinker, an older sister, who was not dependable, and three younger children. Consequently, she had to assume some of the most important family responsibilities. Judy had many tasks. First, she was in charge of the family finances. She was assigned this responsibility by her mother, who, in spite of her considerable intemperance, wanted to ensure that some of her weekly wages would be spent for the basic necessities of the family. The mother never cashed her own paychecks; instead, she made arrangements with a small storekeeper to make Judy the payee. Judy did all the food shopping each week. She knew where to find quality items and the best prices. Before Judy purchased the week's groceries, she always went to the liquor counter and priced a fifth of her mother's favorite whiskey; she then deducted the cost of the liquor from the money she had to spend. Judy managed the money so that she could buy clothing and shoes for the younger children at irregular intervals. Whenever the rent was several days overdue, the manager of Blackmoor or one of his representatives would contact Judy. In school, this eight-year-old girl who could handle the budgeting, purchasing, and dispersal of the family's finances was considered poor in arithmetic.

Judy had other tasks. She kept the clinic appointments that were made for her younger siblings but that her mother ignored. She prepared meals, saw the younger children off to school, and protected them. Everywhere, the people knew Judy—at the laundromat, at the grocery store, at the project rent and administration office.

After four and a half years of this activity, Judy began to behave differently. She stayed out very late; occasionally she spent a night away from home; finally she began to spend whole weekends away from home. The parent attempted to stop this behavior but was unable to cope with the child. Neither Judy's teacher, the social worker, nor the counselor was able to handle her, short of recommending her confinement to a correction home for girls. Because Judy was a twelve-year-old juvenile who knew she was the only cohesive force in the family, being told that she would be confined did not even represent a threat. As more and more people worked with Judy, they discovered that she had functioned as an adult for so long that she felt that she had earned the right to control her own behavior like an adult. This was a case in which early independence and responsibility had made a child into an adult who demanded all the rights and privileges pertaining thereto; Judy was only twelve years old but was the most efficient person in her family.

In spite of the early independence of disadvantaged children, these children have certain needs that could affect their lives in a positive way.

The disadvantaged child needs a warm and friendly environment. This does not mean that the environment must be one that is economically solvent or middle class in its values. Even a poor community can be a responsive and cordial one for the child, particularly if the home is intact and each member of the family can extract from others in the family certain stimuli that will help him function more effectively in society. Moreover, a ghetto, in the generic sense—which is isolated by some impoverishment, by social class, and by ethnic characteristics—can be imbued with pride, can be close-knit and productive, if the individual family or the individual within the family can provide for his needs. Poor people have frequently developed unity and a sense of purpose when they had some cohesive force to hold them together. A proud tradition, religion, mores, and history have often provided that cohesiveness when the people involved had some opportunity and ability to work and sustain themselves. Children just above the poverty level even today grow up in homes where they do not have excessive freedom and money and yet do not show overt hostility to adults. These children do not plan or expect to go to college, do not expect to own a new car before they are adults, and do not expect to live in the suburbs. Nevertheless, these young people and their parents are respected, enjoy human dignity, and have a positive view of themselves. In these homes the members of the family laugh, work, play, and pray together. A considerable number of these families do not appear to be interested in the pursuit of a middle-class life style. Half of America's population was poor during the great depression of the 1930s, yet the basic institutions of family and home remained, for the most part, strong. There are certain common threads running through all the above examples: in every case, the traditional role of breadwinner was handled traditionally; the family had some means providing for its needs; there was at least some opportunity for mobility; and the child was in an environment that offered him enough of the basic necessities and emotional support to cope with the mainstream of society.

However, for the disadvantaged child who lives in a slum, the examples above do not apply, particularly if he is black. The examples do not apply to the slum child because his family does not meet the criteria: the family is probably not intact; it provides few services and produces fewer goods; it does not have a strong religious affiliation; there is not a proud tradition for the child to follow; and there is neither the opportunity nor the ability for the family to sustain itself. Moreover, people in the slums are not respected, are not shown much human dignity, do not have a positive image of themselves. Their lower-class status, impoverishment, and ethnic characteristics help society keep them powerless, divided, and unable to provide for their needs. It is true that the disadvantaged child needs a warm and friendly environment, but one is not likely to find it in many homes in Blackmoor.

A child in Blackmoor needs someone to emulate, a good model to observe, someone to teach him by example how the appropriate roles in the home are traditionally assumed and fulfilled. A boy (or a girl) could learn responsibility from watching a father provide the basic necessities for his family; he could profit from hearing a father make a decision or repair a broken window sash; he might learn more about the father role if he could see how a father fulfills the role both in times of triumph and in times of adversity. The same applies to the role of mother. The disadvantaged child could profit from seeing these simple day-to-day habits and routines of the adults in the family that spell out the sex roles. This does not mean that the roles the disadvantaged child observes should be labeled middle-class values or behaviors, although they might. Whether a child lives in a tribe, village, or city, an apartment or grass hut, he normally learns his role and the function of his sex from watching and being taught by the adults in the family. There are, of course, indistinct behaviors that he observes on his own. The quiet and beguiling glances exchanged between his parents, the tone of finality in his father's voice, and the many other antics of human interaction, understanding, and affection that are part of the telepathy of family living are among the challenges to his sensibilities. The child feels an ambivalence of loyalty when his parents or his siblings disagree or have problems. He needs to have many occasions to watch a variety of satisfactory ways in which these problems in the family are met and successfully resolved. The child must learn subtle ways to handle feelings and alternatives necessary to help him learn his role and function. Most of these things he learns from example.

Our lives are largely a mixture of successes and failures, perhaps more of the former than the latter. With the balance tipped in the direction of success, we can be optimistic about the world. The balance in the life of the disadvantaged child is tipped more toward failure except in his own environment. One of the great ironies of Blackmoor is the fact that while it does not enhance the child's success for living in the mainstream, it is remarkably successful in producing a child who can develop all of the skills of survival and who is an exemplar of "copability."

This child learns to fight before he learns to play an organized game; he learns to curse more effectively than he learns to read and can conform to his gang's code and demands while he rejects the regimentation of the school. Whether it is fighting, cursing, or conforming to a slum code, this disadvantaged child is a success in his own insular society. It is in the behavior found in the mainstream that he enjoys little or no success. The normal kinds of activities for which many children are praised, such as learning to go to the store alone or to care for oneself, are expected of children in the slums without any reward. As a working mother in Blackmoor puts it, "If that store across the street separates him from his breakfast and he goes over there and buys it, ain't nobody going to stand up and cheer because he did. He ate it didn't he?"

When the disadvantaged child goes to school, his chances for success begin to diminish. He frequently encounters incessant failure. The language he uses seldom, if ever, evokes praise; his habits, behavior, and values do not receive understanding or endorsement from the school, and the experiences of the child have come from a small corner of the total culture that the school does not support. Consequently, the child is frequently consumed by a lack of success. There are, in fact, so many failures in the life of the child in Blackmoor that failure itself becomes a psychological expectancy.

The child in Blackmoor has a need to release aggression, but he does it differently from a privileged child. Observe the nursery school playground or public park in an affluent community. There one observes that even the play activity of the small children has a kind of organization. The children stand in circles, squares, and other formations as they prepare for play. Even as they play with a kind of reckless abandon that only a child knows, there is still a semblance of order. Adults are often available to guide and direct the play of middle-class children. Much of the aggression and competition inherent in the play antics of the young child is absorbed by the games and activities. When the play becomes too violent and physical contact is made between players, nondisadvantaged children are willing to relinquish their desire to strike back to a mediator—a father, referee, or teacher.

In contrast, deprived children play in a no man's land—in the streets, on the stoops, and in the alleys. If they live in Blackmoor, they play in the elevator, stairwells, washrooms, galleys, and every other available space. They make use of every found item to enhance their play. There is rarely organization or direction. Even the play yard at school has two to three times more pupils than it was constructed to handle. There are few places to run and no place to sit. Disadvantaged children, too, play with reckless abandon, but most of their games involve physical contact. They tussle, push and strike, and kick each other, each to his own special brutality. Most of their games are, in reality, practice for fighting. Because the children play in congested areas, they frequently collide with one another; when this happens, they fight. In the disadvantaged environment, no one has taught them alternatives to fighting—not their peers, parents, or neighbors. Anyone who would teach a child in the ghetto not to fight would have less than a sharp eye on reality. For this child to make a prompt retreat when he is confronted only increases the number of his confrontations. Yet the deprived child needs to learn how to control his aggression and to release it through acceptable channels.

The small child in Blackmoor has little or no opportunity to participate in any organized and supervised activity where he can learn some of the approved ways aggressive and competitive behavior are exemplified. Physical aggression is a part of the home and community where he lives. Thus, the approved ways the deprived child learns to handle aggressive behavior in his own community are contrary to the ways that a child would handle it in a privileged community.

Middle-class values, standards, and opportunities may appear to be the criteria necessary for the disadvantaged child to grow and relate effectively in the mainstream of society. If one accepts them as being solely middle-class criteria, then they are what the disadvantaged child needs. On the other hand, if one considers the critical needs of any child, many of those things that have been labeled and publicized as middle class are, in fact, classless. Every child needs a father to relate to, whether he is called family head, breadwinner, or some other label. The role of the father in the family is not one that emerged with the middle class. It is a role that the middle class incorporated, made a few modifications in, and absorbed as its own. In fact, the peasants and other members of the traditional working class define the male position with much more precision than does contemporary Western society. In like manner, whether the male is a native and brings his kill to his grass hut in the village or an executive who brings his paycheck home to a split-level home in the suburbs, he is serving the same function. All children need to have sufficient food, clothing, and shelter and to learn to adjust to the society in which they live. If the skills they need are labeled middle class, then we accept the label.

The disadvantaged child in Blackmoor is a child of poverty. He lives in the midst of roaches, rabble, and ridicule. The longer he remains in this environment, the more he is affected by the conditions that will eventually mold him into a wasted American; that is, one of a growing number of persons whose lives are filled with poverty, hopelessness, conflict, dilemma, and failure. "Baby—it's enough to scoop out your insides."

This child lives in a community where more than half of the families do not have adult males in the home; more than 60 percent of the families are on welfare, and more than 70 percent of the adults have not finished high school. On one or more of these counts poverty succeeds in alienating the child from society—and convinces him that the road to the mainstream is impenetrable. Against this debasing picture of poverty, the child has no defense; he knows—or he learns early—that the picture is authentic.

Low income and chronic unemployment in the child's home are symptoms of poverty. Among Blackmoor households as a whole (excluding those over 60 and minors), 79 percent of them have incomes of less than $4,000 annually. Only one father in four has a job. Those who do work do not earn enough money to take care of their families adequately. Unemployed fathers desert their homes so that their families can receive welfare. The disadvantaged child also lives among thousands of teenagers, high school dropouts, and high school graduates who cannot find employment. They are restless and rebellious at a crucial stage in their lives, and they try to soothe their tensions and turmoil with deadly and deceptive escape therapies: narcotics, alcohol, and crime. These latter problems only accentuate the myriad other problems that permeate the life of the disadvantaged child and provide patterns for his future behavior.

Along with his poor and insufficient diet, the child of poverty is ill-clothed and lives in overcrowded conditions; in his community nine out of every ten children sleep with one or more persons.

Repeatedly, in public and in private, with a seeming sincerity and even a certain passion, the parents of disadvantaged children insist that they want an education for their children. The fact remains, however, that the deprived child is without much educational stimulation. Little is done with intent or by chance that will help him function well in a school setting. Educational retardation starts early in the ghetto, and there, where poverty achieves some of its most deleterious work, many people come every year to conduct research and observe it. When these visitors come to Blackmoor and look into the incredible self-contained world of the disadvantaged child, their reaction is seldom mild. They had not known previously the extent of the chasm in the deprived child's learning environment. It is hard for them to conceive that in the twentieth-century United States there is a child who has never owned a book, drawn pictures with crayola, or manipulated a pencil. They are even more astonished to find a home where the child may never see a newspaper or be delighted and enchanted by the pictures and symbols in a magazine.

Rarely does the disadvantaged child have an educational tradition. There are many families in Blackmoor in which no single member has a high school education. If one reaches back three generations, the same statement applies to elementary school education.

The deprived child is socially inept in a middle-class world. He is a child who may never sit at the dinner table with his entire family and use either the tools or the amenities of dining. Many of the skills that will facilitate his social integration into the larger community are unknown to him. He sees the well-developed value system related to social behavior in our culture rejected by his own community. Consequently, he often defies the code in manner, dress, and behavior.

The child in Blackmoor is one who learns the reaction of people to him and his condition of poverty. He recognizes both the public and the private contempt of him by his observers long before he is able to verbalize his knowledge. The social rejection he sometimes encounters contributes to some of his problems of adjustment. Sometimes he meets the repugnance from the outer environment by developing an attitude of hostility and aggression.

The disadvantaged child is a child like many other children. He has the same basic needs as any other child and matures, physically, at least, along the same dimensions as other children. Quite apparently, he must be different in some aspects from the privileged child. What, then, are the characteristics that distinguish the culturally disadvantaged child from his higher-class counterparts? In a word, what is he?

The disadvantaged child is one who has had limited experience with the mainstream of society. If he lives in Blackmoor, he may never have crossed the boundaries that encompass it. Frequently, this child has never been to a supermarket or a movie. He may never have seen a strawberry or eaten bacon. He may never have had a bath towel or a toothbrush of his own but may have shared them with others. He has had limited contact with the tools of education and with people who speak the language correctly.

The parents of this child may not have taught him the value of cleanliness, and his physical development may reflect the indigent quality of his diet. His reaction to authority is hostile. None of the prescriptions for success in society is readily observable in the life of this child. What, then is the culturally disadvantaged child? He is a child who has not had the opportunity to partake of the psychological, physiological, sociological, and educational opportunities that are found in the mainstream of culture—opportunities to which he is entitled as a human being.

He has a right to protest!

V - Who Am I?

The family remains one of the most essential forces in the development of the human organism. Few aspects of the child's life are left untouched by this institution. The effectiveness of the family lies in the fact that it receives the child first, and from conception to burial he is inextricably pinioned to its influence. This is no less true in the impoverished family than in the more affluent family. It is also true regardless of the racial identification or whether the family is intact or broken for some reason. However, for three decades, men like E. Franklin Frazier (1939), Gunnar Myrdal (1944), and Daniel P. Moynihan (1965) have cited the dissolution of the Negro family structure as a problem of major magnitude in all black ghettos of America. *The Report of the National Advisory Commission on Civil Disorders* (1968) further emphasizes the problem of the broken Negro family.

Blackmoor is noted for its "BB" families—black and broken. In fact, 63 percent of the households in this housing project are fatherless. Because a fatherless home is a prerequisite for receiving relief, the large number of broken families is dramatized by the equally large number of mothers who apply for welfare. Therefore, Blackmoor has an unusually high concentration of families that are not only poor but also female-centered.

FEMALE-CENTERED FAMILIES

In sixty-three of the families sampled, the mother is the head. In some of these families the father is present in the home but is totally disabled. Unlike mothers in more privileged households or in those with functioning adult male residents, most mothers in Blackmoor assume responsibility for every function that is normally carried on in the home by members of both sexes. They are expected to provide the basic necessities, to protect the family against adversities, and to aid in the development of the values, attitudes, and behavior of the other members of the household by using the same overt and subtle tactics used by any leader. In his discussion of the black matriarchy and the distorted masculine image, Kenneth Clark (1965) talks about the role of the black woman: "The Negro woman has in turn been required to hold the family together; to set the goals, to stimulate, encourage, and to protect both boys and girls." Her compensatory strength tended to perpetuate the weaker role of the black male.

There is a lack of legal divorce; however, it is not uncommon to find mothers whose husbands have deserted them but who have several sexual partners. Nor is it uncommon to find a child who may know his own father but may have shared the home temporarily with several "visiting" or "acting" fathers. The school records of a large percentage of lower-class siblings will reveal several family names. Basically, this behavior on the part of the female, as well as the male, can be economical. For example, a mother who receives aid to dependent children (ADC) cannot, in many cities, have a husband in the home unless he is totally incapacitated physically or mentally. Transitory illness and unemployment of the husband are not sufficient criteria for welfare assistance. Ironically, the father who is unskilled, unlearned, and unemployed frequently must "desert" his wife and children in order to provide for them. In like manner, a divorced mother, receiving subsistence, may take a male companion who will assist her financially. Such behavior is common in Blackmoor. Moreover, it is acceptable behavior in the environment without loss of status.

Grandmothers were at the head of one-fifth of the families included in the sample. In fact, more grandmothers than fathers were family leaders.* A grandmother would become the household head when she had the only consistent and guaranteed income (old-age assistance, OAA); when a mother or a father or both had deserted their children; when a family was broken by divorce and she moved into the home; when a father was incarcerated; when mothers of illegitimate children had rejected them; or when a parent was deceased. Finally, some grandmothers became heads of the home because they had the more dominant personalities. Frequently this strong personality challenges a daughter or a son or an in-law who also has a strong will, and conflict arises in the family.

Certain features characterize the family structure of all the public housing projects in such major cities as Chicago, St. Louis, Detroit, Cleveland, and New York. After the age of twenty, females outnumber the males 2 to 1. This figure tends to remain stable up through the age of sixty. Therefore, during the adult years, the residents of a housing project live in an edifice inhabited primarily by women, dominated by women, and sustained by the efforts of women. The number of children in housing projects exceeds the number of adult men by a ratio of 7 to 1.

ROLE OF THE FATHER

The father is really peripheral in Blackmoor. All the forces in the community place him outside his family. If he is not one of the few bona fide family heads, one who is disabled but receives compensation or a pensioner, he is one who meets his family by appointment. He keeps this appointment only after the time when the caseworker would be checking to see if his wife is keeping him or another man in the apartment. He is a man who has access to the home but can assume the role of

* Only seventeen families had a father at the head of household.

husband and father only on a part-time basis. The father stands outside and watches the state feed his children, sees his wife go to work when he cannot get a job, and cannot stay close enough to defend his family if something happens to it. He comes home after dark to be told that the sleeping baby needs shoes or that his son wants to attend a father-and-son dinner. He reads about what others say he needs and listens to others talk about his apathy or action. He has no job, no money, no power, and no influence; but he has all the ingredients to compound his frustration. So at day's end, the father in Blackmoor goes home to play house.

In homes where there are male spouses, the mothers in the families perform the traditional tasks of homemaking even if they are employed outside the home.* They never expect the men to do housework, go shopping, make clinic visits, and perform other such tasks. Few such duties are mutually assumed. In like manner, women who have husbands are never expected to do "a man's work" unless they live alone. Accompany a family to the laundromat and you will see this clearly defined division of labor. A project woman may be escorted to the laundry by her spouse, who will carry the bundle; however, she will expect no further assistance. While the mother washes the clothes, the father will read a magazine, leave the building, or hold a conversation with other males who are following the same pattern.

The ideal husband in the project environment is expected to be, as much as possible, a provider, sex partner, and protector. The father in the project is expected to be worldly, not in academic and intellectual profundity but in ways to beat "the man" —that is, "the system," his employer, or any other white or black man who he feels is of higher status and class than himself. If he fails in any one of these areas, he loses status in the family and environment. He is seldom viewed as an emotional, loving, and understanding individual who may have the same needs and require the same support as a woman. A man seems to get respect when he exhibits physical prowess and is impervious to the emotional binges that may characterize female behavior.

* For a more complete discussion of attitudes of task expectancies, see John A. Williams' *Sissie* (1963).

He develops a philosophy that compensates for whatever loss in status and self-esteem his behavior has incurred and thereby avoids becoming submerged in society's built-in moral conflicts.

SIBLINGS' ROLE

Children in the disadvantaged family are exceedingly close. The closer together siblings are chronologically, the more they seem to assume responsibility for each other. Seven- and eight-year-olds can be seen caring for a preschool or kindergarten child, as is most discernible at school. At the noon hour, and during recess, the young protectors watch over their brothers and sisters in the kindergarten and can be seen braiding hair, fastening clothes, and tying their shoes. One of the best and most accurate ways to observe such relationships in a disadvantaged setting such as the one studied is to watch an older child protect a younger sibling who is being intimidated by some other aggressive child. Such an aggressor will, without doubt, incur the wrath of a young protector.

Mothers expect older children to assume responsibility for younger children. There appears to be little or no resentment from the older siblings for being shackled with such a responsibility. The older children often show more concern for the smaller child than the mother shows. Some mothers in Blackmoor seem somewhat ambivalent toward their children and do not employ the resources and talents with which they should be distinctively and instinctively qualified. It is often said in Blackmoor that "Mothers bear children, but children raise them."

Few sibling rivalries exist in the disadvantaged home, because no one child appears to receive a monopoly of parental love, time, or praise. Expediency in the housing project tends to prevent much of the sibling rivalry that sometimes characterizes more privileged children. Early emancipation from the parents seems to be another factor that tends to influence closer sibling relationships, and mutual security is still another variable that appears to contribute to desirable interaction between brothers and sisters. Finally, the cultural framework, to some degree, must provide the matrixes out of which disadvantaged siblings develop their close relationships. None of the young children questioned felt that caring for his younger brothers and sisters was an imposition. However, one teen-ager in five felt that caring for his younger brothers and sisters was a burden.

DISCIPLINE AND MANNERS

Children in the family are not intimidated and threatened with the withdrawal or the withholding of parental love as punishment. When mothers in Blackmoor were asked if they ever told a child that they would not love him if he misbehaved or was disobedient, nine out of ten said no. They further related that they simply whipped the child when he did wrong. During the interview with these mothers, the same question repeatedly occurred: "What does loving or not loving him have to do with punishing him?" As one mother summed up, "The little scamp would probably laugh in my face and think that he had put something over on me if I told him I wouldn't love him any more if he didn't be good. Then I *would* have to crucify him."

Love is not questioned in the disadvantaged family. It simply goes with membership in the family. It is not an essential tool consciously used in the rearing of children, as it appears to be in the middle class. Although the withholding of love may be a more sophisticated approach, from a psychological point of view it has a much more deleterious effect upon the personality of the young child.

Ghetto parents do not tolerate insolence or tantrums from children until the children are too large to punish physically. The child learns early that crying cannot be used as an instrumental function to obtain certain rewards. He may, more often than not, incur wrath, hostility, and physical punishment rather than sympathy, reward, and fulfillment.

One of the ways adults control children in this community is with the use of force. When they threaten punitive measures against the child, they never break the promise. They use force. Some mothers carry a worn ironing cord in their purses and are always ready when a child misbehaves. And mothers do not isolate themselves when they punish children. Whether in the presence of a minister or principal, in a supermarket or a crowded department store, the parents reprimand their children wherever the misdeeds are perpetrated. They claim no embarrassment and do not construe their behavior as being undignified. One mother said:

> As long as I feed him, I don't plan to use no psychology. I going to use this [ironing cord]! . . . and when he gets too big to whip he can get out and feed hisself. So why should I be embarrassed about where I make him mind. I'd be more embarrassed about standing up in front of some judge somewhere begging him not to put him where his oldest brother is. When I was a child I got whippings and they didn't hurt me. Everybody in the neighborhood got on you, the teacher, the principal, the neighbors, and a lot of other people who you didn't even know.

Project mothers do, however, seem inconsistent in their discipline. At one time, they may be very harsh and inflexible. At other times, the children run wild without direction or punishment.

Children in the family learn early that they may be punished by several members of the family: the right of the mother, of course, is unquestioned; however, she shares this power with the grandmother and other children. The power is then shared in descending order. It is indeed common to see a teen-ager responsible for an eight- or nine-year-old child in Blackmoor who, correspondingly, has almost complete responsibility for rearing a preschool sibling, including physical punishment. In like manner, it is common on the playground, at school, or adjacent to the project for a primary school child or preschooler to inform his older sibling of aggression toward him by another child instead of informing the teacher or his parent. The sibling acting as protector will avenge the transgression against the smaller child. The behavior of disadvantaged siblings transcends paradox. The same older child who takes his little brother's ice cream would become extremely hostile to anyone else who perpetrated the same behavior.

The punitive behavior of deprived children is the modus operandi in this culture. The children employ force with their own siblings, and they use it with other children. Some 87 percent of the parents use corporal punishment as a punitive measure. It would seem to follow that the children *learn to use force, live with force,* and *respect force.*

In the housing project environment there is a marked absence of the spontaneous, intimate friendliness characteristic of a warmer home environment. Many people move away, and there are frequent evictions. It is a mobile community, and few families really get to know each other. No one cares about who you are and where you are going, but everyone knows something about you. When families come to live in Blackmoor, its members must quickly find peers who have similar interests and cultivate their friendships. For the preschool child, these are children with whom he can play. For the older child, the cultivation of friends is for survival and safety. The children make these judgments and decisions. Parents in the slum culture take little part in the selection and approval of the friends of their children, nor do they have much influence in the choices that their children make. Only twelve mothers related that they tried to seek out the children of desirable families. Seventy-four of the parents did not know the children with whom their own children played, and fourteen only *thought* they knew their children's playmates. Ten knew the families of their children's friends well enough to visit them. In cases where children do not know the parents of their peers and parents do not know the peers of their children, this condition can be regrettable for both parents and children.

Parents never know where they can find the friends of their children when an emergency arises. There are many cases where this lack of information has proven to be detrimental to the health and well-being of one or more members of a family. To illustrate: Allen and his good friend, whom he knew only by the name of Bubbles, were inseparable. Both were nine years of age. Neither had ever visited the home or knew the parents of the other. One day Allen was severely bitten by a dog belonging to Bubbles. At least the dog always followed and responded to Bubbles' commands. Allen ran home while his friend attempted to control the dog. Later at the hospital the police and health authorities wanted to locate the animal to make a test in order to determine whether or not the dog was rabid. Failure to find the dog would result in Allen having to take a series of extremely painful shots as a precaution against the possibility of his having contracted rabies. Neither Allen nor his mother could provide the authorities with the full name, address, or phone number of Allen's friend. Since no dogs were allowed in the housing project, the management was not obliged to even consider going through the files of 11,000 people looking for a boy whose name they only knew as "Bubbles."

After Allen had taken the shots and was released from the hospital it was discovered that Bubbles' real name was Phillip Washington and that he lived with his mother in a project building one street away. It was later determined that Phillip's father who lived a few blocks from the housing project kept the dog and the animal had been properly vaccinated and licensed. There was some good to come out of this incident: Since it is common for project children and other children to only be known by their nick-names, the management began recording their nick-names on their files.

In middle-class homes, the evening meal has traditionally been a kind of clearing house where a diversity of stimuli are presented and the child can extract certain samples of his environment for further investigation. In the ghetto, however, the dinner table is not a communication center where each member of the family contributes and exchanges his own ideas and experiences. Little in the mainstream of culture is transmitted to the disadvantaged at mealtime.

Good manners and other social amenities are practically non-existent in the housing project. Although the family is very verbal, the language that is used and the number and kinds of words used at the table are not the kinds for which children are rewarded.

The semantic conditions that exist in the disadvantaged family provide few stimuli for linguistic development. The disadvantaged child must learn most of the acceptable communication skills and social behaviors on his own or after he goes to school. Even his older school-age siblings, who theoretically know some of the appropriate behaviors, know that such behaviors, in reality, will not "work" in his home. For example, a ghetto child would not forgo taking the last piece of meat on the platter, because there may not be anything else until the next meal and then there may not be any meat. The child in the project is *here and now* oriented. Mealtime in Blackmoor is simply what it implies, a time when one cares for his nutritional needs by consuming as much food as he can as quickly as possible. It is not a time to try to develop his social graces. The next meal is frequently too uncertain.

A FAMILY OF UNCERTAINTY

The family in Blackmoor is one in which uncertainty abounds; parents and children alike live a hand-to-mouth existence. The family is frequently without enough food or money to plan from one meal to the next. Eighty-nine of the family heads found it necessary to go to the grocery store at least once daily—in some cases, several times. Many mothers and children agreed that children left home in the morning without assurance that there would be dinner when they returned in the evening.

This uncertainty in the family is seen everywhere. In some households where there are fathers, other members of the family never know what to expect when he is away from home. There are always persistent questions: Is he coming home for dinner? Will he still be employed? Will he be intoxicated? Has he been picked up by the police? Will there be an argument? Such are the conditions in Blackmoor that do little to provide stable family relationships or a feeling of security.

A minister who works in the project comments:

People here aren't secure. I know that they go around with the façade of being callous, but few human beings are really like that. People need to be able to plan and dream. They can't just go along in this constant limbo of not knowing where they're going, what they are going to eat, wondering what new adversity will affect their lives each day, what new ingenuity will be necessary for them to make it through the day. They don't worry about getting sick because they can't afford it; they can't worry about dying because death gives respite. Under the circumstances how can we expect them to function at a human level? Certainly we can't expect them to be secure. Actually they live in a kind of withdrawal.

Even the preschooler learns early never to count on what is not in hand. Unlike his more privileged counterpart, the promise of reward is not enough. The child has experienced far too many disappointments to accept readily verbal promises. He also learns not to postpone gratification. Of the fifty-three five-year-old children included in the study, thirty-nine did not believe in Santa Claus. Disadvantaged children seem to learn never to expect too much; then they can be pleasantly surprised.

In addition to the uncertainty, there is an air of irregularity in the family in the housing project. Children stay up very late or until they fall asleep. Only eight families had established routines about mealtimes, bedtime, grooming, and recreation. Thirty-four of the mothers said that they had established plans to handle meals and bedtime but they had no routine or plan for recreation or bathing. Children are expected to handle these situations themselves. It is not surprising for a schoolteacher to find a child who has not combed his hair. He may not have a comb, or, being left to his own devices, he simply has forgotten. Parents seldom inspect the grooming of the children. Such things as teeth, ears, and neck are never checked in the morning. Children come to breakfast without washing. Some 63 percent of the children had never owned toothbrushes. In most cases the same bath towel was used by the entire household.

Several factors contribute to the habits of irregularity observed in Blackmoor's families, especially in the behavior of many children. Children are left alone a great deal, and peer-group activities are influential in the patterns of behavior evolved in the children. Numerous children are free to roam the project area during the day and early evening, and 118 preschoolers found playing in the project area were questioned, 21 of whom were a part of the sampling. The inquiry revealed that approximately one-fourth of the children were "locked out" while the mother worked. They and their siblings were expected to shift for themselves. Few of them had adequate food. None had adequate supervision. A total of 61 were locked out while the mother took care of some business; older children were expected to keep an eye on the younger ones. The remaining children were—as well as could be determined—those who were "in the way" of teen-age siblings who wanted to entertain boyfriends while the parents were away. The children were not on the play areas. They were found playing in elevators, on landings and stairways, in the washrooms, and in buildings other than their own. Many of them used the recreation and administration building as a kind of refuge because it was air conditioned and had an ice cold fountain—two luxuries not in abundance in a housing project in the month of August.

Because of the power of the ghetto forces, project parents generally yield much of their influence to the peer group of the child. This contributes to the early emergence of his independence. The common attitudes of his parents sometimes seem surprisingly cold. In spite of what appears to be emotional and social distance, parents, when their children are threatened or are the recipients of aggression, strike out with a vengeance— usually without thought, without good reason, and without all the facts. They strike out with violence and bring to bear all their pent-up hostilities on the situation. They are not discriminating about the chronological age, status, class, race, or position of the person they attack. The parents' behavior is parallel to their inconsistent punishment practices; that is, the parent may do nothing or he may exaggerate the incident all out of proportion.

THE FAMILY: A SOURCE OF PROTECTION AND SECURITY

The disadvantaged family is close. It is large, noisy, ungrammatical, and economically insufficient. Nevertheless, it provides protection for its members and minimizes the conditions that produce excessive competitiveness. It understands, accepts, and helps those members who make mistakes. For example, a girl who becomes pregnant without the benefit of marriage is not sent abroad; the pregnancy is rarely aborted; at birth the infant is not offered for adoption, nor is the girl disinherited. People who suggest such activities only accrue the hostility and contempt of the disadvantaged group. In the sample 96 percent of the mothers said that they would be embarrassed if a daughter became pregnant but none would subscribe to the suggestions previously mentioned. There were, in fact, three pregnancies among the daughters of the ninety-six mothers responding. Rarely does the family put undue pressure on the boy involved. They insist that the infant belongs to them and not to the boy's family. Kenneth Clark (1965) calls this "total acceptance of the child." He goes on to say:

> In the ghetto, the meaning of the illegitimate child is not ultimate disgrace. There is not the demand for abortion or for surrender of the child that one finds in more privileged communities. In the middle class, the disgrace of illegitimacy is tied to personal and family aspirations. In lower-class families, on the other hand, the girl loses only some of her already limited options by having an illegitimate child; she is not going to make a "better marriage" or improve her economic and social status either way. On the contrary, a child is a symbol of the fact that she is a woman, and she may gain from having something of her own. Nor is the boy who fathers an illegitimate child going to lose, for where is he going? The path to any higher status seems closed to him in any case.

The attitude of the disadvantaged family is one of helping each other. A mother in this subculture would not give a second thought to sending a child or children to a relative to be cared for, especially if the relative lived in a rural area. This would not necessarily be true if the relative lived in an urban area. A relative of a housing project tenant can move in at any time. Although there are rules that govern the length of time a guest may remain in the project apartment, the family involved, as well as the neighbors, is usually successful in preventing the management from securing this information. Children are trained never to reveal such information. There are few "grapevines" superior to those found in a public housing project for circumventing the management.

Quite apparently, then, the disadvantaged family is an intrabulwark against the outer society. This, of course, is for its protection. It can maintain itself because of the attitudes, values, and behaviors embraced by both the members of the family and the subculture. Economic and social imperatives force the deprived family to remain in this position. In like manner, the family, in turn, cannot provide the disadvantaged child with the knowledge, tools, and experience that will bring about a social metamorphosis in his development and orientation toward society.

VI - Masculinity Without Status

A MAN AIN'T SUPPOSED TO CRY*

*How can you have any pride? I'm a part-time worker—a
part-time husband. I guess I'm really a part-time man.
I can't find enough to do to keep food on the table. Guess
some people would think that I'm the sorriest man that
ever wore out shoe leather. It ain't that I don't have no
get-up, it's just that I can't find nothing to do. I had to
leave home so the children could eat. While I'm sitting
here with you, they're out looking for me. That ain't so
bad—what really hurts is that my wife is going to tell
them people down at the welfare that some other man
is the baby's daddy or else she thinks she can't get no aid.
If they take her off the welfare she'll starve. So every
time she has another baby she gives a different guy's
name—excuse me for bawling, man, I just can't help
it—but it sure ain't no justice when a man's got to make
his own children bastards in order to feed
them.* —Man, age thirty-nine*

*Help yourself? Is that what you said, baby—help yourself?
I went to that Office of Economic Opportunity and tried
to tell them that the poor people who lived in the ghetto
needed to work in the poverty program because they
understood the problems of the people. I ask you who
else could understand a soul brother better than another
one? But one of them young Ph.D.s sat across his long*

* "A Man Ain't Supposed to Cry" is the title of one of the "soul" recordings
that have been played by ghetto residents for years.

*mahogany table with too much power and too many
henchmen and started running it down to me about
being poor. All I could do was look at him—sitting there
zipped up in his white skin, flashing his big class ring of
1965, and brushing lint from his $150 vine [suit].
Maybe the stud was all of twenty-five. He leaned back
in his big leather chair and as he relaxed on the poverty
gravy train, he told me about public welfare and how
the poor live. He said I needed a degree to do the kind of
work I wanted to do in the poverty program and that
the proposal I sent in wouldn't be funded because it
wasn't written well enough.*

*As I watched this young college boy and his four assistants,
I got mad. But, baby, I wanted to laugh. Anybody could
see that he wasn't too swift and his helpers were just
like him. There sat $60,000 worth of college-trained
personnel to deal with one high school graduate. Can you
imagine that $60,000 worth of employees who don't know
their asses from a hole in the ground running it down to
me about living with the poor? That young white boy
talked about poverty like he invented it. All the time I'm
sitting there in the middle of my wardrobe, fumbling with
this scar from a rat bite on my cheek. Somebody needs
to wise him up. He's still reading the script and I have
already been through the first two acts. I just couldn't take
any more and I stood up and said, as loud as I could, "Go
to hell!" And before they got over the shock I said it
again. That young "so and so" with all of his Harvard
education couldn't survive three weeks where I've lived all
my life. The stupid bastard don't know—he is because I
ain't.*—Former recreation worker, age twenty-four

You just can't win.

*Every time I try to get a job they ask me how much did
I go to school. Son—going to school for me was something
you done in season. First you went to school in August,
then you was out of school during cotton chopping and
cotton picking season. You was back in again until planting
and plowing season, then you was out again.*

*I never went to school all total five months connected
together in my life. Even the little ones had to tote their
own load. They couldn't go to school because the big*

ones had to work and couldn't take them. Besides—we
had to walk eight miles to school—it was easier not to go.
Nobody seemed to care then. It really didn't matter until
they started using machines on the land.

Still they always telling us that we need to do something
for ourself. They say we always want something for
nothing. "Pick yourself up by the bootstrap" they say—
but it's like that Martin King fellow says, "How you going
to pick yourself up by the bootstrap if you ain't never had
no shoes?" They always talk about what we done to the
city by crowding it, breaking the law, being on relief,
and all that—but what is the city done for us? The
city don't do no more for my children than it did for me,
and I been here thirty years. You'd think they'd learn
something by now. When I come here, I didn't know
nothing about no city living and nobody told me about it.
No matter what people say we try to help
ourself.— Former tenant farmer, age fifty-six

The anguished pleas of the Negro male in his quest for identity
and pride have echoed down through the decades. This search
for himself has been documented by historian, novelist, poet,
and dramatist. Both the scholar and the man on the street know
about the problem, and it is now being distilled from its psychological jargon. From Alexis de Tocqueville (1956 ed.) to Whitney
Young (1964), men have penned their observations of the
Negro male's struggle for identity. James Baldwin (1963a)
writes about it passionately and with caustic bitterness; Abram
Kardiner and Lionel Ovesey (1962) record it clinically; E.
Franklin Frazier (1962) ruthlessly strips away the middle-
class Negro's façade and exposes the male's feeling of inferiority;
Stokely Carmichael (1967) sees it as a part of the black man's
ineffectiveness in politics; and Kenneth B. Clark (1965) sees
this problem of identity in all facets of social needs: in education,
in economics, in politics, and in racial integration. The black
male himself, affluent and impoverished, now recognizes the
problem. It started below the Mason-Dixon line, where the
slave quarters on the plantations were the hothouses for breeding
human beings. And the law was used to deprive the black male
of his manhood. In the North, the castration was more subtle,

but it was complete. The black male in Blackmoor is a contemporary of his grandfather and is heir to this legacy of male castration. As a result, after a hundred years, he is still the man called "boy." He left his homeland by force, the plantation by edict, and his family for welfare. He is still on the move.

The average male in Blackmoor is one or two generations from the soil. He thought when he left the hen houses, hog pens, and backbreaking toil in the fields and brought his family to the North that he was finished with poverty. He discovered, however, that in lieu of his chicken feed, slop, and barnyard feces, he has roaches, rats, and no work. Conditions in the North forced him to break up the family he had brought with him intact. After being forced (economically) to live apart from his family, he soon discovered that he had exchanged a grim past for a debasing future. This is certainly true in Midwest City.

THE MALE DILEMMA
IN THE DISADVANTAGED CULTURE

The newspapers and other news media in Midwest City label the acute absence of adult males in Blackmoor and the concomitant behavior and conditions that encompass this absence as the "male crisis" or the "masculinity crisis." Such labels seem to be misnomers. A crisis usually denotes an acute condition within a relatively short time interval; moreover, a turning point is implied, the culmination of which is always adjustment or exhaustion. This is not true of a dilemma. A dilemma is a choice between two alternatives and cannot necessarily be terminated with dispatch. Here the "male dilemma" lies not in the lack of males present in the lower-class home but in the predicament of the male who, when illegally present, dares not openly assume true responsibility of the masculine role in the family.

In thirty states law prohibits the presence of the male spouse in the home where the mother is a recipient of aid to dependent children unless he is physically and/or mentally incapacitated. If the unemployed father in Blackmoor is at home, therefore, his family is denied welfare aid; if he leaves home, not only can he not function as the father but a warrant for his arrest may be issued for desertion. State law dictates that the authorities (office of the district attorney and so on) must be informed if there is a father alive who has deserted the home. Actually, mothers rarely initiate such an action. This attitude can be summed up in this statement of a mother facing such a situation:

> Why should I fat-mouth on him? Don't see how putting him in the workhouse will help us. All it does is give him a record. Then he can't never get no job. If they wants to put him in jail, let them find him. I ain't going to fat-mouth on him. Why should I make his life harder just to make their job easier?

Thus, the father encounters a dilemma. If he stays home, his family may starve and be evicted; if he leaves home, he cannot provide a consistent male model for his children, and he goes to jail if he is caught. He is devoid of desirable alternatives. The mother has the same dilemma, although not to the same degree.

The absence of the father in the home in this environment has a net worth of $43 per month each to his wife and first child and $24 per month for each additional child. The children must be under the age of eighteen. Unfortunately, but practically, the father is often evaluated not in the human terms to which he is entitled but in terms of the dollars and cents that his absence earns. He is an exile by consent without the immunity that the sanctuary of exile sometimes provides. He is well aware of his own shortcomings as well as the prevailing social inequities.

Children who live in such families and homes do not perceive the father as the breadwinner. They have very few, if any, opportunities to see the father in the various roles that society has traditionally assigned to him. They know him as a "backdoor companion" to the mother and an absentee father. He does not represent the mountain of strength and security that characterizes "fatherness."

Twenty-three of the preschool children included in this study whose mothers received aid to dependent children did not know the identity of their fathers, although, in some cases, he slept in the home every night. In those cases, he came home after the preschool children were asleep and left before they had awakened in the morning.

We don't really have to worry about getting caught by welfare people—they work banker's hours. They are always trying to get rapport or whats-a-never it is. That's the stuff that telegraphs every move they make. Every kid in the place warns you that they're coming. They're never here during the swing shift.

The father who made the preceding statement was known to the six- and seven-year-old children who saw him as the mother's "boyfriend." Older children knew better; however, they are not normally informed until they are old enough not to reveal the information to the "wrong source" or authority.

In some cases, the father is employed, but the constant threat of unemployment prevents his taking the active, legal, and appropriate position as head of the household. The threads of a socioeconomic dilemma are woven herein. Should the father in the disadvantaged home take his rightful position and become a full-time father to his children and a person of personal worth or should he continue to submerge his personality, disregard his integrity, and risk his mental health for economic expediency? It is difficult to make the judgment. When living with the disadvantaged, one learns early that many of the judgments of the more affluent classes about the poor are based on standards of behavior and values that could hardly apply in Blackmoor.

THE INFLUENCE OF THE MALE DILEMMA

The mother in Blackmoor sometimes has several children by as many men. Each child in such a family unit may bear a different family name, and such a family composition can create extreme traumatic experiences for children. On some occasions, the respective fathers of different children may have access to the same household. The relationship of each father to the mother and to his own child can provide tension and conflict in the family.

It is also somewhat common to see several preschool children within the same family who do not suffer the same degree of deprivation. For example, the father of one child, who is not the father of other children in the family, may provide adequately for his own child's care. The provision is often with the stipulation that his child, and only his child, receive the benefit. Consequently, one child in the family may have experiences provided by his own father that other children in the family with a different father do not enjoy.

> I don't mind looking after my child—he's mine—but I ain't going sponsor nobody else's. Would you? Once last winter I came here and Jay [his son] was running around in his socks while one of the other kids wore his shoes to kindergarten. Now, how would you feel? You know some fellows don't bring their kid nothing—but I ain't like that; I never miss a week. I don't always care about the little money I put here, but when she takes Jay's things and lets the other kids wear them out—that's it! Jay ain't got no aid but them other kids that live here do.

The mother says:

> I know Leo [Jay's father] don't want me to take Jay's things and let the other children use them, but what can I do? He's got everything and the rest don't have nothing. After all, they protect Jay and look after him, so I have to do what I think is best. I have to love them all. Leo seemed to think the other children were all right when I was going with him. Besides, I got to teach Jay to share like I teach the other children.

Clearly the mother faces a dilemma. The condition is most discernible on such special occasions as birthdays and Christmas. One child in the family may receive gifts for these occasions while other children in the same family are deprived of the same kinds of experiences. Families were observed where one child in the family had pajamas, robes, a raincoat, and other clothing while other children in the same family had never possessed such items. In terms of desirable family relationships, the mother and children inevitably experience conflict. Children who observe this plurality sometimes view it as the preference of the mother for one of their half-siblings. Jealousies are evoked. The attitude of the more fortunate child is sometimes one of superiority and arrogance. Therefore, he is frequently the object of aggression. One family was found in which two fathers were almost in open competition. Each father provided for his individual child, while four other children in the same family, whose fathers were not so generous, were practically destitute. The mother of this latter family reports:

> I almost wish none of their fathers did nothing for the children. When Walter and Norman's fathers bring them things it only makes it bad for the rest of the kids. They want nice things, too—especially the girls. I don't get no aid for Walter and Norman and I can't retire on the twenty-four dollars apiece I get for the other four every month.

The male deficit is noticed in the lack of father-son (or-daughter) activities. Young children do not have bedtime stories read or told to them by the father, and the children are not kissed goodnight by him. Only two respondents reported the father doing these things. Twelve mothers reported that they performed the task of reading bedtime stories to the children. Usually, school-age siblings accept this responsibility. Fathers rarely bathe or dress the younger children or perform any of the tasks that exhibit emotional warmth.

In this housing project, half of the male children under five years of age had never been to the barber shop with the father. Nine out of ten had never been to a circus or a similar extravaganza. Less than 1 percent of the school children had accompanied the father to a movie theater, although many had attended the drive-in movies. More than 60 percent of the preschoolers had never been on an outing with the father. Whereas baseball appears to be the most popular spectator sport among the lower-class adult males in this housing project, only six boys (21%) between the ages of twelve and sixteen had ever attended a baseball game with the male parent, and only three of the fourth-grade boys (8%) (age nine to ten) had accompanied him to a baseball game. The three younger boys were siblings of two of the older boys mentioned above. None of the preschool boys was reported to have been taken to watch any spectator sport.

Disadvantaged children are not oblivious to the absence of the father in the home, nor are they insensitive to the experiential value of a father image. The forty-one fourth-grade siblings of the respondents were asked, "What one thing do you think would make you happiest?" Only 6 percent said money. Some 38 percent related some material object. The remainder indicated in various ways the desire to have the entire family unit together. Because the father in most cases was missing, his return was implied by this response. More than half of the junior high school siblings revealed this same desire. All the mothers who were household heads felt that a father who could assume this function adequately would not only stabilize the home economically but would add a positive force to the desirable growth and development of the children.

Mothers say:

You need a man in the house when you try to raise children. Even animals keep a mate.

Any kind of man is better than no man in the house. Boys need a father—girls too, but especially boys.

In spite of all the arguing, fussing, drinking, and fighting that goes on sometimes, a house without a father is worser.

When I was a child in the country, we didn't have much either—none of the folks I growed up with did—but we all had a father.

THE BLACK BOY: A SPECIAL CASE OF
FATHER-SON RELATIONSHIP

The black boy in the disadvantaged urban culture seems to manifest extreme difficulty in developing a positive relationship to the father. He often views his father as an individual with a low-status job who does not exemplify the culturally projected image of the fathers he views on television or sees in his textbooks. He constantly sees his father as an object of derision and indifference and not as a desirable figure to emulate. Perceiving his mother in an essential role in the home and his father as one who cannot adequately assume his position, the black boy sometimes develops a kind of role blur that makes nebulous his perception of what his own role should be:

All we hear about is how important a father is, about going to church together—but that don't mean us. My daddy says the bosses on his job call him boy and he's forty-five years old. My mamma can make more money than he can. He gets so mad that sometimes I don't see him for weeks. I don't know what they want you to say when people ask you, "Don't you want to be like your daddy?" *I don't know what he's like.*

This condition plays havoc with good emotional adjustment.

Recognizing the boy's dilemma and his own, a father in Blackmoor sometimes is extremely harsh to the mother and children. He seems to feel that such behavior will provide him with a position of stature. He attempts to demand respect from the family instead of earning it. The mother sometimes presents the absentee father with the welfare check and lets him pay the bills or purchase the food. Such activity at least allows him some measure of status and face saving.

You can't make a man feel like a dog all the time and expect him to do the good things other men do. Sometimes he's mean and nasty to me and the children, but I know he's sad inside. Always after he's mean he goes into the bathroom and stays a long time. His eyes are always red when he comes out.

The mother in the case above was a good amateur psychologist. She understood her husband's plight, behavior, and temporary withdrawal. In *Crisis in Black and White* (1964), Charles Silberman highlights this situation further:

To survive the blows to his ego and potency, the Negro must erect a number of defenses. The most common is withdrawal. Low self-esteem quite naturally produces a fear of failure in any new or un-familiar situation: school, job, marriage. But if you do not involve yourself in the task in the first place, you can excuse your failure very easily: you failed because you did not try, not because you were incompetent; if you had really cared, you could have succeeded. This tendency to withdraw affects not just the Negro's capacity to compete but his ability to relate to other people. Negro men have much greater difficulty than white men playing the usual male role. Partly because of prejudice, partly because of their own lack of education and training, they have difficulty finding work that will enable them to support their families. The result, inevitably, is a feeling of shame and failure. But the man's ego is too frail to withstand any further blows; to avoid hating himself still more, he turns his hatred against his family, or simply cuts off any feelings for them at all.

Kenneth Clark (1965) pursues this same situation:

Negro boys had the additional problem of finding no strong male father figure upon which to model their own behavior, perhaps one of the reasons for the prevalent idea among marginal Negroes that it is not masculine to sustain a stable father or husband relationship with a woman. Many young men establish temporary liaisons with a number of different women with no responsibility toward any. Among Negro teen-agers the cult of going steady has never had the vogue it seems to have among white teen-agers; security for Negroes is found not in a relationship modeled after a stable family—for they have seen little of this in their own lives—but upon the relationship they observed in their own home: unstable and temporary liaisons. The marginal young Negro male tends to identify his masculinity with the number of girls he can attract. The high incidence of illegitimacy among Negro young people reflects this pervasive fact. In this compensatory distortion of the male image, masculinity is, therefore, equated with alleged sexual prowess.

The father is told constantly by the dominant culture to improve his lot, to pick himself up by his bootstrap, and to know that he can do better if he wants to. His problem: he has forgotten how to "want to."

LACK OF MALE MOTIVATION

In the housing project, a family without an adult male member is deprived of some of the common experiences helpful to the growing boy. Few boys in the project environment learn to use such a common tool as a hammer correctly or to manipulate a screwdriver. They have little opportunity, except in the upper elementary grades, to use most of the other common household tools that characterize the male stereotype. No boy in the group discussed here, regardless of his chronological age, had been taught by the father how to build such things as a playhouse or how to fly a kite, to build a skate truck, or a push car. Unmotivated, boys in the public housing projects do not use their natural skill to prepare themselves for adjustment in society. They do not see the simple behaviors in the home that theoretically separate maleness from its antithesis.

Forced Masculinity

The disadvantaged boy lives under conditions of sparse masculinity. He is surrounded and dominated by females at home, taught (in most cases) by females at school, and consistently subjected to the influence of the female role. Yet few cases of effeminate proclivities and homosexual activities in disadvantaged boys are discovered. Any boy displaying feminine mannerisms in this environment incurs extreme hostility among other boys in the peer group. Boys here respect physical prowess; those who fail to exhibit it encounter not only disrespect but physical aggression. One mother said:

> We want to make men out of our boys but we don't have nobody to teach them how to be except what they learn in the streets. If you want him to be a Boy Scout, you gotta have a fortune in the bank just to buy the uniform; and they want men to volunteer to help them. If we had men to volunteer to work with the boys, we wouldn't need the Boy Scouts. But the streets do a pretty good job keeping them from being sissies.

Peer-group pressure, at least, controls overt homosexual expressions in disadvantaged boys, even if it does not prevent them.

The behavior of the disadvantaged child, as with all children, is culturally defined. It follows that there are certain expectations—family group and environmental—that the child must live up to and, in turn, demand and expect from others. Most of the habits of the disadvantaged child are developed and controlled at first by the family; however, the peer group takes over early and then holds a much tighter control and influence over him than the family. Fathers and older male siblings are sometimes extremely mean to preschool and preadolescent boys. Such behavior is designed to prevent the younger boys from becoming "punks" (effeminate boys).

"We don't want no punks around here," an eight-year-old boy told another boy about his age whom he was collaring. An adult relates: "They [effeminate boys] will last around here about as long as you-know-what in a wind storm. These kids will wipe up the ground with them."

An upset mother explains: "Carl worries me. All he wants to do is play with his sisters' dolls and play house. Every time he leaves the house the other children jump on him. I guess they know he won't fight back."

The problem of masculinity is persistent.

Adults and teen-age males in the family apply pressure to the younger boys in the family in the form of dares and threats. Rarely is direct physical aggression used to accomplish this particular task unless the child is a crybaby. The threat of aggression is usually enough. However, the peer group applies direct pressure and always uses physical aggression. Blackmoor's environment dictates that young boys must be physically strong and almost emotionally detached from many of the more sentimental responses that appear to characterize middle-class boys of comparable ages. Little children are taught by older children to be realistic and vindictive. If a large child takes something from a smaller child, the smaller child must learn to imitate the same behavior. All the techniques employed by disadvantaged boys have the same objective: the development of masculine behavior, conceived primarily in terms of aggression and detachment from emotionality.

Neither all boys in Blackmoor nor their fathers are physically adept. Here, like everywhere, some boys prefer to read books or visit museums rather than play football or break windows. Nevertheless, they must live in this subculture. If they follow their own desires, they incur if not the wrath certainly the lack of approval of the peer group. If they follow the dictates of the peer group, they experience inner conflict. This becomes another one of the ever present conflicts in the disadvantaged community. Many men attempt to eliminate conflict by speaking the vernacular of the street and the prose of a profession—whichever is appropriate.

The Double Standard and the Disadvantaged Male

The adult male in the housing project is constantly subjected to a double standard of evaluation employed for identical behavior he observes in others. This double standard is first and poignantly noticeable in its semantics. A man from the deprived culture who steals is labeled a thief; if a bank president steals, he is called an embezzler. Similarly, if the male project dweller has a mistress in the ghetto, she is designated a prostitute; if his middle-class counterpart has a mistress residing in a fashionable area, she is classified a call-girl or a companion. Three essential differences emerge: who it is, where it is, and what it costs.

The black male in Blackmoor has learned that to be considered for employment, he cannot be merely as good at his skill as his white counterpart; he knows that he must be better. He knows that he must pay more for his possessions and be satisfied with less. He is aware that if he commits a crime against society he will be severely punished while other more "significant" individuals go unpunished or receive minimal punishment. As one resident noted, "It seems like it's all right when rich people do wrong if they got a good lawyer."

The lower-class male constantly observes persons of local and national prominence who exhibit the same behavior that is attributed to him without the accompanying loss of status. The double standard is operative and the dilemma is never terminated.

Similarly, the disadvantaged male must resolve the conflict that exists between the expected behavior patterns of society and conformity to the standards of his subculture. There are some project fathers who do not drink, gamble, or neglect their families. They represent the rebels or nonconformists in this subculture and are part of the "respectables" described in Chapter III. Many other males envision themselves representing such a position, but few exhibit the strength of character and internal motivation that enables them to achieve this goal. The approved patterns of behavior transmitted to them by the community permit them to disregard, without loss of status, the desirable behavior of the larger society. However, they know what the behavior should be. Consequently, they can vacillate between the two alternatives, rarely developing the skill that would enable them to adapt to both social situations. Society expects one behavior from the disadvantaged male; his peer group and subculture expect another. He, of course, must choose:

> This is where I live. You can't wallow with pigs and look like a prince. It's plain enough to me—if you lay down with dogs, you get up with fleas. Most of us are forced to live with our heads in the garbage can; naturally we smell like garbage—but some people expect us to come up smelling like roses.

The prevalence of conflict for the male in the disadvantaged environment is indicated by his acceptance of antisocial behavior. Men who do not possess sufficient education or skill to earn a living have two alternatives. They can beg or steal. The former is not acceptable to lower-class men and the latter is norm-violating behavior. Stealing, however, appears to have some therapeutic value in the disadvantaged culture. Stealing provides an opportunity for men to show their rancor for the larger society; it enables the male to satisfy his need for excitement; and it provides a temporary satisfaction for some physical deficit or economic lack. However wrong the act of stealing is, it gives the disadvantaged male a sense of dignity. It is one of the few times when he feels that he has beat "the system." When asked about the alternative of begging or stealing, a man answers:

> Begging or stealing—that's a choice? That's like asking a man do he want to get killed or would he rather die. If you can't work, you got to do one or the other. Let's look at it in another kind of way. When you beg for the heart fund, or TB, or something like that— that kind of begging has dignity and respectability. They don't even call it the same thing—they call it charity. I can't get no job. If I go out and beg, folks would think I'm strong and healthy enough

to be out working and would look at me and treat me like I'm dirt. At least you can hold your head up when you steal—even if you get caught. You'd rather not have to beg or steal.

Such conflict is rarely resolved. It tends to extend and deepen with time. Where there is bitterness and hostility accompanying conflict, it can encompass other individuals. For example, few men in the deprived culture who become involved in criminal activity work alone. They tend to work in pairs or groups. Most of the unskilled and unemployed males encounter the same conflict; they have the same bitterness toward society and employ the same hostile behavior. Therefore, it is relatively easy to recruit an accomplice in crime. To put this more succinctly, one never has a rival in hating—only in loving.

Often the attempts to correct or rehabilitate some of Blackmoor's residents are met with resistance. Fallaciously the task is begun by trying to change the behavior of the persons involved without first attempting to understand it. The means to improve the economic conditions that surround the disadvantaged individual are not always available—so society preaches morality. Whereas improved behavior is desirable, the techniques employed to bring it about need critical examination: "Preach to the ones who keep us this way. Maybe I do need to change, but they do, too. I'll tell the grocery man that the Lord loves a giver—maybe he won't charge me for my meat and bread."

A hungry man doesn't listen to the preacher and he stops thinking in terms of right and wrong: "Damn right and wrong. I'm trying to feed my family and I'm gonna do it any way I can. If that means stealing—I'll steal; and believe me, buddy, I've learned how."

The male in Blackmoor wants to survive, but he wants to maintain his dignity in the process. He often knows his deficit but he resents others who tell him what he should do or be: "They're always tellin' us what we want or need, like we ain't got sense enough to know."

Certain behaviors seem to follow a normal progression. Theoretically, a man who has better job security will eat better. He will dress better and will provide for his children. He will begin to compare his home with that of others. As his economic conditions improve, there is usually a corresponding change in his attitude, values and behavior. Some respondents noted:

> *During the war we lived good. We had plenty of food, nice clothes, and we really started to get ahead. Even after the war we did good; at one time we had a car. We started buying a house; then I started losing one job after another. Every time they cut back, they cut me out. I don't think the same way any more.* —Man, age fifty-five

Put money in my pocket by letting me work. I'll put food on the table, clothes on our backs and find a decent place to live. These damn projects ain't no place to live. Just do that, let me work. I'll do the rest. —Busboy, age thirty-four

> *One reason you get so many separations [broken homes] is because there ain't enough bread [money]. You gotta have bread; once you get that you can hold your head up—then, food and clothes, a good house and all that jazz just follows.* —Janitor, age twenty-two

Get me a gig [job] that pays a decent wage and I'll put food on the table and shoes on their feet. —Man, age twenty-three

> *I don't belong down here. I'm not use to living in filth. I guess you got to do what you can. It wasn't that way when my husband was working steady. Now Herbert just don't seem to care any more.* —Nurse's aid, age thirty-seven

I ain't had a hustle [job] in nine months and you talking about how I feel. I feel like I want something besides beans on the table, a $6 secondhand coat, and my wife working while I take care of the kids. —Man, unemployed, age forty-two

> *Money in the bank ain't good if you can't never let it stay there. Ain't no use in taking it down there if you gotta keep taking it right back out. We don't never have enough to buy the things we need.* —Mother of five, age twenty-nine

The above statements indicate that changes are initiated by the individual himself when he has the means. When he needs assistance he will seek it. Because our society usually accepts the acquisition of material objects as a legitimate criterion for success, the more the deprived individual can accumulate, the more likely the social distance between himself and the larger culture is narrowed.

Many of the techniques that society has initiated to combat poverty and deplorable living conditions among slum dwellers in large urban areas have become cures worse than the disease. Urban renewal is a case in point. In most cases, it represents two things: Either it is the exchange of horizontal sprawling ghettos replete with human congestion for vertical ones that in many ways are worse or the black people in the slum are displaced and the slums torn down; when new structures are built, the blacks who were removed cannot afford to live in them. This is what John A. Williams, in his book *This Is My Country Too* (1964), calls "the old story of urban renewal."

There is little doubt that the physical structure of housing projects is better and is more in keeping with the minimum standards of decency and is more functional; however, the physical structure was the only change. The standards, values, attitudes, and behaviors of the tentative inhabitants apparently were not considered in the planning, as one project resident noted: "People who build hog pens know about people better than the bastards who built this place."

Men who live in high-rise public housing resent being told how long their house guests can remain, having their homes inspected, and having the paint on the walls chosen for them, regardless of the reasons that may support these rules. Few men readily accept the regulations governing their households that they themselves did not formulate or, at least, help to formulate. Men in the disadvantaged culture believe that "resident advisers," "project commission" and other such titles are nothing but fancy terms to cover up snooping or deceit: "They're about as useful as tits on a water moccasin—and just as deadly."

Most behavior is a reflection of the environment in which the individual is placed. An impoverished environment restricts the growth of "good" behavior, and a more affluent environment stimulates good conduct. All about him the disadvantaged male observes how the community evaluates him. He goes to the corner or neighborhood store, where he is treated as an urban sharecropper. The common social amenities used in the transaction of business such as "Mr.," "thank you," and "sir," are almost nonexistent unless they are called to the attention of the proprietor.

The emptiness of the Negro male image is ever present at home, where he works, where he shops, and with the people he meets outside of his immediate group. Traditionally, the home and family have been a refuge in times of adversity. Such a tradition does not characterize the sanctuary of the disadvantaged "project male": "My house ain't my castle. It's more like my cesspool. I ain't important to nobody—here or any place else. The rest ain't worth crying over."

This male is frequently absent from the home for too long a time to establish relationships that provide comfort. Adversity for him is not temporal but habitual. To the degree that environment determines behavior, his behavior is appropriately exemplified in the environment where he operates. However, he is also judged by a larger environment. The incompatibility of the two is the source of his conflict. If one directs his attention specifically to the man in Blackmoor, he finds that the "project male" represents a unique typology.

THE "PROJECT MALE"

There appear to be four basic types of adult males in this housing project, whose labels here are assigned by the author for the purpose of delineation. Type 1 is the *paternal transient*. He is married and is the legal father of the children in the family, but because the family is the recipient of aid to dependent children, he cannot legally reside in the home. Type 2, the *employed resident,* is also married and the father of the children in the family. His earnings are high enough to support the family but low enough that the family qualifies for residence in the project. Type 3 is the *"free floater."* He is not married. He attempts to use society in general and the project community in particular. In this latter case, he tries to prey on the unmarried or the deserted recipient of ADC. Seldom employed, he prefers unemployment to hard or dirty work. For this reason, his "jobs" are frequently criminal in nature. Type 4 is the *handicapped resident*. He may be married or single, and he may or may not have children. He may previously have been in one of the other classifications of males who live in the project. The handicapped resident is unique in that he is the only adult "project male" who can legally reside in this community while unemployed and receiving some type of welfare assistance. Of these types, 2 and 4 are the only legally authorized tenants. All welfare assistance is immediately terminated if 1 and 3 are found in the project.

Type 1: The Paternal Transient

On an application blank, the paternal transient will circle "unemployed." In reality, however, this resident works harder and under poorer conditions than most other urban dwellers. In the lives of his children, he comes and goes, because he must constantly elude the welfare authorities and project management. He does not even dare acknowledge his paternity if he meets his child on the street, lest he risk loss of the life-sustaining, hated, "crippling" ADC check. He's "home" from dusk till dawn. Daylight hours never reveal his presence in the project community. He works at odd jobs when he can find them. His lack of marketable skills, his membership in a minority group, and his lack of education work against him to the point that he cannot support his family without outside help. He recognizes his inadequacy, and, because of it, he sometimes comes to resent the social agency—usually the state division of social welfare— that is trying to help his family. He and the members of his family often view the welfare worker as an adversary to be outwitted. No information is volunteered, and questions are answered in monosyllables for fear of betraying the father's presence in the home. Sometimes information is withheld that, if known, could enable the agency to give more help. On the other hand, "Those people don't care about us; all they care about is *eligibility;* that all they talk about is eligibility. I don't know what it means to them, but to us it means how many reasons can be found for not helping us."

Because criteria of eligibility for welfare apply primarily to women and children in the family, the male must adjust his existence to fit the situation. The life of the paternal transient is a hard and consuming one. He leaves his family just before dawn, and each new day presents the almost insurmountable task of survival. He misses the morning affection and minor family disturbances that are encountered by other husbands and fathers. He loves his wife and children, but this very love sends him out before they are astir. Lingering sentimentally could cost him a job that a less emotional man in his community might get. He leaves.

The transient is a walker. He buys heavy shoes because some days he may cover as much as twenty miles, walking to save bus fare. If he knows that he has a job for the day, he may ride. On the other hand, he never invests bus fare on a mere possibility. He cannot risk the futile expenditure of even this small amount: "It's this way, son, a long time ago a fellow name E-sop said, 'Don't chance what you got for what you might get.' "

Early morning finds the transient making his rounds of the small merchants in the neighborhood. He goes to the grocery store first, looking for trash to empty, floors to sweep, or any other work he can do. If the grocer doesn't need him, he waits there for the produce truck and tries to get the job of unloading it. Many taverns in the area do not hire regular janitors. The proprietors simply wait for persons such as the paternal transient and barter for his services. He may be offered $2 to mop the floor, wash the windows, clean the toilet, fill the beverage coolers, and stack the empty beer and soft drink cases. He returns to the larger taverns in late afternoon and repeats these services, having in the interim worked at several other odd jobs. Thus, some tavern owners get janitorial service for as little as $12 or $14 a week, and they can even get it for less if they are willing to risk the ineptness of a wino. Consequently, in terms of a minimum wage, the worker is grossly underpaid, but the "project male" has become so accustomed to exploitation that he expects it.

This odd-job man eats on the run. He purchases a loaf of

bread and some cheap lunch meat and eats in an available doorway, at the home of a friend, at the poolroom (the only sanctuary left "for men only" in this community), or on the bed of a parked pickup truck. Not infrequently, he purchases a hot meal from a small neighborhood restaurant. He eats heavy meals. Because of the nature of his work, such items as legumes are the mainstay of his diet. This was the diet of his forefathers, and he appropriately calls it "soul food,"* fulfilling the quotation he has always heard: "Food to keep body and soul together." There are times when this worker will exchange his labor for food. At other times, he purchases pigs' feet, a pig's snoot, or a Polish sausage sandwich from a sidewalk vendor. Whatever the food, he eats it on the run.

Midday never finds the transient standing still. He walks across town to a residential area looking for lawns to mow, basements to clean, cars to wash and wax, or a service station that may have automobile tires to repair. Sometimes a transient develops steady customers. He is only competing against himself and the proceeds of the preceding day. If formerly a union worker, he still hangs around the union hall and pays his dues. He cannot run the risk of getting a call to work and being ineligible, so he proudly and conspicuously displays his union button. If he has been a construction worker, habit and the possibility of employment draw him to excavations and new construction projects. Although this worker will not invest in bus fare, he buys a newspaper every day. He must be aware of any jobs available that he can do. He can and will do almost anything to make a few dollars. Because of the nature of his employment, he does not venture too far during bad weather. Yet because he must leave home, he may spend inclement days at the employment office, the bus depot, or the tavern. Usually, however, his day ends only when everything closes down. He goes home too late and too tired to enjoy his family, looking and smelling like what he is—a man who has worked hard.

To the casual observer, the paternal transient has an odd sense of pride and a peculiar sense of values. He would rather

_____
* This term is frequently and jokingly called "culture food" by more sophisticated Negroes.

"hustle" day by day than accept a $30-a-week job except during the winter months, when he must readjust his habits. This transient's mathematics tells him that although some days may be lean, on the average he can make more "hustling" than on a steady salary. He will not hesitate to clean a toilet but will resist any attempt to make him into a male nurse. Emptying bedpans and ministering to the sick is "woman's work." He sees the need to buy his wife a new dress but will not allow his money to be spent for a girdle—"Who sees it or knows you got it on?" He bathes but seldom buys or uses deodorants. He drinks beer only when he cannot buy the most expensive brand of whiskey— it's a matter of status in the project community. Although absent most of the daylight hours, he makes decisions in his home; and in this way, he can still hold his head up to some degree. He still demands, "Squaw walk behind brave."

Unemployment is not the transient's paramount fear. He is afraid of arrest. Usually dirty after working or looking for work all day and having no visible means of support, he is often arrested on suspicion, although he may or may not be jailed. The paternal transient commits few crimes. Nevertheless, he may have a record of numerous arrests. Indeed, a transient who has *never* committed a crime may have a police record. Upon being arrested, if he has allegedly deserted his family and this fact is discovered, he is detained. This situation creates a further hardship for his family. It follows that the transient attempts to avoid arrest at all cost.

One cannot say that the paternal transient is irreligious. He can better be characterized as being indifferent to religion, or at least passively religious. He cannot accompany his family to church, so he rarely attends. In fact, he has lost the churchgoing habit. Besides, Sunday is his only day of rest. He can quote the Scriptures because he heard them as a child. Yet he is not an avid Bible reader, and one is not likely to find a small catechism on his person. In this matter he is not unlike many other Americans of contrasting social strata. The transient will give his children dimes to put in their Sunday school envelopes, but he will not put a dime in a blind man's cup unless he knows him. In the transient's life, each man bears his own misfortunes. He fears the Deity and shows respect and reverence for places of worship.

The paternal transient knows from experience the value of education. Although he takes a passive role in the lives of his children, he wants them to get an education. He admonishes them to heed the advice of their teachers. He uses himself as testimony against failure to do so. He is not intellectually competent to provide much educational guidance, but he encourages them. His arrival and departure times are such that he does not have an opportunity to play his father role actively. He retires as soon as he reaches home. In many cases the older children may not be at home. Usually the mother must see that the homework is done, sign the report card, attend the PTA meetings, and visit the child's teacher. No father is in the home "officially." So while the paternal transient respects and values education, he gives the appearance of indifference to it. His children are hurt most by his absence because most project children follow the educational pattern of their parents.

The paternal transient is quite worldly compared with members of his family. He knows about revolving doors, mechanized parking lots, power mowers, dishwashers, and electric mixers. All these items are foreign to his children, and some of them may never have been used by his wife. Although he buys a newspaper to check the want ads in the morning, he seldom has it at the end of the day. For obvious reasons, he is not a registered voter, but he may be on a man-to-man basis with his committeeman or drink beer with his precinct captain. His wife may never know these persons. On the other hand, he never knows the minister, social worker, and school personnel who deal with the children. His bank is the pawnshop, but his wife never accompanies him there. He has seen the interiors of modern skyscrapers, and the sculptured lawns in the subdivisions are often his handiwork. Many of the jobs that he secures, particularly in the area of domestic service, are through referrals. Consequently, he has opportunity to meet many people in varying fields of endeavor. He knows the city, but his preschool children may never have crossed the boundaries of the project where they live. He has chauffeured families and driven trucks, but in some cases his children have never ridden in an automobile. He has window-shopped at the downtown stores and used the bus and train depots as places of refuge in inclement weather. He knows how to survive. That he is a jack-of-all-trades is more than a cliché; he has mastered most. He is a true sophisticate of urban life. Yet his children, for the most part, are naïve. He imparts little worldliness to them. They live under the same roof, but they are largely their mother's concern and their lives are her domain. He does not always know what they think and feel; they are equally ignorant about him.

Nevertheless, the paternal transient seems to be an optimist. He can be described in this way because he leaves home each day never knowing what it will bring in terms of employment. Yet he believes in himself, and his approach to each day is one of faith in kismet. He does not necessarily believe in the American dream, but he holds enough of its vision to feel that he will make it. He drinks, smokes, cheats, and lies enough to hold the respect of the male members of his subculture, but he also recognizes some responsibilities and virtues. There is a new emphasis on pride in the black community and he now has a positive sense of group identification, but he does not seem to feel self-conscious when a member of his group gets into trouble. He is realistic enough to know that he cannot disavow his membership in the group. He is willing to accept an inferior or submissive role for economic expediency. This does not mean that he capitulates totally.

The transient sympathizes with the Negro revolution but is frightened by the riots taking place all over the country. Still, the new militancy of younger Negroes gives him a sense of pride. He does not have the time to devote to sit-ins and other types of protests, nor is his name likely to be found on the roster of civil rights or militant groups. He would never admit it publicly, but he lives vicariously through the words of Huey Newton, Ron Karenga, and Eldridge Cleaver when they "tell it like it is." Some of the goals of some civil rights groups are not his goals. For example, eating in the best restaurants or getting the best public accommodations are goals that are inevitably denied him because of his financial status. He is likely to show more interest in the batting average of Willie Mays than the next speaking engagement of a civil rights leader.

There are times when the paternal transient encounters difficulty. He is unsuccessful in his quest for employment, or he is not as resourceful as he might be. When he has exerted all effort and goes home to a wife who may be hostile and indifferent or who fails to understand the stress he is under, he may take refuge in liquor. After a while, even this depressant is not a sufficient opiate. Then he uses what seems to him his only defense. He stays away from home. At first, he may stay away part of the night; later, the whole night; then, several days. Finally, he does not return at all. He truly becomes a deserter.

There is another paternal transient. He refuses to accept responsibility but he does not desert. He may find enough employment to provide for himself and will use the income on drinking and gambling. He goes home drunk without funds or with few funds to assist in the care of his family. The wife usually takes him in, but his life at home can become a "living hell."

The transient lives life as best he can, considering his circumstances, and respects it enough never to contemplate suicide. His day of pleasure is either Friday or Saturday night, sometimes both. He can go to the tavern with the express aim of getting drunk and does not have to fear social disapproval from his peers. The fights that frequently erupt in the taverns are soon forgotten. If the results are tragic, more is the pity. Life is difficult for him, but he "asks no quarter and gives none." He is wise because he must be and shrewd because he has to be. He does not worry too much about death and tends to be more physically fit at the age of fifty than more affluent men are at thirty-five. Illness seems almost foreign to him. He cannot afford the time or the money to be ill. He ignores minor discomforts that may be forewarnings of more serious illness. As a result, when he does break down, he goes all the way from Type 1 to Type 4. He finally becomes an "authorized" resident of the project. Basically, however, he is an "unauthorized" resident, going his way, moving in and out of the lives of the members of his family, not legally sanctioned.

Type 2: The Employed Resident

The employed resident is an authorized resident of the project. His family is intact and he is not the recipient of any welfare assistance. This project male has few financial assets. There are really two distinctly individual types in this classification: the aggressive and the passive. The aggressive resident uses the project as a stepping stone to better things for himself and his family. He remains a "project male" only for the period of time that it takes him to secure "better" housing for his family. In the project studied he is usually holding a civil service or city job. His family lives in Blackmoor but is not "of" it. His home is a typical middle-class home though located in the project. His family has the morals and mores of the middle class rather than the lower and working classes. His children may play with the neighboring children, but they do not use the vulgar language or indulge in much of the sex play that is common in this project. So much that is degrading seems not to touch his family. What is taught in the home seems to have a good effect upon the children. As soon as possible, this father removes his family from the project. He leaves no mark on the project and it seems to leave little or no mark upon him and his family; they are almost transients for the period of their stay. The father plays his role as strongly as the father in any other section of urban life. His is the motivating drive. He sets goals, and he and his wife work together to attain them for the family. Because of his strength, his children never fall heir to the awful legacy of project dwellers. Because this aggressive resident follows the normal middle-class pattern, it is not necessary to delineate his behavior, attitudes, values, or outlook.

In contrast, the passive employed resident has a semiskilled job and could, conceivably, move upward in the class structure, too, but he lacks ambition. He is not competitive and appears to be content with the status quo. He neither seeks nor expects promotion on his job, but he hopes for it. Living in the project for him is an "end" in itself.

Frequently, the passive resident is one who married early and started a family that multiplied faster than his assets. His early marriage contributed to his interrupted education. Because of this and his lack of ambition, the job ceiling for him is just below the semiskilled class. This resident may be a dropout or a high school graduate. In some cases, he may have even attended college. However, for him the amount of his education is of no consequence. He feels trapped in menial employment.

Daybreak finds the passive employed resident getting up, breakfasting, and leaving for work. En route to the elevator he sidesteps myriad objects: toys, beer cans, and empty cartons on the landings. On the way to the bus stop he waves to other early passers-by, kicks an empty liquor bottle from his path, and encounters the same merchants as the paternal transient. However, the employed resident does not stop. He has a job.

He goes to work as a janitor, stock clerk, dishwasher. All the jobs that he secures are of the same caliber: unskilled, monotonous, routine, and vulnerable to extinction. He has many bosses: the department head, the foreman, the secretary, and the delivery boy.

During the noon hour, he eats lunch brought from home for economy's sake. While eating, he may window-shop or tune his inexpensive transistor radio to a local Negro disc jockey. If the employed resident is a young man, he may carry a paper-back novel in his pocket. Often he sits on the sidewalk or on crates in the stockroom and argues about sports, women, and politics.

At quitting time he may "moonlight" on essentially the same kind of job. He never has respite from the pressures of the time clock, the bus schedule, the finance company, his wife, and too many children. If he does not have a second job, he frequently stops by a neighborhood tavern on the way home; if he is well known, he is allowed to drink "on the cuff." Like the paternal transient, he goes home tired—but earlier. His day ends as routinely as it began. He arrives home, washes himself, and dines on the enduring legacies of starches, legumes, greens, and corn-bread. After dinner he has several choices: watching television, listening to his wife enumerate all the things they need that he knows they cannot buy, involving himself in the play antics of his children, or going to bed. Looking at his day in retrospect, he finds no feeling of accomplishment, no ray of hope, no pro-pensity toward wit or humor. He goes to bed as a defense. His impasse is highlighted when he says:

One day is pretty much like another. Nothing ever happens—not to me anyway. Other people get new things, go on vacations, get better jobs, and do things like that. Me? Man—I'm just here.

The passive employed resident can salvage some pride in the knowledge that he lives in a community of broken homes but his is intact. He resides in a milieu charged with excessive crime, but he is not a criminal; he abides among the unemployed, but he has a job. He accepts responsibility; many men cannot. Many illiterates inhabit his urban colony, but he is literate. At the tavern, patrons defer to his judgment. He buys and reads the newspaper, a behavior that isolates him from most of his neighbors. If he is a young man, he is as fashionable as his assets will permit. If, on the other hand, he is older, cleanliness is more important than style. He participates in some family activities and his children are usually in school. He points to another fact with pride: "If somebody in my family dies, we've got enough to bury him."

Both the passive and the aggressive employed resident are concerned with religion. They usually have church membership. Their children attend Sunday school, and the whole family may worship together. The families are not unlike many others in their churchgoing habits. The aggressive resident, as might be expected, takes a more active role in the church. Teaching Sunday school, accompanying children on outings, and accepting leadership in church organizations are activities that characterize him as a dynamic participant in church affairs. His children are instructed in some religious dogma; they say grace before meals and are taught to respect the minister and to show reverence for places of worship. The passive resident may take part in some of the same activities but rarely assumes a leadership role. He is not likely to be as regular in attendance as his more ambitious counterpart. For the most part, both residents are Protestants.

To the passive employed resident, life is not to be enjoyed or destroyed but endured. He believes in luck. He expects to succeed through some stroke of good fortune, not necessarily through his own effort. He knows life owes him nothing, but he feels it will give him something. The arrogance of youth and the fire of competition have deserted him. He expects too little of himself.

This resident has ambivalent feelings toward his family, perceiving it as a blessing and a burden. The ambivalence is unmistakable. He sees the joys that his family can bring but is distressed by trying to satisfy its needs adequately. This perception binds him in an approach-avoidance conflict. Like most men who suffer adversities, sometimes he feels obliged to grasp at some pleasure, such as drinking, as a remedy for despair and an opiate for his frustrated hopes. Because this behavior is inconsistent with his dubious income and his duty as a father, neglect of his family can be the penalty for his folly.

The employed resident plays his role more as a spectator than as a participant. Fear of losing the esteem that he has *where he is* prevents him from competing in the larger culture. He would rather be a lifelong marginal spectator than have the tensions and troubles of a contender. This is the pattern of his existence. He doesn't pour himself into life; he drips into it. He has the same bourgeois lust as others without the accompanying drive toward fulfillment.

Perhaps one can conclude that the essential difference between the two employed residents is that one resides in the housing project and dreams, while the other merely lives there. The latter has forgotten how to dream; perhaps he never learned.

Type 3: The "Free Floater"

The "free floater" is not a legal resident of the housing project. His name will never be found on a lease, *but he is there*. He neither has nor seeks employment. No job is good enough for him. His aim is to avoid work but to reap its rewards. His premise: collect from the world. He accepts responsibility only for himself.

The free floater is a guy with a trick, a get-rich-quick scheme on another's investment. One knows the type by different names: the gigolo, the slickster, the fast talker, the name-dropper. Reckless and contemptuous of authority, he is cruel, arrogant, irresponsible, and dangerous. This resident is not opposed to aggressive behavior or crime. Many people like to see him coming, for he is colorful, and he is missed when he leaves the neighborhood. He is always watching others to see if they are watching him. Charm is his only commodity and pleasure his only visible goal. He is able to manipulate people because he knows human nature, or, rather, human weakness. Lonely, frustrated women are recipients of his favors and endure his hostility. The hard-working, steady, inept "project male" (employed resident) accrues only his contempt. He hates discomfort and is not willing to delay any satisfaction. He is too busy scheming to be lonely, but he does become moody. Many see through him, but almost all are fascinated.

The free floater has acquired a good self-image. Unlike the passive employed resident, he is aggressive. Few people are important to him. He looks up only to the guy slicker than himself. He feels he is the greatest. Other people are to be used and tolerated, not respected and appreciated: "Man, don't tell me 'bout people. They don't mean a damn thing to me."

As fate often dictates, this urban sycophant is the one who can frequently get a good job. His dress and verbal acuity are likely to catch a prospective employer's eye. Yet he rejects employment. The ability to avoid work is an attribute among his peers. He brags about soft hands and clean fingernails: "Work is for suckers. I live by my wits."

The free floater is an optimist about himself; still, he is pessimistic about the world. A psychologist would probably suggest that he has a character disorder.

The free floater frequently lives with an indulgent mother, aunt, or grandmother. He sleeps late and arises only when he chooses. This illegal resident is one of the "night people" in the project. The older women in the home are slaves to his desire. He lives royally in the midst of poverty. Administering to his own appetites consumes his interests and energy. His day begins innocuously; most of it is spent getting ready for the evening. His breakfast is prepared about midmorning and, while he eats, he listens to his "box" (record player). He is an authority on contemporary "sounds" (jazz). His possessions must be of the best quality. For example, the record player must be the most expensive model. But he did not buy it. Someone whom he has long since abandoned may still be making payments on it.

As his day progresses, the free floater watches television. He attempts to keep abreast of what is going on. Similarly, he checks the latest record releases and practices the newest dance steps. There is a telephone available to him, one of the few straight lines in the neighborhood. A considerable amount of his time is spent making contacts for the evening. He constantly develops his technique for "confidencing" others.

This quasi-resident is a meticulous dresser and worships clothes. Accordingly, he spends a major portion of the afternoon preparing his apparel. Clothes, to him, are a visible measure of his success. His hair, which was likely to be processed* three or four years ago, may now be worn *au naturel*. His nails are manicured. To his peers, he is pretty to look at, but to some others, a fastidious misfit. Paradoxically, he is one of the few project males who can use cologne and not be considered effeminate. He can often be identified by his "shades" (dark glasses), which are worn even at night.

The free floater moves into the surrounding community. He knows the narcotics pusher, the prostitute, the wino, the burglar, and other slicksters like himself. He visits the billiards parlor, the cocktail lounge, and the barbershop and may pass the time of day with the pawnbroker. He eats his lunch at the home of an admirer and borrows from anyone who will lend. He is the only individual in the tavern who tips the barmaid. He knows the racketeers. Anything he wants—he knows where to get. The petty thieves and others in the community fill him in on which neighborhoods are ripe for burglary, who has gone to jail or has been released, and what public dances are planned. In the latter case, he knows women will be found at a public dance without an escort. From returned convicts he can gain important information.

This project dweller has no compunction about how he gets his money. He asks only that the means not be hard or dirty work. His audacity is amazing. He has been known to excuse himself from a party, commit a robbery, and return to the festivities and to have gone into the room where the wraps of guests have been placed and to have thrown the wraps out the window to a waiting accomplice. The free floater "cases" every home he visits in affluent neighborhoods. He may talk about his love of dogs in order to find out if his host has one. His motivation is personal gain. The inept individual who wanders into this project resi-

---

* Straightened by the use of chemicals and then finger-waved. The hair is then tied in place with a silk scarf.

dent's bailiwick is flirting with disaster. The free floater is watching the braggart who pays for his drink with a large bill or who freely makes change on request.

The free floater lives incognito. Few know where he hangs his hat. Messages for him are left at the tavern, barbershop, and newsstand. More often than not, he gives the address of a law-abiding relative. If required, he could not produce receipts for the items he owns. Therefore, he limits knowledge of his residence to a few chosen persons. He may have a girlfriend in the project and can be seen going in and out of her apartment. In reality, this may be an attempt to establish a façade or diversion that will hide where he actually lives.

After his afternoon of "briefing," the free floater returns home, more knowledgeable, if not wiser. He may take a nap or watch television. Later, he dominates the telephone. While talking, he maneuvers an invitation to dinner. It has been suggested that he is an asset to a party. Older women in his home wait on him hand and foot, much to the distaste of the older men in the house. Sometimes the slickster is forced to leave home as soon as he returns to escape the sharp tongue of a pensioner father or uncle who damns his idleness and who threatens to put him out. The women in the home will not allow such an alternative.

Nighttime finds the floater in pursuit of amour, visiting parties, and going to cocktail lounges. He is always "cool" but the life of the party. He "hits on" every woman who will listen, usually married ones. His rationale: she dare not tell, someone else is financially responsible for her, and her friendship will only be an affair, an interlude, another conquest for him. He feels sophisticated enough to outwit the husband. He postulates: "All husbands are stupid. They had to be stupid to get married."

Although the free floater will spend time with a "project mother" in his community, he will never escort her to a "nice" party among his more affluent social contacts. He may spend the night with an "old" conquest or part of the night with a married woman. In either case, she pays the bill.

Sometimes a part of the free floater's evening is spent in criminal activity. Except for burglaries, most of his crimes are not planned. Rather, an opportunity is presented and he takes advantage of it. This may run the gamut from acquiring another hustler for his stable (if he has one), to narcotics, to extortion. Anything for a buck. He may or may not go home at night. Often dawn finds him in an all-night restaurant. He has no responsibilities at home, no real reason to go there—unless he wants to change his clothes. Only time, involuntary confinement (prison), and dissipation shake him from his pinnacle.

The free floater never attends church. He spends Sunday in bed. He detests the loudness and rigor of spiritual singers and is uncomfortable in the provocative silence of the more dignified congregation. He does not have the intellectual sophistication to deny the existence of God; nevertheless, he seems to reject the pageantry and ceremony in the church as being meaningless. He is impatient with the behavior and verbalizations of older members of the family and their preoccupation with "going t' heaven." His life is here and now. He points out that the poorest people he knows are "foot patters and hand clappers." He feels that religion is for other people who need it. Not only does he not attend church, he would be one of the first to burglarize it if he felt there was something of tangible worth to be found there. Even the Sunday morning religious broadcasts irritate him.

> You can't get nothing decent on the radio on Sunday morning except some damn fool yelling sin and Amen. Some of the biggest "con" men I know are yelling, sweating, and leaning over the pulpit preaching to others about righteousness. If you go to one of them fancy churches, all they do is kneel a half a dozen times, have drinks, and go home. Church? Who needs it?

He is quick to point out that we have too many Sunday and holiday Christians.

> A lot of the people you don't ever see in church—until Christmas and Easter. A lot of others go through the whole week lying, cheating, and doing everything to people and then try to look pious on Sunday. They're nothing but a bunch of hypocrites. The preacher gets up and talks about all the things we are not supposed to do. Don't gamble, don't drink, don't do nothing. If you do, you're a sinner. But they don't pass the sinner by with the collection basket.

There is a church up the street that has a bookie joint in the back
and the pastor knows it; while they're raising hell up front, the book-
maker is quietly raking in the chips.

Everybody that's trying to beat somebody is found in church.
People go for status. They even hire professional fund raisers in
some of them. If people are supposed to be so righteous, you'd think
they wouldn't have to do that.*

This project male views education neither as a real need nor
as a panacea. He knows many with academic training who have
low incomes. They fail to impress him because they do not have
the ornaments that, to him, denote affluence: big cars and expensive clothes; nor do they give fancy parties. He considers
the time needed to get an education too long and the remunera-
tion too small. Most educated people he views with contempt;
he has been able to outwit most of them. He considers them
dull. The free floater would rather be head of a dope ring than
president of a university. He gives more credit to the "break" one
gets than to one's academic preparation. He values only educated individuals with money; and he uses education only as a
means of establishing contact with persons in the class hierarchies above him.

At a party, the free floater is likely to change the subject when
educational topics are discussed. One approach is to remind the
conversationalists that they are spoiling the party, talking intellectual shop, or guilty of snobbery. He suggests that education
may be all right, but "mother wit" (common sense) is more
important. The floater knows enough practical psychology not
to preach his contempt for education and the educated overtly.
He uses inference and other subtleties. The irony is that frequently he has more education than any other male resident in
the project, excluding the aggressive employed resident. It is
only when the free floater begins to age that he reevaluates
education.

At one time the free floater may have shared the American
dream that education is important and necessary in order to
move up the social and economic ladder. However, when he

*These extracts are a composite made from tapes by four free floaters. These
statements summarize candidly the free floater's attitude toward religion.

discovered that academic training was not the only requirement for getting ahead, he became disillusioned. Education would not open all doors to him, so he rejected it. He still does.

The resident has few involvements that tie him directly to education. He has no spouse, no children whose paternity he admits, no family responsibilities, no civic ties, no intellectual pursuits. Consequently, the common, everyday educational concerns that may touch the lives of most people are not a part of his life.

Type 4: The Handicapped Resident

The life of the handicapped resident does not have the drama and optimism of the paternal transient, the security and potential of the employed resident, or the glamour and deception of the free floater. This resident is one of the forgotten people in society. Hidden from the mainstream of culture and limited in contact with his own subculture, he is tolerated by some and ignored by others. Several conditions qualify him for residency and welfare assistance. Age sixty-five, a chronic illness, or a serious injury are criteria for legal tenancy. The deserter can now come home. He becomes, as a project resident, one of the human statistics who is characterized by poverty, isolation, illness, and fear. He finds little pleasure in books because he is undereducated, small comfort in friendships because most of his friends have either died or moved elsewhere or, like himself, live in anonymity, surrounded by the black ghettos of urban America. He is older than most male residents in the housing project.

Unlike the younger project or slum dweller, this resident has no corner society, no partners in crime, no stomach for rebellion. His appetites are simple, and he lives in a climate of withdrawal. The petty irritants that disturb younger men no longer evoke the same hostility in him. Material possessions and excessive entertainment are not his paramount pursuits.

The handicapped resident has few visitors. The social worker makes routine calls, an occasional insurance man chats with him, and if he is a member of a congregation, a parishioner may remember him and visit. His adult children, looking for a baby-sitter, come to see him and leave their children. He loves his grandchildren, but he neither has the patience nor the stamina to cope with their play antics. The handicapped resident knows he is being *used* by his children, but he prefers this exploitation to loneliness. This tenant rarely leaves his apartment. He lives looking out his window.

There is an atypical handicapped resident who is younger and who has more contact with the day-to-day world; he rarely lives alone. He is the young man who was wounded in military service, has a cardiac condition, or sustained a permanent injury in industry. Sometimes he is married and has a family intact. Generally, he has more education and can often be a part of the activities taking place in the home. He gets to know the people who come to see other members of his family. A younger handicapped resident ventures out—leaves the apartment and goes down to sit on the benches. He sees people come and go, talks to them, and plays with the children. He is both a resident and a participant in the project activities. Further description of this younger resident is not germane to a delineation of the representative Type 4 project male.

The elderly tenant arises early. Unless he is bedridden, no one greets him, prepares his meals, or administers to his other needs. He has no job or other outside responsibility. His task is to prepare a small meal for himself. After breakfast, he sits in his chair by the window. If he is situated on a lower floor, he waves to the paternal transient, the employed resident, and any other early riser that will respond to his greeting. If he fails to exercise this ordinary aggression, he simply sits and watches the events and dynamics that take place in this project society. He has no place to go, nothing to do, no appointments to keep. He sits; time is of little consequence. He leaves his place by the window only to eat or care for other natural needs or to escape the sun's glare and heat. Sometimes he stops a passer-by that he knows and asks him to read some correspondence or to fill out a form that he doesn't understand. He waits for the mailman, the tenant relations adviser, a member of the tenant council, and other persons in the project community who may help to blunt his loneliness. He says:

If it wasn't for the mailman and one or two other people, I'd go through the whole day and never talk to nobody. If I died in this room, it might be days before they found me. Old folks like me don't have nobody . . . nobody pays me any mind. One of my grandbabies said to me the other day, "Hush your mouth, grandpa! You don't know what you're talking about." He's just seven. I used to think that old people that had to live in the old folk's home was to be pitied. I don't feel that way no more; at least they got somebody to talk with.

The elderly male tenant attends to his priority of worries, his health, the arrival of the welfare check, the weather, the loss of his few possessions. He meets the postman on the day his check is due. Fear of robbery and an empty cupboard motivates him to pay his rent at once, then go to the nearest market to purchase food. Replenished, he returns to his vigil by the window. Except for his clinic appointment, seldom does he venture farther than the corner store.

Distinct from other project dwellers, the handicapped resident never misses his day at the public clinic. There he finds others like himself. He never complains about the waiting or the lack of courtesy from the clinic staff. There are people to talk to. Other patients reminisce with him, compare adversities, and share laughter. One finds an interesting contrast between the young and old in a public clinic. The old laugh and enjoy the opportunity to be with others and assume such minor responsibilities as minding a baby momentarily for a weary mother. The young, on the other hand, show impatience, become irritable, attend to their own needs, and express hostility. The clinic visit for the aged is truly therapeutic.

Inclement weather affects only the handicapped resident's physical comfort, never his routine:

I do the same things I do when the sun is shining. I can't remember the last time I walked in the rain. I ain't had a raincoat in years— my old joints couldn't take it no way. Funny thing about things like that—you don't appreciate them till you can't do them.

The handicapped resident is up early enough to see the paternal transient and late enough to glimpse the free floater. The hours in between are uneventful. The tools of idleness, solitaire, crocheting, knitting, and embroidering are usually diversions of the opposite sex. Sometimes this tenant occupies himself by reading the Bible—most of the aged handicapped claim this skill whether they are literate or not. On his infrequent trips to the barbershop, he has an opportunity to play checkers. Most of the time, he simply stays out of the way. He is so accustomed to the noise and daily chaos that false fire alarms, fights, and other types of melee do not hold his attention. Even the tragedies that he witnesses are common and a part of his day. He is more in search of a kind face than another bizarre incident.

> From this window you can see everything—fights, robberies, shootings—you name it, I done seen it. But you don't see much as the paper says. You see some nice people, too—don't you forget it! Most of them gotta be nice, otherwise with as many folks as live here it'd be like a war all the time.

A housing project never completely quiets down. As the pressures of idleness persist more and more, the handicapped resident goes to bed out of boredom or fatigue—perhaps both. "Lawd today."* He makes his final appeal.

When the handicapped resident needs assistance, he often tries to conceal the fact. He takes pride in his own proficiency and is embarrassed when he must prostitute himself as a ward of society. He introduces the social worker to his neighbor as a relative, to hide his dependency. The neighbor usually knows better but will not expose his little charade. He carries the deception even further; the offer of food from a sympathetic tenant may be declined, even when he is hungry. Money is accepted from people he knows with the explanation that he will "put it in church," and he confesses that he wears worn-out shoes because his good pair hurts his feet.

> It's hard to take handouts and save face. You offer to work for what you get, but you know you can't. Them that gives it know it, too. Then—God forgive me—you start lying. You say you ain't

---

* This term, indigenous to the black culture, particularly the aged and rural black, means comfort, resignation, surprise, an appeal to the ultimate authority.

hungry when your belly is touching your backbone. You lie about money and say it's for the church. Nobody questions that!

The handicapped resident's sense of pride also manifests itself in a different way. If he can read and write, he is proud of his literacy; and if he is considered a man of his word, this gives him pleasure. When his children are law-abiding, he exudes enthusiasm when he talks about them. Occasionally, they come to him for assistance; when he can give it, he is gratified.

Social security and old-age assistance afford this tenant a steady income that he does not perceive as charity.

When I draw social security I don't feel "shame" at all . . . Didn't I work for it? . . . All them ditches I dug, paid for it—cold mornings when my hands nearly froze, paid for it—my back aching on scorching summer days paid for it, and all them little paychecks paid for it. Shame? Naw, I ain't "shame"! What for?

Life is precious to the handicapped resident because he knows it is slipping away. He is preoccupied with death; much of his time is spent preparing for it, living a Christian life, acquiring religious trappings, purchasing burial insurance, and attending church regularly if his health will permit. He is increasingly concerned with life after death, although he is frightened by the prospect of dying. Nevertheless, he has ambivalent feelings about life. He struggles to hang on to life, but he knows that death would bring an end to his misery.

The handicapped resident's arrogance is now diluted, weakened by time, experience, maturity, and dependency. Every day is more important to him. Consequently, he attempts to live each day without antagonism toward another, through his presence, his deeds, or his words. The disregard for life and limb shown by the young disturbs him. He would rather be left alone than be victorious in an argument. If he complains, it is likely to be about his health, not his other adversities.

By contrast, when one observes the wives of the handicapped residents, he is immediately aware that the women exercise more alternatives in their activities than do the men. They are the regulars at church who are members of the church choir, ladies auxiliary, and usher board. They are the volunteers who nurse the communicants who are ill. Many of them still work as domestics in the suburban areas around the city. They work as babysitters for working mothers who live in the project and elsewhere. They visit with friends, sew, read, maintain flowerboxes, and find many other things to do with their time.

The women appear to be in better health (mentally and physically) than their spouses. They appear to be more optimistic and do not seem to be as preoccupied with themselves as the men. They are much more likely to be involved with their children and grandchildren. Like the men, however, they are afraid to come and go in the project, especially at night. They are also preoccupied with many of the same concerns as the male but, perhaps, not to the same degree.

VII - Room at the Top

Through boom and depression, the bleak economic facts of life remain the same for Blackmoor's tenants. More than 63 percent of the homes are without adult males who bring in income. Those tenants who do find work (male and female) work at menial tasks, for minimum or subminimum wages. The unemployment rate for the city's Negro population as a whole is about 12 percent, but Midwest City's housing authority says that the adult male unemployment rate in Blackmoor is over 40 percent. Every resident in the housing project has heard the reports and statistics about his economic plight and has stopped listening to them. He is more sensitive to his stomach, which tells him he is hungry. His baby's crying is the biting rhetoric that holds his attention. His empty hands clenched in his empty pockets tell him he has no money for adequate shelter or decent clothes or health service.

The lack of employment and its consequence, the lack of money, is the problem of major magnitude in the disadvantaged home. This home is characterized not only by financial deficit due to insufficient income but also by a lack of skill to increase the income. Moreover, employment opportunities for the disadvantaged are fragmentary and tentative. If there is room at the top in employment, the tenants in the housing project know that it is not intended for the rank and file, which they represent. Most of Blackmoor's tenants are denied access to

---

* Class motto: THERE IS ALWAYS ROOM AT THE TOP—Tuskegee Institute, Class of 1886.

employment because of inadequate skill, social stigma, and racism, with all its attentive inequities (discrimination in hiring, bigotry, denial of entrance into labor unions and apprenticeship programs, crippling schools that do not offer adequate training). These are the reasons why tenants have come to regard the pronouncements of the alleged room at the top as being inundated in hypocrisy.

The traditional idealism of honor in poverty has been refuted by today's needs of poor people. Poverty and pride in contemporary society have been assessed by Blackmoor's residents as two separate entities—one, primarily physical; the other, primarily emotional—and they see little reward for having them coexist. The economic inequities encountered by the disadvantaged wage earner in the housing project are never corrected. Many things about Blackmoor describe the economic frustrations of the people. The fact that a person lives in the housing project in the first place reveals that he is a person whose income falls within certain limits. Only 12 households in 1,700 earn as much as $7,000. In the sample of the 100 families used in this book, only one family had an annual income of more than $3,999 (see Table 6).

Table 6. Income of 100 Sample Families

Income	Number
Under $1,000	1
$1,000–$1,999	32
$2,000–$2,999	46
$3,000–$3,999	20
$4,000–$4,999	1
$5,000 and over	0

Families have very small incomes in Blackmoor. Fifty-five of the households had no earning power; they were recipients of aid to dependent children. In no case did any family's income exceed an annual salary of $4,600. The total number of children reported in these families numbered as many as fifteen and as few as two. In view of the income limitations and the family size, the poor economic conditions that prevail in most families create situations that make desirable adjustment in the family and society a monumental task and survival a difficult and uncertain goal. Dorothy Rogers (1962) contends, "Economic frustrations have serious detrimental effects upon personalities of adults and children." These frustrations often destroy rather than strengthen character and appear to have a particularly deleterious effect upon the black father as a wage earner.

THE FATHER AS A WAGE EARNER

The father in the disadvantaged home is usually a sporadic wage earner. Possessing few skills, he is forced to take whatever kind of employment is available to him. In the labor market, he is expendable. He is never in a position to bargain. The few skills that he has to market have long since reached the point of diminishing returns in the technological stream of our culture.

Historically, the Negro male has not been the source of complete support of his family. There have been working wives in these families for generations. As Maurice R. Davis (1949) noted, "Negro working-class women always hold the purse strings. Ill-paid and irregularly employed, the masses of Negro men have not succeeded in becoming steady providers for their families . . . Negro women are actually or potentially economically independent."

Lack of adequate employment is one of the many sources of psychological stress for the father in the slum culture. This father rarely establishes or maintains a position of respect in the family; furthermore, he seldom becomes a good model for his children, especially the boys, and finally, his stimulus value seems so low that his own ego structure is in constant jeopardy. Israel Woronoff (1962) summarizes these observations effectively:

> The husband, if present, is often an ineffective family leader. The boy growing up in a Negro family frequently perceives his father with a low-status job, who is regarded with indifference or varying degrees of hostility by members of the outgroup. In short, the lower-class Negro adult male is seldom regarded as a worth-while masculine model for the boy to emulate.
>
> This problem of identification with a sound male model is of the

utmost importance to a male youngster. Emotionally the boy who grows up surrounded and dominated by women readily develops a sense of role confusion which is often crippling. Such a youngster has problems of handling aggression, making decisions, accepting responsibility, and executing leadership, in addition to syndromes of neurotic behavior (i.e., panic, extreme self-centeredness, hypochondriasis, irritability, depression).

A strong back and a willingness to work are no longer adequate criteria for employment for culturally disadvantaged males; skill is also necessary. Most men in the ghetto are willing to do almost anything, but they are without skill. There are some men in this housing project who work from day to day when they can find work. They can frequently be seen distributing handbills, working on coal trucks, unloading produce, and "junking" (selling rags, glass, bones, and paper). They work as janitors, dishwashers, and shoeshine boys.

Many of the traditional jobs done by unskilled men are now gone. Midwest City has not kept pace with other urban communities of its size in industrial expansion or in attracting new industry—and thus new jobs—into the area. In fact, there has been a decline in the textile, apparel, stockyard, and warehousing industries in the Midwest City community. These were the industries that were low paying and labor intensive and required relatively unskilled workers. It was to these industries that historically, immigrants and other minorities initially tended to attach themselves. The demand for unskilled labor has been declining in the inner city, while the size of the work force has increased. The suburban communities surround Midwest City like a white collar around a dirty neck. Unlike the city, the suburbs have experienced a rapid expansion in transportation, electrical, chemical, and service industries. The skills required in the *growth industries* and the amount of training necessary are considerably higher than in the *declining industries*. There are, however, some job opportunities for the unskilled and uneducated individual. The problem is that workers in the city have no way of getting from the inner city to the suburb. The cost of public transportation is such that the small salary that they could earn would become even smaller. (This condition exists in several major cities: Los Angeles, Chicago, and St. Louis.) Even when the unskilled do secure employment, it is frequently terminated after a few days, sometimes a few weeks, at most a few months. It is therefore understandable why a group of unemployed men sitting in a state employment agency made these remarks. One said:

> I'm the best hod carrier you can find—but who needs a hod carrier? I've been carrying hod since I was fifteen. I don't know how to do nothin' else.

Another, obviously trying to preserve his dignity, related:

> I set here day by day—I know I ain't going to get no job but I keep on coming and setting. _I have to keep going through the motions of being a man._

And another tried to explain or rationalize his lack of skill:

> I didn't get no education because I didn't need no education then— in Mississippi—what for? Down there they had more college-trained elevator operators than they did professors.

Still another said:

> I have been from one end of this city to the other—walking. I'm willing to do any kind of work. I'll do anything short of stealing, but it looks like I'm gonna have to do that.

The depth of another's feelings are characterized in this statement:

> I used to hate the alarm clock because I knowed I had to meet "the Man." Now it'd sound like Gabriel's horn. If I could just do it a week, so I'd know how it feels to get up and go to work again, to smell stinking, sweat and joke with other fellows, to draw down a paycheck. I'd rather hear the old lady fussing because I had spent part of the money on whiskey than to have her go along and just say nothing.

Only three of the husbands in the families surveyed reported knowledge of some special skill. Out of the three, one, a tailor, was actively engaged in his trade. Another, a baker, was employed as a cook; and the third, a mechanic, was employed as a janitor. The majority of the males in the families surveyed worked in some type of janitorial service. Five of the husbands were employed as day laborers in construction work. These workers *did not* live with their families. Their salaries were well over the limits set by the housing authority and thus would render their families unqualified for residency in public housing. The rationale for separate residency of the men was simple: it was better for the male to live away from home and let the family continue on the welfare rolls than it would be to go back home and have their families removed from the welfare rolls. The men knew that construction work for them was seasonal and unstable; therefore, they could not run the risk of being laid off and moving away from home again so that their families could receive relief. Four of the five did contribute significantly to the mother for the care of the children. These four fathers became transient or visiting fathers.

Many men physically withdraw from the home although they *have not* deserted their families. They exhibit all the behavior of the deserting husband, but they frequently leave by mutual agreement with the mother for the economic benefit of the entire family. The father will rarely be seen in the project community; nevertheless, he is "there." Although there are many women without husbands, there are fewer divorces among project residents than any other group in the city as a whole, and legal separation is seldom requested or authorized.

The social worker is often the only one who is expected to believe that the husband has deserted; and he knows better. He may also know that a man is employed and his family is still receiving welfare payments. He has heard the following type of statement many times.

> We don't desert our families—we hide. I probably spend more time with my family than a lot of other men. It was real hard at first for a man like me to see his family take handouts and couldn't do nothin' 'bout it. But then I learned how to act like I don't give a damn. That helped a little.

He has also heard the pragmatic view:

> Don't make no kinda sense to go running back home soon as you
> draw one paycheck. You know you ain't gonna be drawing it long.
> So, you better off to pay five bucks a week for a room somewhere
> and help your family out all you can while money is coming in.

Whereas some may consider some of this activity as having
really dishonest aspects, many men say that the economic practi-
cality dictates their behavior. Each male the author talked to
indicated that he would rather help provide for the family
the way he was doing it than have his wife be the lone breadwinner all the time.

THE MOTHER AS A WAGE EARNER

The mother in the disadvantaged home does not encounter the
same employment problems as the father. She can usually do
domestic work or "day work" if she has someone to care for her
children, although she usually expects her children to care for
themselves. In like manner, if she is without a husband, she
can apply and qualify for aid to dependent children. One young
mother's response to "Do you have difficulty finding employment?" was

> Naw, I don't have no trouble finding work—none of the women do.
> It's the men and boys that can't find nothing to do. Our only prob-
> lem is to find somebody to take care of the children.

An older, rather candid mother who "tells it like it is" explained:

> As long as folks are too lazy to clean up after themselves, I'll have
> a job. Have you ever heard of a status symbol? Well, I'm it. I heard
> Mrs. J. talking to a friend of hers on the phone and she was saying,
> "Well, darling, you know that we really can't afford her, but she's
> one of the status symbols that we all have to ad-here to." That _her_
> that they was talking about was me.

Numerous women in this environment work as waitresses, barmaids, hotel workers, and nurses' aides. These jobs provide more

than salary. The mother can frequently bring foodstuffs and other items home that will help her provide for her children. She is also in a better position to save her own money for her own entertainment. Her sex is also an important fact in her securing employment, because employers do not have to pay women the same salaries as men, although the women are frequently expected to do the same job.

The mother in Blackmoor who is compelled to work to augment her income seems frequently to encounter family disorganization. Robert C. Weaver calls the incidence of family disorganization to urbanization an indicator of social disorganization. This disorganization permeates the entire family. School-age siblings are expected to get their own meals and take care of the needs of the smaller children. Older children frequently do not attend school regularly but remain at home in the mother's absence to entertain friends in the apartment. An investigator in the project environment can pick almost any building at random and find groups of elementary school children and teen-agers assembled at some apartment during school hours playing the "soul sounds."

Disadvantaged preschool children get very little attention when the mother is employed. After work, parents rarely have the time or energy to provide desirable training and experience for the small children. Except in families where there was a grandmother, there were only nine cases where the female parent was employed and the children had a hot breakfast prepared for them. The parent who must report to work early frequently leaves her children in bed and expects the older ones to arise and care for the younger ones. Many older siblings perform this task well. Others neglect the small children. Many mothers recognize this problem. As one said:

You know, mister, it's really a matter of choosing; what I mean by that is, I've either got to go to work and feed them or stay home and watch them hungry. Some folks wouldn't even call that a choice. There is a lot of things I'd like to do for them and with them, but I got to depend on the big children to do it. You know how children are—they don't always do what you say. When you get right down to it—they ain't responsible for them. I just found out that when I go to work in the morning and leave money with my oldest daughter

to buy food and cook breakfast for the little children, she doesn't
do it. She has been giving the little kids a few cents and they have
been buying donuts, potato chips, and candy bars for breakfast
from them street peddlers and them little gyp stores up and down
the street in the neighborhood and eating on the way to school.

Mothers who have children too young to look after themselves
often leave them with relatives and friends while they work.
Others sometimes keep school-age siblings at home to care for
the children. One employed mother of ten rotated her children
as baby-sitters by keeping a different one home from school
each day to baby-sit with the three preschool children. No one
child was absent from school enough consecutive days to attract
the immediate attention of the welfare authorities.

There is little doubt that some working mothers in this environment neglect their children, for there is constant evidence
of this neglect. It is common to see preschool and some young
school-age children without socks and with shoes unlaced. One
observes the comedy of dress as he sees children with their
shoes on the wrong feet. This lack of attention would not, in
itself, be unusual for many preschool children. However, the fact
that some school-age children receive so little attention that they
reach school in this condition provides an example of neglect
and lack of parental supervision.

Items of clothing such as sweaters may be worn by children
until one side is filthy and then turned and worn on the reverse
side until they develop offensive odors. Some say that these
examples definitely indicate neglect. Parents say, however:

> When they ain't got no clothes—that ain't neglect. Have you ever
> tried to get six children out in the morning without a good suit of
> underwear among them? Half of them can't find their shoes. You
> need to wash every day with a family this big, but you got to wash
> when the schedule says—so if the children don't have changes of
> clothes, and you can't wash them they got every day, they just have
> to wear them.
>
> Lawd today! Here we go with that again! Expecting us to do with
> seven or eight what a lot of other folks can't do with one—and I
> leave mine at home to go there and help them with that one. I expect
> they would be in the same fix without a husband, with one bath-
> room, six kids, and poor. They probably couldn't do as well.

Many mothers apparently do not have the skill, know-how, or desire to develop routines and schedules designed to make their families function more effectively; yet some try. Others simply do not accept parental responsibility. The household tends to fall apart from lack of leadership and direction.

Although the mother in Blackmoor must assume many responsibilities that are not normally undertaken by a woman in a privileged home or in a home where there is a male spouse, she does not always develop good qualities of leadership. Many things happen to her as she plays the numerous roles incumbent upon her. Frequently, she has had too little education to deal with some of her children intellectually. Sometimes she has encountered many frictions and abrasions in dealing with merchants who have attempted to exploit her. These encounters make her skeptical and suspicious; thus, she may fail to instill in her children a sense of trust. If she lives in a house without an adult male, her children will have little or no opportunity to see her react emotionally to a member of the opposite sex. She recoils at the moral myopia of people in the mainstream who criticize her and expect a code of behavior from her that she feels is too difficult and too absurd for her to follow. Consequently, she may not always set a good example for her children. Many mothers fail to become effective leaders because they do not know what their rights are and what resources are available to them. Mothers in Blackmoor have lived with the many and varied evils of the ghetto—human congestion, filth, crime, exploitation, low income, lack of dignity—which have made them cynical. Too many are hostile. Hostility in a mother does little to develop in children a positive attitude.

Household heads in the housing project spend their time providing for the basic needs and have little time to devote to developing their own leadership or to giving direction to their children. Being poor is an all-consuming and full-time job.

ECONOMICS AND LEARNING

Economic poverty is a major barrier not only to securing the basic physical needs but also to the conditions that provide for learning. Three-fourths of the children included in the sampling had never ridden a train. Some 68 percent of the children under eight years of age had never ridden a public bus. These facts would not normally be surprising when we consider the large number of people who travel by automobile. However, only 7 percent of the families interviewed owned automobiles. One resident asked, "Ride the train—what for? We ain't got nowhere to go. What has riding the train got to do with the price of butter?"

One child in ten among preschool children in this project has been to the city zoo. Families cannot afford the cost of transportation to convey the entire family to such places of interest as the zoo. Most of Blackmoor's preschool children have never been in a supermarket. Seventeen of the hundred families did not own a television set, and a third of the families did not have telephone service. Only one in five of the respondents reported ever buying a book for a child's birthday or Christmas. Many families said that the money could be better spent for food or clothing. Disadvantaged parents are impatient with what they consider frivolity. Typically, only forty-three of the families had had a Christmas tree each year. Thirty families reported having a tree occasionally. The remaining families had never had a Christmas tree. The primary concern of many disadvantaged families is not the abstract, symbolic, and traditional significance placed on such objects as Christmas trees but the real object and its practical value. The children learn early that fairies do not put money under their pillows when they lose a tooth and that Santa Claus may not come even if they are "good." Project parents attempt to avoid projecting such middle-class values. They do not promise gifts from fairyland. Children know where their goodies come from. Parents resent some of the things told children by school people, as the following statements illustrate:

The children seem to get more dissatisfied from going to school. They don't teach them nothing there but how things ought to be. They don't ever teach them how to live with things the way they is—especially when they ought to know that you can't do no better.

My little girl came home and cried her eyes out because she didn't have a washcloth of her own. She told me that the teacher said everybody in the house ought to have his own.

We use salt and baking soda to brush our teeth—and I sure wish that over at that there school they would stop talking about using toothpaste and tooth powder. They see that stuff on TV every day. I got them to brushing, haven't I? Pretty soon they'll be ashamed to use salt.

In spite of the assumption that education in America is allegedly free, the cost of providing the experiences that enhance the educative process can reach staggering proportions. The contemporary home and family in today's culture can rarely provide the diversity of experiences adequate to meet all the needs of children. Therefore, the family must go outside the home to meet many of these needs. Unfortunately, this movement out of the home frequently incurs expense.

In the past, many of the activities and experiences that contributed significantly to learning were free or of minimal cost. Paradoxically, many of the established places of interest in Midwest City were more accessible to disadvantaged children years ago than they are today. Twenty years ago, thousands of children participated in "streetcar riding" as a Sunday afternoon activity. A child could purchase a 25-cent Sunday pass, which would enable him to ride all day at no additional cost. Parents purchased passes for their children, who spent Sunday afternoons riding about the city. Many children "learned" Midwest City using this method. In cases where there were several children in the family and both adults worked, the children could borrow the weekly pass of both parents and perhaps the passes of employed relatives. When this procedure was used, the children did not incur any expenditures. It was common to see groups of children ride from one end of the line to the other on one streetcar, transfer to another streetcar or bus, and repeat the same pattern. They were also able to get off and visit the points of interest. They did not have to be concerned with zones, transfer points, transfers, or additional cost. Some 91 percent of the respondents said that they had learned most about Midwest City in this way. None of their children who were sixteen years of age or younger reported learning anything about their city in this manner.

My social-science teacher said that people sort of live in little pockets around the city, so it ain't as important as it used to be to know where everything is. Everybody just stays in his own little pocket.

Streetcars are now extinct. Other public transportation is too expensive to ride for fun, and the city has gone through many changes. At the same time, these changes have strengthened and influenced at least one of the barriers to learning, namely, the lack of familiarity with the larger environment. It is also discernible how seemingly unimportant and prosaic behavior in the culture can provide techniques and conditions for meaningful experience. One of the main things that changed the behavior of the disadvantaged persons involved has been the cost factor. On the other hand, although lack of money and low income may affect the family as a whole, one frequently finds an economic paradox within the family. Some teen-age members of the family can secure money while the family as a whole remains destitute.

TEEN-AGERS' MONEY

In spite of what has been said about the closeness of siblings and how they help and offer mutual support to one another, teen-age boys in the disadvantaged family sometimes exhibit behavior that is contradictory. They frequently do not experience the same impact of economic poverty as their younger siblings. If they are fortunate enough to secure employment, they will spend $45 for a pair of shoes while their parents do not have enough food at home. They will keep up the payments on a hundred-dollar suit while a younger sibling is compelled to go without a winter coat. They will involve themselves in felonious activity to pay for exorbitantly priced clothing. The label in wearing apparel is a status badge for the teen-ager in this slum culture. In a survey taken by a collection of men's apparel shops in Midwest City, it was found that 63 percent of the boys in ghetto high schools wore shoes that cost more than $35 a pair. Teen-age boys, in particular, measure many kinds of relationships in terms of dress. One teen-ager explained his idea of a good friend as follows: "A good friend is a 'stud' who you can ask to wear his Bannisters [expensive shoes] and he lets you have them without a lot of lip."

The teen-age boy in this environment learns early to live by his wits. He does not have an adult male model in the home. And he lives in a hostile aggressive community where he must have not only the ability to cope with his own milieu but also the flexibility to adjust to situations in the broader culture. If he is really skillful, he must be able to protect himself from physical aggression. The teen-ager in Blackmoor must also be able to communicate at several levels, from the gutter to the personnel office. He must get his on-the-job training in the streets of the ghetto while learning to adjust to a world that is not a slum. A social worker reports:

> These kids have to live by their unique talents which they learn in the streets. Otherwise I'm afraid they wouldn't make it.

A policeman says:

> There are really two types of kids down here. They both live by their ability to cope; one does it and doesn't break the law, and the other seems only to exist by breaking the law.

From a teacher:

> When a child, from a very early age, has to live by his wits without the benefit of guidance or wholesome direction, he will undoubtedly encounter situations where he has neither the skill nor the knowledge of the resources available to him that will help him make a desirable adjustment in school.

From a judge:

> Most of the kids who come into my court have had to live by whatever devices they could conjure up. In most cases, they have not had a good home, family, and school experience. This is true not only of disadvantaged children but also of children from more affluent environments. However, the majority are from disadvantaged backgrounds.

A teen-ager says:

> I got to make it. I can't get a job, I can't expect no help from my people, so I got to do it the best way I can. Really.

The teen-age boy frequently leaves home about midmorning and does not return until the early hours of the following morning. He learns to shoot pool and other such activities where he can obtain money to purchase food and other items that he may desire for himself. Many parents report that their teen-age boys rarely come home for meals. Nevertheless, they may enjoy better food, be better dressed, and be economically more independent than the rest of the family. Teen-agers around Blackmoor often identify with criminals and other such people adept at "beating the Man." If an investigator approaches the right teen-ager, he can order almost any item (or buy back his own) that he wishes and expect to have it delivered. For example, if a prospective customer wants a special kind of hub cap for his car or a transistor radio or a tire, these teen-agers will get the items according to the customer's specifications at a small fraction of the actual cost. The purchaser, of course, in all probability, is receiving stolen, or "hot," goods. The teen-agers are well aware of puritanical hypocrisy. They do not hesitate to proclaim: "Our best customers are the law-abiding citizens—nobody else has any money."

Frequently these teen-agers exhibit blatant behavior with little compunction and apparently no fear. Two teen-agers were observed playing a pinball machine in a building just opposite a high school. A third person, an adult, joined them. He asked these boys to get him a tire for his automobile. One of the boys asked the man for his car keys. After obtaining the keys, the boy went directly to the man's car, opened the trunk, and took out his bumper jack. After getting the jack, the first boy was joined by the second one. In the meantime, the man moved the car into a nearby alley. The two boys moved up and down the row of parked cars in front of the school until they found the one desired. Without hesitation, they hoisted the car, removed the wheel and lowered the car to the rim. They then picked up the jack, rolled the wheel and jack into the trunk of the man's car, and closed the lid. They unhurriedly walked back to the man, returned his keys, received their pay, and resumed their game. Such behavior seems unbelievable; however, the unbelievable is commonplace here.

Many teen-agers in this environment are "legitimate" business-men. They operate with an uncanny knowledge of human nature. They know that many people want something for nothing. Because they know this, teen-agers may obtain a peddler's license and buy merchandise wholesale. They later approach an unsuspecting customer in a suspicious manner and offer the supposedly "hot" wares to him. The customer, feeling that he is being offered a bargain, will often buy what he thinks are "hot" goods. Later he frequently finds that he has paid more for inferior merchandise than he may have paid for a better-quality item in a legitimate retail store. If the customer complains to the police, the seller has legal receipts to show that the goods were purchased from a reputable firm and that he has a license to sell them.

Some teen-age boys in this subculture are often economically more independent than their fathers or other members in the family. Whether they obtain money legally or illegally, they are more affluent. This is the economic paradox operative within the same household.

Girls in the household can be economically independent also, but rarely to the same degree as boys because they do not always have the freedom that boys have. Whereas most teen-age girls in Blackmoor are not often involved in assaults, do not commit felonies with deadly weapons, and rarely if ever are convicted of a crime, some are shoplifters. Infrequently, they are involved with narcotics. Most often, however, their unlawful conduct is centered around sexual activities—they may become prostitutes or procurers—but they must leave the project area to do it. Regardless of where such illegal acts take place, most of the time these acts are done for money, rarely "for kicks."

FINANCES AND FAMILY HARMONY

The lack of economic solvency in the disadvantaged home seems to be the focal point of much family discontent. Everything appears to change in the home with relation to available money. The number and intensity of adult arguments and disputes seems directly proportional to the earning power and employment status of the father. Similarly, mothers who receive aid to dependent children tend to scold and nag the children more during periods of the month when the relief money has been exhausted.

It seems like we spend all our time trying to make ends meet. Hungry children are sad to look at and a husband that can't get a job is hell to live with. I'm doing better than most—at least, I have a husband. But the end of the month without money makes our house a battleground.

Fifty-three of the mothers reported that there were more arguments and family discord when the father was out of work or when family funds were depleted.

Some of the employed fathers in these families did not bring their wages directly home. They stopped to drink and gamble, sometimes losing their entire salary before they reached home. After a few such experiences, eight mothers reported that they met their husbands at their place of employment on paydays. This procedure was used in order to secure money to provide for the family before the husband had an opportunity to spend it drinking or lose it gambling. Other wives had agreements with the husband's employer whereby the wife would pick up the husband's paycheck. However, the majority of husbands would not agree to such arrangements. One man voiced his resentment: "No woman's gonna draw my paycheck. That what's wrong now. They run everything."

The lack of money touches the father, as we have seen, but more significantly, it touches the entire family—from the oldest member of the family to the preschool child who is constantly subjected to the discord in the family over money, as well as the physical and psychological impact this deficit propagates. Because additional money is hard to get, children in the disadvantaged home are sometimes harshly punished for tearing some article of clothing or "kicking out" their shoes.

A minister working in this area reports: "I've seen them beat their children with animal fury for tearing some article of clothing. Many parents do this at the slightest provocation."

One mother says: "I guess the only way to make them take care of their clothes is to beat them. It might be the wrong way, but it works."

In some project families, children must remain at home because they do not have proper clothing or shoes to wear to school. Because preschool children usually remain at home, many parents do not recognize the need to provide them with the same care and experiences that they provide for their school-age children.

> The little children don't do nothing but stay around the house—so it seems better to spend money on the children that have to go to school.
>
> Let's look at this like it is—which one of them is going to school? Which one of them is gonna be at home all day? Who gonna see this here one staying at home but me and other children just like him? Well, that ought to explain why we spent more time watching the children that goes to school.

Thus, the preschool child's clothing and grooming receive less attention. Most of his clothing has been handed down from older siblings. Many three-, four-, and five-year-old boys receive a haircut only about four times a year. There are other male children these same ages who receive a haircut only for such special occasions as Christmas and Easter. Occasionally, small boys are seen dressed in female apparel, such as blouses, particularly blouses styled like a boy's shirt. They have also been observed wearing girls' coats. This is very common in a family where there are several girls in the family and only one boy. If the child is a preschooler, he may not encounter much difficulty. However, if he is a school-age child he will not wear such clothes. He may be forced to leave home dressed in some items, but as soon as he is out of the view of his parents he removes the item. Sometimes he "loses" it. This is a boy's only alternative to fighting. So dressed, from the time he left home until he returned, he would be ridiculed. Many boys would rather play hooky than wear such items.

In many project homes, the smaller children soon learn to eat first or find themselves without sufficient food at mealtime. Disadvantaged children know that there are rarely "leftovers" and "second helpings." Consequently, the problem of coercing smaller children to eat is never acute in most project homes. Some 94 percent of the respondents reported that they never had difficulty in getting preschool children to eat. As one said, "I don't have time to wonder about what he likes and don't like— if he wants to eat, he'll eat what's on the table."

Because they live in such economic destitution and frustration, it is not difficult to see why there is an overemphasis on some material things by older children and sometimes their parents. Teachers who work in this area have an expression that appears, at least, to be valid: "If you want to see how destitute or deprived the children are, look at how well the mother is dressed." Some mothers, like their teen-age sons previously described, wear the best clothing. They also eat and drink the best food and beverage away from home while their children are inadequately and improperly fed and clothed. Although it seems contrary to the image of motherhood for a woman to act this way, it is understandable when we consider that she is fulfilling a need and buttressing her self-esteem. This disadvantaged mother is meeting some of the same needs as the middle-class mother who buys a hat to "lift her spirits." The stimulus may be the same for both; the behavior may be the same; but the consequences of their actions are quite different. However, because of the deprived mother's failure to project the traditional mother image —that is, depriving herself for her children—she finds herself in conflict with self and community. Thus, the very esteem that she strives for eludes her.

SKILLFUL MANAGEMENT IN A HOUSING PROJECT

There are families who are skillful in budgeting, family organization, and management. Such families are well aware that money alone is not the critical factor in establishing a desirable economic climate. Rogers (1962) emphasizes this position: "The economic climate of the home is a function not so much of actual cash available as a sense of economic well-being derived from wise management and healthy family attitude."

The author came to know quite well one family of eight that exemplified the economic climate and family attitude characterized by Rogers. This family had a $202 per month income derived from ADC. There was no father in the home, and all the children were under sixteen years of age. The mother managed to prepare three meals a day for her children, to send the school-age children to school regularly, clean and on time, and to maintain a stable household. The mother made most of her own clothes and those of the girls in the family. She purchased clothes for the boys from the Goodwill Industries. The mother was skillful in the planning and serving of meals and had a well-developed and functioning family routine, including church, recreation, and personal habits. Each child in the family, including the three-year-old, had a specific task to perform in the home. A climate of cooperation permeated the entire household. Obviously, the family described is one of the many exceptions. The mother was so adept at home management that she received requests from the project management to explain her organizational and management methods to other groups of project residents.

Children who live and grow in the kind of family environment illustrated will find their training and experiences exceedingly valuable in their everyday social relationships at home and at school.

The mother in the home described considered neither herself nor her skill unusual. The monologue that follows was extracted from tapes and personal conversations over a three-day period.

> *I don't really see nothing so different 'bout me. I just use plain old common courtesy, hard work, and common sense. When you really think about it though, I guess those things aren't too common—like they used to be. They got all those old sayings about the birds of a feather, laying down with dogs and getting up with fleas, and the like—well, I just don't believe them. If you lay*

*down with dogs you won't have no trouble if you got
flea powder. So, I just keep my flea powder handy, so
to speak. My mother always told me that cleanliness
was next to godliness, and my mother was a God-fearing
woman, so we keep clean—there are no two ways
about it. If some of the rest of these people would quit
trying to buy everything they see, they could probably
do a little better too. But deliver me from throwing
stones, there are probably some things I need to stop
doing, too. I guess it kind of boils down to caring about
yourself and having patience.*

*They [social workers, resident advisers] are always sending
women to me and I'm supposed to show them how I keep
house or prepare meals for my children. That's a joke!
The average one of these women can cook me under
the table and knows more about keeping a house
clean than I will ever learn. Trouble is—they are always
talking to the people down here and* nobody ever listens
to them. *Most of the people here can help you more
than you can help them. You forget—these are the
women who have kept the city's homes clean for
generations; they have fed the most prominent citizens
and have kept the clothes on their backs starched and
ironed. The crowned heads from the world over have
eaten menus prepared by them. They have had closer
contact with the children of their employers than the
parents have. Trying to tell these people about things
like that is like telling fish how to swim. No, it's something
else these people need—and it's not telling them how to plan
a menu. Seems to me you got to find some kind of
way to make them take pride in themselves and what
they do. You also got to find some way to keep the human
scavengers from taking advantage of them. Look at all
them little Jew credit stores up and down O Street—
they take advantage of the people. A $5 pair of shoes cost
$10, and by the time you get them paid for they cost $15
and they're already worn out.* —Maggie T., age forty-four

Maggie T. put her finger on one of the central problems found
in the housing project. The merchants on O Street hold a chattel
mortgage on the belongings of 80 percent of Blackmoor's tenants
who have anything purchased new.

Most furniture, however, is usually purchased "used" from a secondhand store, the Salvation Army store, or the Goodwill Industries. In the latter two stores, one sees a blending of social classes. The rich are searching for antiques, the middle class are looking for "conversation pieces," and the poor are looking for anything that can be used: an article of clothing, a piece of furniture, an appliance, a wall decoration, or any one of the thousands of unidentified miscellaneous objects found there. Generally, however, the poor purchase used furniture or clothing. For those people who do purchase articles new they are caught in the vise of the credit store.

A DOLLAR DOWN—A DOLLAR A WEEK

Household furnishings that have been purchased new come from the small installment credit stores found in every ghetto and poor community in the inner city. It is easy for a project family to buy on credit: a dollar down and a dollar a week is the only requirement. If the purchaser fails to meet the payments, the merchant has several legal controls* over his customers to ensure that he will get his money. Items are sometimes repossessed and resold as used furniture. Few individuals in Blackmoor pay the last installment; when the balance of his note is within one payment, this buyer frequently makes another purchase and adds it on to the previous contract. If he later has financial difficulty and cannot fulfill his contract on the second item, the seller can repossess both. There are individuals who have traded with the same store for ten, fifteen, and twenty years who have never fulfilled a contract. Many stores encourage their project customers to "add on" rather than completely pay for the first item.

> Mrs. ——, you can add this bedroom suite on to your old bill and walk out with it tonight. But if you make a new bill, you have to establish your credit.

There are times, however, when the customer's business behavior is equally as questionable; he takes advantage of the

* For an excellent and exhaustive study on consumer practices of low-income families see David Caplovitz's *The Poor Pay More* (1967).

repossession policy. An individual has been known to have his furniture repossessed and then have a friend purchase it as "used" furniture for less than the balance he currently owes.

Don't do no good for 'em to raise sand; you can't put a man in jail for being in debt in this state. Let 'em sue me! I ain't got no wages to garnishee and they can't take back what they done already took back. They *did* sell it again. This is just the poor man's bankruptcy.

In conclusion, it is obvious that family finances can be formidable pressures exerted on the family or can serve as a motivating device offering many and constant opportunities for the development of initiative and creative tension. Consequently, some families learn to solve their problems and fulfill their needs in ways that the society deems acceptable. Others choose different behavior. Regardless of the method used by the family to solve its financial problems, economic poverty ultimately takes its toll in many aspects of human development and social interaction. The writer would hesitate to predict a one-to-one relationship between norm-violating behavior and economic poverty, but these two social conditions do seem to have a high positive correlation.

VIII - Say, "Ahhh"

A definition of "health" is usually restricted to the physical dimension. Such a restriction expresses an incomplete definition. Health appears to involve three other aspects of the individual: mental, social, and emotional. Therefore, an adequate definition of this term must encompass all three of the dimensions cited above. It follows, then, that to be considered in good health one must be free of illness in all dimensions.

The soundness of the definition given above establishes on an equally sound basis the corollary that good health is the same for all people, irrespective of the social structure in which they find themselves. In point of fact, the attitudes, values, techniques, and behavior employed in establishing and maintaining good health in all its aspects may be radically different among different groups or classes of people. It seems probable that the emergence and integration of some health habits are more heavily influenced by example, while others are more dependent upon deliberate training. Economic conditions are a salient factor. The health practices and patterns that characterize the home and family of the child in Blackmoor form the focus of the present concern.

GOOD MEDICAL CARE AND THE DISADVANTAGED

Contrary to what may be generally thought, the urban disadvantaged in Midwest City can receive fairly good medical attention. Although only four of the families studied reported having the services of a family doctor, the other ninety-six reported some public clinic affiliation. If one has such an affiliation, the cost of providing medical care and drugs is not always as formidable for the deprived family as it can be for other groups and social classes, but the cost in human dignity to get this care cannot be tabulated. The disadvantaged family that can satisfactorily establish that it cannot assume financial responsibility for medical care usually receives it at very little cost. For this reason, therefore, it is possible for Blackmoor's children to receive fairly good medical attention. Nevertheless, the U.S. Department of Health, Education and Welfare (1965a) notes that "the mark of poverty is often stamped upon a child even before he is born. His mother is less likely to get good medical care. He is more likely to be born in an over-crowded public or charity hospital and discharged to a sub-standard home one or two days after birth."

Medical attention, however, does not necessarily mean that disadvantaged children are healthy. They are not. Such things as malnutrition, poor sanitation conditions, poor hygienic practices, and undesirable psychological conditions prevailing in Blackmoor can have serious and undesirable effects on the health of children. There are many project children who never have an opportunity to see good health practices in the home; children who not only do not drink orange juice but also have never possessed or even seen a real orange; children who cannot remember their last hot breakfast; children who have never tasted butter; and, as was pointed out, children who have never slept alone.

HEALTH RESOURCES

Project tenants utilize several medical resources in the maintenance of good health: the public clinics, including the municipal hospitals, which are "free of cost," and the medical-school clinics; the family doctor; health insurance; and the public schools.

The Public Clinic

There is really no such thing as a free clinic in Midwest City; every patient pays something. The cost of a clinic card is 25 cents; the holder of the card pays 10 cents per visit. This minimum fee actually obscures the total costs of visiting the clinic. The patient who is employed loses one or two days' salary. Although his weekly income is reduced when he visits the clinic, he still must pay for a baby-sitter and transportation. As a consequence, a given clinic visit may cost far more than the cost of visiting a private physician, but most tenants do not visit a private physician simply because they do not have the ready cash. A procedure as simple as renewing a clinic card can be costly; a patient who wants his card renewed may be forced to wait all day and return the following day before it is issued. He then makes an appointment and uses still another day to see the doctor. If the patient is employed, he loses work. University clinics screen applicants closely. In these clinics the patient pays about $3 per visit plus the cost of medicines, X rays, and so on. The admitting officer of medical-school clinics refers welfare patients to the municipal hospital because their income is so low that likelihood of being able to continue to pay is slim.

The patient is expected to pay an amount commensurate with his income. When he makes his first appearance at the public clinic, the social-service division of the hospital sets about to determine his ability to pay. He reports to a social worker, who interrogates him about his job, the size of his family, his bills, and other information to determine his eligibility for medical attention. The interrogation of the patient is not to determine ways to serve him but to find ways not to serve. As one patient noted, "They want your pedigree before they wait on you. I don't expect nobody in his right mind would come here if you could afford to go someplace else."

The individual is allowed to suffer during this routine procedure. It is not likely that he will be served on his first visit. Most prospective patients make the initial visit one in which to establish eligibility and then go back later for service.

There are cases where one agency attempts to shift the responsibility of caring for patients to another. The medical-school clinics may send the patient to the city hospital, and the city hospital may send the patient to another private agency, such as the Society for the Blind in the case of a child who needs glasses. After this "round robin," the patient may find himself back at his point of origin. In the meantime, his condition is aggravated and is allowed to deteriorate from lack of attention.

A slip bearing his name, the date, day, and hour is the appointment notice given to the clinic patient. The designated time is often meaningless; the patient arrives at 8:30 A.M. for his appointment and waits to be served, sometime between the time of his arrival in the morning and 4:30 P.M., if then, or at all. If he is not served by the end of the day, he is handed another slip and asked to report another day. He is not given much choice, nor is the individual issuing the appointments much concerned with his prior commitments, his means of returning, or the urgency of his medical needs. Older patients do not seem to mind returning if they have transportation available. Younger persons, however, profess a tighter schedule, and their temperaments are not usually as accordant. They protest.

You go set up out at the clinic all day long and they talk to you like you some kinda dog. Your appointment is for 8:30 and they wait on you at 4:00 if you're lucky. Say something, they remind you you ain't paying for it—like they is.

The patient arrives at the clinic, checks in (shows his clinic card, pays a fee if necessary), and sits down. The person next to him may be younger or older, one with his head bandaged, one in a wheelchair, one whose illness is apparent, or one who can hide his affliction, a person with a chronic or an acute ailment, one with a contagious or innocuous disease. They sit together. The patient may know his clinic peer and talk to him, or each may sit in mute preoccupation with his own suffering, afraid to venture even to the restroom for fear of losing both his seat and his turn. He waits and listens for his name to be called. Sometimes the deaf or hard-of-hearing patient will bring a school-age child with him to listen for his name. As the patient waits, he is surrounded by the discord of crying babies and the monotony of the public address system. His peace is disturbed. The incoherent mumble of many voices is only stilled by the abrupt silence when a nurse or some other staff member suddenly appears and prepares to call the next patient.

The first patient to arrive at the clinic is not always the first one served. The doctor who handles his particular ailment may report two or three hours later. Finally his name is called and the process of being shuffled from station to station begins. There are patients who appear to get prompt attention: some because they are clean and seem intelligent, some because they know members of the hospital staff, girls who are young and pretty, and, of course, the cantankerous and demanding patients.

There is also the patient with a rare disease—he gets the red carpet treatment. For example, Alice Y. is married and has one child and a husband. Her husband earns about $50 a week. She works when she is able. The family has a small vintage car, and the child is fairly well kept. But Alice Y. has a rare blood disease. She was taken into the clinic without much difficulty. She is the darling of the supervising physician and fourth-year medical students. Alice goes to the clinic; she rarely waits, is always treated, and never pays.

Mary X, on the other hand, is the mother of six children, whose ages are one, three, four, six, nine, and eleven, respectively. The three older children suffer from malnutrition. There is no adult male in the home. Mary X. lives in a housing project and is the recipient of ADC. Her income is $181 per month. Of this amount, $43 is spent for rent. Each member of the family has less than 64 cents per day. Mary X. has no other income. This patient depends on the clinic and emergency room for medical service. She has no means of transportation and no money to pay a baby-sitter. She walks to the clinic and takes her preschool children with her. Mary X. has diabetes. Hers is a common case without any unusual complications. The disease is under control. She reports to the clinic for checkups and drugs. Mary X. goes to the clinic with her children; she waits; she is usually served. Mary X. always pays.

Most patients are dealt with dispassionately—some with paternalism and some with contempt. Many who are treated on an outpatient basis because of overcrowded conditions in the hospital feel that they would probably progress better if they were hospitalized. Each week they return. One noted:

The doctor in the "B" clinic sends me to the one in the "L" clinic who is already gone somewhere when I get there. I go back to the "B" clinic and stand in that line all over again, and the doctor tells me to come back next week. I don't mind coming back so much, but I wish I could put all my pain into one big sick spell and get it over with.

Courtesy and respect in dealing with the poor seem to be lacking among the clinic staff:

They come out and look at you first and then decide whether they going to call you "Mrs." or not. The dirtiest people always seem to get waited on last, no matter when you come. I guess they postpone touching you as long as they can.

It is purported that hospital personnel are trained to be scientific, objective, and impersonal in their interaction with patients. The staff member who achieves this skill has probably learned his lessons well. Nevertheless, most of the project persons and others who are served want not only a scientist and technician but also a human being to listen to them and talk with them. In many cases, the cold detachment of the hospital is compounded by a lack of courtesy when staff members respond to disadvantaged people. Time after time a member of the hospital staff passes by and is questioned by a patient. Infrequently the patient is answered; more often he is ignored. Though the people resent the discourtesy, they resent being ignored most: "We got pride and we got feelings, too, but they treat us like we ain't here. I know folks who'd rather stay sick than come to this place."

As the patient moves through the various stations for his examination and treatment, he is constantly confronted with situations that deplete his dignity. Urinalysis is a case in point. At station 9, he may be presented with a bottle and asked for a specimen of urine. He looks around for the restroom and sees it a fourth of a block away near station 1. He walks the length of the clinic to station 1, carrying the empty bottle. Everybody knows what the bottle is for. On the way back from the restroom, he carries the bottle wrapped in a paper towel, a tissue, or a discarded paper bag—anything to hide his embarrassment. His fellow patients are not deceived. He knows it.

The clinic patient learns to wait. In spite of the claim that the hospital is understaffed and overworked, members of the staff spend considerable time in idle chit-chat, smoking cigarettes and gossiping while the patient waits. "It wouldn't be so bad if they didn't stand right up in front of you and smoke and act cute while you been waitin' for hours. You'd think they would go in a back room somewhere."

The examination of the patient is prolonged because the examining intern is interrupted by another doctor who stops by for a chat; the examinee waits. If one of the interns has not arrived, the patient waits. At the clinic pharmacy, the patient waits. At lunchtime the patient waits. If the clinic-goer is not served today and still wants to be tomorrow, he waits—and waits—and waits.

"Nurse, I've been here since this morning: what can you tell me now?"

"Wait!"

The Emergency Room

A siren wails, an ambulance deposits a DOA, a child screams, a woman yields to the pains of labor, a baby pukes, blood spurts from a gaping wound. There is also the bewilderment, anguish, silent suffering, and apathy. Here, too, the patient waits. This is part of the emergency-room syndrome. Although every situation is a crisis to the individual involved, for the personnel in this receiving room a crisis situation is routine.

A serious accident can make the emergency receiving room of the municipal hospital the setting for a melodrama. The patient is the principal character, and every action revolves around him. The supporting players have a vested interest in him, yet he is almost anonymous. From the time he is left near the hospital by the cab driver who doesn't want to get involved with the receiving-room bureaucracy to the day he walks or is carried out, he has the spotlight.

If the patient is brought by ambulance, he may find the business card of an attorney in his hand or on his person. How it gets there remains a mystery.* The receiving clerk and the social

* It is said that some ambulance drivers work with lawyers of dubious integrity. These drivers are reputed to solicit business for the lawyers on a commission basis.

worker are only interested in the patient's vital statistics and his ability to pay. The policeman is there to determine if the law has been violated and to provide constraint if necessary. The van for the undertaker is close by. The last person on the scene is the intern. This is the irony: his services are needed most, yet he is the last to come. He, too, needs the patient; he needs the human specimen in order to learn his trade. Most of the agents and agencies necessary for birth, life, and death are present. But the patient is almost a nonentity.

All classes and peoples who are injured or taken suddenly ill on the city streets are taken to the municipal hospital, which is well equipped to handle emergencies. Thus, the municipal hospital is probably the only true melting pot of a city. The patient can refuse treatment. Those who can afford to go elsewhere do so. If the patient's condition is such that he cannot make the decision to remain at the time of his admission, his family may make arrangements to have him transferred to a private hospital. The poor, however, are without choice.

The deprived individual who is admitted to the hospital may find his bed next to that of a prisoner who is shackled and guarded by a policeman. There are some municipal hospitals without prison wards. Teen-agers find themselves in wards with adults. It is fair to say that all are treated with the medical service that is available. Most types of medical specialists who can be obtained are called, from the pediatrician to the psychiatrist. However, when the patient's condition is one that requires a specialist who is not available and the cost to bring him in from elsewhere is prohibitive, the patient again falls heir to the legacy of poverty: hopelessness, suffering, and sometimes death.

The Family Doctor

A family doctor is rarely used by project residents. Only four families identified a family physician, and the persons who identified him admitted that he would not make a house call at their apartments. The private doctors who serve the poor provide their services on a pay-as-you-go basis. The poor cannot expect to pay the doctor by personal check or to be billed at the end of the month. Under these conditions, some persons who may prefer a private doctor are forced to use the public clinic. These same doctors *do* make house calls, accept checks, and bill patients in more affluent neighborhoods. Some physicians have established their practices in poor neighborhoods, gained wealth serving the poor, and, once well established, moved on.

There is a new trend among black physicians in the inner city; they work together in groups of four or five and establish medical associations or centers. Each individual doctor promotes his specialty. These centers are equipped with a pharmacy, X-ray technicians, pathology laboratories, and other medical services. They provide luxurious waiting rooms, complete with air conditioning, soft music, lounge chairs, current magazines, lollipops for the children, and, in some cases, birthday cards for the patients. The medical centers can, in fact, provide complete medical service. This service, however, is frequently priced out of the range of most project dwellers. These associations appear to be monuments of status for the middle-class black and not designed for the poor citizen or project resident. The more affluent patient may have his case diagnosed and treated and have his prescription filled all under one roof. Frequently, he can be handled in one or two visits. The doctor usually knows his patient, attends some of the same social functions, goes to the same church, or has children attending school with the children of his patient. They may be friends. Conversely, the project resident who goes to a private doctor in his community is likely to be served in a small dingy office with few, if any, of the comforts, conveniences, and services mentioned above. He makes several trips to the office and must go to the corner drugstore for his pharmaceuticals. The doctor may never really know the patient. There is little likelihood of their ever having cocktails together or of their children attending the same school. The patient pays for a service and the doctor provides it.

> When they come to me, I treat them. I use all of the skill I have and try to make them as comfortable as I can. I'm not interested in their problems; I don't want to live next door to them. Because I treat them doesn't mean I have to take a bath with them. I'm sorry— that's the way it is.

The image of the sympathetic physician is rarely exemplified in the project community. People being attended by a doctor while not paying their bills is a myth, and the legend of the dedicated doctor fighting the elements to reach the door of the ill is just that —a legend. The doctor in the inner city is not paid off in eggs and preserves. Patients are even exploited.

> It should be called the Oath of Hypocrites. That's what most of them are. I been going to that bastard every week for six months and he's been giving me a play-bo—a play-sebo—a damn sugar pill. Then I went to that little Jew doctor and he took some kinda graphs and told me nothing was wrong with my heart.

Health Insurance

Hospitalization plans and other types of group health insurance are not used much in the project community. The prerequisite for this type of medical coverage makes it inaccessible for most project residents. First, group insurance plans require that the insured be employed and that the employer be a participating member of the plan. This first requirement, then, eliminates the ADC mother and the woman who works as a domestic. It also eliminates the paternal transient, the free floater, and the handicapped resident. Second, some tenants cannot afford the cost of hospitalization insurance even when it is available. This passive employed resident makes the case in point: "It would take too much of my pay to buy that kind of insurance and still it wouldn't be enough. The free hospital has to be good enough for me; I don't have a choice."

Most of the project residents buy the small industrial-type policies sold to persons who are not good insurance risks. Premiums are paid weekly. This is the type of policy that insurance agents label nuisance insurance. Some of these policies have sick and accident provisions that will pay the insured a small compensation should he become ill or injured. The compensation is usually less than $15 per week. In order to receive the payment, the person must file a sick claim, which must be completed by a physician, and in most cases the claimant must be confined to bed. After the patient pays a doctor for his treatment, he has little or nothing left. There is no provision for loss of income, no provision for drugs, special doctors, or hospital confinement—"If you ain't dead, this stuff ain't worth the paper it's written on. They ought to write it on toilet paper, it would be more useful."

It appears that project residents are better insured for death than life. It is common to find families who have burial insurance—a small, relatively inexpensive policy that provides no financial dividends to the insured while he is alive and no benefits for his heirs after his death. However, it can (although it rarely does) eliminate the burden of the final expenses of his interment for the survivors. Many undertaking establishments underwrite this type of insurance in poor neighborhoods and hire high-pressure salesmen to sell it. Project residents, particularly the aged, are no match for these glib salesmen; the sales pitch is always emotional and psychological:

If you should die, *God forbid,* we will take take care of everything. Your family won't have to go out and beg to bury you. Your children won't have to look down at you, *God forbid,* and be ashamed of the way you are being put away. It is better to have it and not need it than to need it and be without it. We all die. *God forbid* it happening to you for a long time yet, but you know it will happen. Do you smoke, sir? Well, for the price of a package of cigarettes each week, we can provide a complete burial service for you. One of the saddest things I think I ever saw was a group of young children—no sir, they weren't children, they were nothing but babies, and they were out begging money to bury their grandfather. When you die, *God forbid,* I know you don't want to end up in Potter's Field.

The surviving family never receives an itemized accounting of the services rendered. The undertaker handles the complete funeral arrangements. The family never knows whether or not the deceased is getting what he paid for.

Health insurance is rarely used as a health resource for the persons described here except for the aggressive employed residents and a few employed mothers.

The School as a Health Resource

As a health resource in the project area, the school is primarily a referral agency. Except for minor first aid, the medical agents of the school can neither treat children nor prescribe drugs for them. When a school-age child is found to have a physical, mental, social, or emotional impairment, the parent is informed. If the parent has the necessary financial means to correct or arrest the impairment, he is encouraged to do so with dispatch. On the other hand, the parent who cannot afford the various types of medical services may be referred to the municipal hospital or some other agency, depending on the nature of the child's affliction. In the case of a physical illness, the school doctor or nurse makes the referral. When a child is suspected of being mentally deficient by his teacher or other school personnel, the school administrator requests psychometric evaluation. In like manner, the school social worker can make recommendations when a child is neglected or maltreated in the home or shows extreme maladjustment in school. Actually these school agents work as a team, at times one member of the team assuming the responsibility of another.

Every child in the inner city who is enrolled in the public schools in Midwest City undergoes a medical examination* as well as periodic checkups throughout his stay in the elementary school. Many project parents are unaware of afflictions in their children prior to this examination. In performing this service, the school is a diagnostic agency, one that is extremely important to the project community. It also serves as an inoculation station for polio, diphtheria, and other such diseases and excludes children who have symptoms of contagious disease. In addition to these services, the school provides instruction in health and assigns patrol boys and girls to assist in maintaining the safety and well-being of pupils as they go to and from school. This agency petitions the city to provide adequate signals and crossing guards as another safety measure. Pupils are instructed in evacuation

---

* In addition to the routine medical examination, children receive audiometer tests, superficial eye examinations, dental checks, and checks for scalp ringworm and speech defects. The child's inoculation history is reviewed periodically.

procedures in the event of storm, fire, or attack. In this way, then, the school is a health resource.

Realizing that some pupils have individual health problems, the schools maintain special auxiliary services for them. Midwest City's schools provide home teachers for children who are ill for long periods of time. There are also schools for children with varying types of physical and emotional handicaps. Rooms have been established with specially trained teachers for the slow learner. There is a school psychologist and a testing service that identifies the retarded or slow learner, enabling him to be grouped in terms of his ability. All these services are available. The problem, however, is that they are not adequate to meet the needs of the large number of children who require them. The fact remains, nevertheless, that the school assumes many social, instrumental, and residual functions in making health services available.

LACK OF PREVENTIVE CARE BY PARENTS

Except for infants taken to the public health clinic for postnatal care, children are never taken to the doctor or clinic unless something is currently wrong. No parent reported taking a well child to the doctor. Parents do not provide routine checkups for their children or themselves. Some 87 percent of the children observed had never been to the dentist. Statistics taken from the U.S. Department of Health, Education and Welfare Children's Bureau's *Illness Among Children* (1965b) based on data from a national health survey, show that 23.5 percent of all urban children aged five to fourteen have never been to a dentist. This percentage is significantly higher for nonwhite children. A child who may have eye or ear trouble rarely receives any attention if these conditions are not acute and discernible. Such conditions are usually discovered, and if possible rectified, with the advent of school enrollment.

The school health program provides many of the preventive measures, such as immunization, that if omitted would leave thousands of children exposed to communicable disease. When one considers the unsanitary conditions under which many disadvantaged children live, the type of diet to which they are subjected, and the inappropriate clothing they wear, one concludes that if they were denied the preventive measures they receive through the school or public health services, the results would be catastrophic for them and the entire community as well.

GROOMING, PERSONAL HYGIENE, HEALTH, AND SAFETY

Disadvantaged parents manifest attitudes toward cleanliness significantly different from those of middle-class parents. If a child's outer garments are clean, this state constitutes cleanliness to many parents. Only four parents in the hundred families studied reported giving the preschool child a daily bath. In some families where there was more than one preschool child, two or more children were bathed together. Only one child in ten had a washcloth and a towel of his own. Some children bathed and redressed in the same underclothing. In one family, six children were using the same toothbrush. In another home, the bathtub was used as the dirty clothes hamper. This is neither new nor unusual in Midwest City.

Many homes in the slum areas of the inner city do not have heated bathrooms; during the winter months, families must bathe in other parts of the house—usually the kitchen. The bathtub in such homes is sometimes used as a storage area. For years, in many slum dwellings, coal was stored in the bathtub during winter months. There seems to be a carry-over of this behavior by parents who formerly lived in slum areas, but in the projects, other things have replaced coal as the item stored.

It is not uncommon to see small children in the early morning who appear to be wearing a mask. Actually, they have attempted to wash their faces. They have washed from ear to ear and from forehead to chin. The area behind the ears, under the chin, and the neck have gone untouched. Mucus is still discernible in the corners of the eyes, and hands are streaked with soap residue where they have not been completely submerged in the water. Because many parents do not supervise or check their small children in the morning, little is done about these conditions.

In summer, many children who run barefooted are required to wash their feet only before they get into bed.

A general lack of routine permeates the disadvantaged home, particularly in matters of health. Few children have a specific time for bed, meals, or play. There is chaos around the bathroom in the mornings. Some children are trying to wash while others are seeking relief. In large families, physical relief is such a problem in the morning that parents sometimes provide diaper pails and other such receptacles to be used for this purpose until the bathroom is free. Most children dress before they wash. Therefore, if they cannot get access to the bathroom for physical relief, they sometimes leave the apartment and move up or down the steps to a landing other than their own or to the elevator or laundry rooms to take care of their physical needs.

The daily search for clothing, socks, and shoes is a ritual in the project apartment. Smaller children are generally ignored until the school-age children are out of the house. Some children do show industry and prepare for the following day. However, they must arise first or the garments they have prepared may be taken by another child. It is not uncommon to see a project child at school without his socks or some other article of apparel proceed to recover his clothing from another sibling, who had taken it while he was still in bed or in the bathroom. Many young children hide their belongings at night so their siblings will not take them should these older children awaken first.

Few mothers have the insight or, perhaps, the energy to organize the family routine and prevent much of this pandemonium. They seem to develop a closed ear to the noise and go about preparing breakfast without too much concern, or they simply stay in bed until the rush is over. However, if the situation becomes unbearable, a handy ironing cord rigorously applied terminates the problem or at least makes the situation one that can be tolerated.

Not a single project child was found who had a handkerchief of his own. Only five were provided with Kleenex or paper tissues even when they had colds or running noses. Small children wipe their noses on their sleeves. Small children rarely have combs or hairbrushes of their own. Diapers are sometimes dipped into the toilet to remove feces and then rinsed and hung up to dry. In many cases this constitutes the washing of diapers. Diaper pails and other such containers filled with soiled diapers can often be found in various places in the house.

Frequently, the presence of aged persons in the home provides conditions that are not inducive to good health or hygiene. The tobacco chewer or snuff dipper—and there are many in this environment—must have a receptacle for expulsion. These receptacles can be found in many apartments uncovered and without adequate sanitation agents such as disinfectants. These older residents may wear clothes until they almost disintegrate. Because they usually need assistance in bathing, they seldom bathe.

Few parents provide adequate safety measures for the health and well-being of their children. Small children are often exposed to conditions that are a threat to life and limb. Not a single household was found in which small toddlers had a confined supervised place in which to play safely. Three families were even using the bathtub as a playpen.

In Blackmoor the hand rails on the landings outside the apartments have so few vertical ribs that small children have fallen from the upper floors and injured themselves. Further, more than half a dozen children have fallen from windows and been killed since Blackmoor was built.

NUTRITION

Nine out of ten families observed reported never serving fruit juice for breakfast. Although a few families reported purchasing one or more of the traditional breakfast meats—ham, bacon, and sausage—each week, the majority of the families revealed that they never purchased them. In fifty-four cases, the main breakfast meat was salt pork, boiled until reasonably free of salt, then fried. The fat that is extracted from this technique is sometimes poured over such things as rice or grits for seasoning.

Thirty-seven families reported preparing hot meals for the children's breakfast each day. Rice, oatmeal, grits, and pancakes are the foods served most frequently as hot breakfast. Often the breakfast consists of fried salt pork, molasses, and some type of bread.

The disadvantaged family is conspicuous for one-item meals; for example, fried potatoes. In the majority of cases, the primary concern is alleviating hunger and not providing proper nourishment. Consequently, one sometimes finds adequately fed but ill-nourished children in the project. Fortunately, however, preschool children are provided with vitamin and mineral supplements obtained from free public clinics, which help them to maintain some semblance of a balanced diet.

Pork is the major meat consumed in the housing project. Such things as hog maws (hog stomach), tripe (cow stomach), neckbones, and pigs' ears, feet, and skins (the outer rind from a side of bacon or some other such meat) are daily fare in the disadvantaged home. Although many in privileged communities consume some of the same foods, these items are usually camouflaged in specially prepared foods. For example, tripe is found in many commercially prepared soups, chili con carne, and Vienna sausage; and, of course, pigs' feet is acceptable to many if pickled and served as canapes but is unacceptable if boiled with dried beans. The lower-class black family learned long before the meat packing companies did that these items were fit for human consumption. While the more affluent would only eat the muscle of animals, disadvantaged people were eating the entrails and vital organs, some of which subsequently have been shown to be the most nutritious. For example, during the first two decades of this century, only carnivorous domestic animals, rural "poor whites," and blacks ate liver in America. Today, liver not only is considered one of the most nutritious meats but is one of the most expensive. In the disadvantaged neighborhood, tripe is sold in the same manner as hamburgers and hot dogs in other neighborhoods. It is considered a treat when served as a sandwich. Michael Harrington, when describing a casual walk through Harlem in *The Other America* (1962), his classic study of poverty in America, wrote:

> . . . you will see advertised some of these things: chitterlings, ham knuckles, hog maw, pig's feet, pig's tail, pig's ear; and fish is everywhere. This food—and some of it can be fairly costly—is the diet of the poor South, brought North in the migrations. These are the things the white man did not want.

The poor consume large quantities of rice, potatoes, and other starches, a filling and high-energy diet. Whereas in most families members eat a small quantity of these foods as a supplement to the main course, in the disadvantaged home, they *are* the main course.

There are very few meals free of grease or gravy. Few meals are served with salad, and still fewer are served with dessert. Food is rarely, if ever, served in courses. Rather, plates are filled by the mother or a grandmother. If children were allowed to fill their own plates, some would not receive an equal share. Fifty-eight mothers reported that they never set the table but "dished" the food directly from the cooking utensils.

In the project homes there are few hygienic practices that would meet the minimum standards for good health. Although free medical care is available to deprived families, few take advantage of this care unless their health problems are chronic or acute. In addition, many families do not eat the foods that provide the minimum dietary requirements. Cleanliness appears to be a matter of interpretation. Parents frequently do not have the means to provide the simple tools, such as toothbrushes, for maintaining good health or making possible the development of good hygienic habits. Children are not always supervised, and there appears to be a total lack of family organization. The majority of project children learn most about good health and hygiene after they come to school. Parents of preschool children tend to defer the needs of the latter in preference to meeting the needs of the older children in the family. It is therefore apparent why, in this environment, preschool children suffer most.

IX - Cross My Heart

The persistent mass media bombard us with relentless referrals to moral decadence; in literature, the press, television programs, and the pulpit, a barrage of words and actions dramatize a constant spreading of ethical dry rot. From the college campus to the Senate chamber, men are pointing out a need for the members of our society to develop into individuals who have strong personal motivation to make moral decisions. Traditionally, the home was primarily responsible for the development of character; however, the disadvantaged home in an urban setting is without strong leadership, consistent moral guidance, and spiritual objectives.

I guess if you've got plenty to eat and wear all the time and some place to stay, it's easy to think about the rules. But if you haven't got them things, I suppose you look at it different. A lot of them people who talk about stealing haven't ever been in a position to have t'. Even a lion don't go out and look for something to kill and eat if his belly is full. People ain't no different, 'cept it takes more 'n food to make 'em happy.

MORAL LESSONS: A REALISTIC VIEW

Hinduism expresses its version of the Golden Rule this way: "Let no man do to another what would be repugnant to himself." Yet the culture that produced those words contradicts them. And American society, using Christianity's Golden Rule as a point of reference, does not follow it. A tenant in Blackmoor is likely to view such words as empty, because he rarely sees them in practice. Most of his life he has been turning the other cheek. He now questions the values and behavior other people say he should develop.

> Mister, what do people want from us? Work, they say, is good for you and makes you responsible, but you can't get no job. The early bird gets the worm, they keep sayin'; but I'm tired of worms—I want steak. They say we ought to take better care of our house— I don't care how hard you try, you can't make a outhouse look like a living room. Most of all, people just won't let you alone. What's so good about their way anyway?

Immorality is visible in the disadvantaged community, but the people there are no less moral than the people in other social classes. One does, however, see more fighting, hear more profanity, observe loyalties distorted, experience disrespect for authority and the rights and property of others. A lack of cooperation and deliberate untruthfulness are in evidence also. Closer inspection of the above behaviors makes them more understandable to the outsider.

FIGHTING

> I ain't nonviolent. That's the way it is. You got to do to some people *before* they do to you. Everywhere "the man" has been in the world he has goofed. Go ahead—name some place he's been where he didn't. The savages he tried to civilize all over the world got more honor than him . . . at least savages insult you before your face. I guess he thinks cause you wear shoes, that makes you civilized.

Poverty and misery have convinced the disadvantaged persons in Blackmoor to disregard the platitudes and to make their behavior fit the situation regardless of the moral implications. Parents in the projects, for example, agree that children should not fight; however, they are realistic enough to know that the child who will not fight incurs more physical aggression than any other child.

Either the parent or an older sibling has to assume responsibility for protecting the child who refuses to fight. It is easier to let the child learn to fight and protect himself. In a large measure, the success of a disadvantaged family depends on each member of the family's accepting responsibility for himself, with the knowledge that when he is in real trouble the family will be around to assist him.

Fifty-two of the hundred families interviewed tell their children not to fight unless some child is aggressive toward them. Twenty-one said that their children are instructed to fight—strike the first blow if necessary and then explain it later. And twenty-seven tell their children never to fight; however, the small children are usually taught by the older children with the threat of violence if they do not always fight for themselves. Few of Blackmoor's children run home crying to "mama." The peer group forces them to be aggressive. Fighting is necessary for survival in the project community. The school and its agency in the inner city are aware of this situation. A school principal related:

> Let's face it, the cowards down here fight more than the bullies in the neighborhood where my children go to school. They have to.

The social worker continued:

> You're right, and it's ridiculous to tell these kids not to fight. What other way do they know to solve their problems?

From the teacher:

> They start in the kindergarten on the child that won't protect himself. It's amazing how they can detect the child who won't fight back. First, they take his crayola, then they take his milk and milk money. Later they take his gloves, his hat, his movie money on Saturdays, and anything else he has that he won't fight to keep. We certainly can't watch him every moment.

The deprived child sees his parents or other adults use physical violence in attempting to solve their problems. In the forty-five homes where both parents were present, nine of the married couples interviewed admitted some physical aggression toward each other. Many adults are the first to suggest fighting as a way to solve their problems. Everywhere the child goes he sees fighting—on the playground, in the home, in the streets. It is a part of his daily life. Whenever a loud argument starts, a crowd gathers; people hang from their windows to watch. Mothers with babies in their arms are there to watch; children stop their games to watch. It is as if the people enjoy a vicarious release of their own hostility. And yet others are so accustomed to such activity that they continue their tasks, paying little or no attention to the melee. The police arrive, with sirens screaming and lights flashing. The mere presence of police officers further swells the size of the crowd. In such a situation in the housing project where many of the people are poor, angry, and resentful of authority, the conditions are always potentially explosive. Any imprudent behavior on the part of the crowd or the police can trigger an incident. (The Watts riot in Los Angeles is a good example of how destructive such an incident can be.)

The project child fights with a purpose: to "settle his arguments," to show he is coming of age, because it is the prevailing mode of conduct in his environment and few alternatives are tolerated, for survival, and *to save face.* Many would consider these fairly good reasons.

Profanity

Profanity is heard everywhere in the project. The young child hears it at home from his parents and siblings; he hears it in the elevators, on the landings, in the stairwells, on the playground, from older children and adults. When people cuss in Blackmoor, there is little regard for the presence of children. Forty of the hundred family heads reported that they sometimes used profanity around the children although they did not intend to do so. Another twenty-three said that they used profanity around their children but did not permit their children to use it. One mother put it this way: "I'm grown . . . they ain't supposed to do what I do . . . and they better not." The remainder said that they made a conscious effort not to use profanity around the children.

This latter group represented very young mothers or very old ones and grandmothers. The ease of transition in the language used by project tenants is amazing. They go from biblical quotations to dockside profanity without a raised eyebrow. During one interview, for example, a small child persistently disturbed a project respondent. The censuring mother kept repeating, "All right, now, Mr. ——— is goin' to see me have t' get-a-hold of you." The pleas of the mother seemed to fall on deaf ears. Finally, at wits' end, she said in a most calm, unperturbed and angelic voice, " 'Scuse me Mr. ———." Then in the same breath she yelled, "Come here you little bastard! I'm gonna beat the hell out-o-you!"

And she did.

LOYALTY IN DISADVANTAGED CHILDREN

Loyalty is a reciprocal virtue. It carries with it a positive implication and a moral responsibility. Few children appear to manifest the loyalty exhibited by deprived children, who can be trusted and depended upon to support each other and their own cause(s). However, their loyalty is rarely directed toward the dominant culture. They are loyal to their families, their friends, and the members of their community. Many times, deserting a cause would be more advantageous to them than supporting it; however, they tend to adhere to the cause. Frequently, their loyalty becomes a vice instead of its antithesis. For example, deprived children sometimes remain faithful to friends who are committing wrongs to themselves or against society. Many of them do not know when to terminate their loyalties.

Teen-age boys have been known to agree to be sent to training schools (reform schools) rather than reveal to authorities the names and activities of their friends. Similarly, children have been excluded from school because they refused to provide information to school authorities. Teachers, social workers, and others should not expect or encourage disadvantaged children to carry tales. It would be fruitless to try.

Teachers sometimes inadvertently or intentionally contribute to the lack of school loyalties in some of the statements they

make to children. For example, teachers often make such statements as "This is the worst bunch that I have ever tried to teach,"
"Why can't you be like your brother?" "This school is not as good
as the one I left." Such statements show a lack of loyalty to the
school and to the children. Children should have the loyalty of the
teacher.

There is not a lack of loyalty in the disadvantaged culture;
rather, there appears to be a lack of knowledge of the values in
which one should invest his loyalties and the point at which one
should terminate them.

RESPECT

Respect is when you want to do something but it
would make somebody you like feel bad
about you. —Boy, age twelve, ward of the court

In the ghetto, respect is a reciprocal virtue. Here one gets what
he gives—nothing more. Outside the ghetto one often finds that
persons pay respect to entire groups. Germans may be respected
for industry and Jews for their commercial prowess. Inside the
housing project, the resident only respects the German, the Jew,
or another "soul brother" he knows on a one-to-one basis, never
collectively.

Children in the housing project learn at a very early age to
respect the person who is cunning, the one who lives by his wits,
and the one who can "beat the system." They are taught by their
parents to have regard for the church and other places of solemnity. Their peers and others teach them to be tough. The
youthful project dwellers learn to respect force without instruction,
although they see force wherever they go.

Good manners, courtesy, consideration, and other tenets of respect are viewed by project children as clues to weakness. To be
weak in this community is to be exploited by its members. As one
resident said, "What makes you think the meek will inherit the
earth? They never have!"

Showing disrespect for the property and rights of others is
one of the ways deprived children get back at authority and au-

thority figures. This lack of respect is manifested in the behavior of school-age children. They may vandalize schools and other public and private property, costing the public and individuals thousands of dollars. Preschool children show their lack of training and, perhaps hostility, in the things they do at home. They write on the walls, throw debris in the stairwells, spit on the floor of the corridors, deface the textbooks of their siblings, and destroy some of their own things.

Many adults here do not give, receive, or expect courteous behavior from project children. Between adults and children there is a kind of mutual disrespect.

Respect huh? That's pretty good. Friend, looking at the respect from where you stand is different from seeing it at the gutter level. For every reason you can give me for respect, I can give you two reasons against it. "Grant me an ear," friend.

Take a walk down any street in this project and listen to the language the adults use. Is that the way to respect the kids? Listen to the way some of the teachers talk to the children. I bet you can't find a guy in the block that has been called mister in the last six months. I'm lucky. I've been to school enough to know the reason for all this respect jazz you're talking about. What about the poor sap that's on welfare or the one who has to go to the "painful palace" [public clinic] for a headache? He never gets respect.

COOPERATION

Many feel that project children are uncooperative. It is said that they will not work with other children and that they are obstinate. This is not completely true. Disadvantaged children work well with each other toward a mutually acceptable goal. They are quite effective in cooperating to shut out members of the larger culture. They readily accept responsibility for each other in the family, although they strive for self-sufficiency. Most families could not survive without the mutual cooperation of all members of the family.

The children respect and try to enhance the contributions of the members of their own group but must be convinced that others are genuine before they are cooperative. With outsiders, they may combine their efforts to champion the wrong cause. A case in point: the police sometimes have been prevented from carrying out assignments by large groups of persons—adults and children—who have bodily blocked their activities. It has been necessary on those occasions to bring in police dogs and additional personnel to make arrests. Cooperation taking this form is distorted and, as such, becomes a social absurdity.

Children in this environment cooperate for their own survival, not to please others outside their community. They are constantly reminded by social workers, teachers, and other such persons of the value of working together, but they interpret this to mean:

When they say cooperate, they mean "drop lip" on your friend. The only time somebody is interested in our cooperating is when we do what he wants. It doesn't matter what you want yourself. If a window gets broken out in this damn place, don't ask for it to be put back too many times or they will accuse you of being uncooperative. At school, cooperation means sit down, shut up, and don't ask too many questions. If the teachers could half-teach you, they wouldn't have to ask you to cooperate.

TRUTH

Disadvantaged children, like most children, are truthful most of the time. There are times when they are not. Whether or not they tell the truth is often determined by who is seeking it. The truth to them does not always mean the whole story. From a very early age these children are taught to be prudent around people who ask questions. The children rarely become embarrassed when they are caught in falsehood; they react with anger. They are taught how to handle bill collectors, the project manager, and welfare investigators.

Persons who work with children can usually discriminate between the vivid imaginations of children and falsehood. The stories told by the child in Blackmoor seem too bizarre to be true, but they frequently are true. Whenever primary children from Blackmoor relate stories about fights, shootings, cuttings, and other such violent activities in the neighborhood, these incidents are usually true and are told in the particular style of the children.

At the neighborhood movie house disadvantaged children can often be found loitering around the entrance. They use lying and deception to accomplish their objectives. A child will display a few pennies to some individual who looks like an easy touch and, with a face that shows anguish, ask for a few more pennies in order to attend the movie. This activity may continue for hours. The author has never seen it fail to be fruitful. The children will pocket the few pennies, then wait for the next victim. They will swear to anything that will enable them to accomplish their objectives. The tenacity with which they stick to a tale once it is told is amazing. Even in the face of contradictory evidence, they hold fast. However, they do not normally lie to their peers. They are untruthful to most of their teachers and other such authority figures. Attempting to show them the harm that lying can do seems to be a waste of time. Lying appears to be an instrumental function in the disadvantaged culture.

A survey made in four fourth-grade classes in the three schools that serve Blackmoor revealed that only seven students felt that cheating was dishonest. They reported that they had been told that it was not the honest thing to do, but they could see nothing wrong with it if it helped them. They were asked, "If you saw a classmate cheating and the teacher asked the class about it, would you come forth and tell the truth?" Four said, "Yes." It is a little difficult to decide whether the others are being loyal to their classmates or being deliberately untruthful.

Warnings about the deleterious effects of gossip and false rumors seem to fall on deaf ears. In like manner, motivating deprived children to tell the truth by stressing the immorality of falsehood for selfish reasons appears to be a waste of time. Basically, disadvantaged children do not seem to tell the truth for the sake of the truth except to each other. A lie to an authority figure that reaps them some reward can make them kings among their peer group.

Society tries in various ways to guarantee that its members will be truthful. It has tried technological means (polygraph), judicial means (penalties for libel, slander, and perjury), symbolic techniques (the hand placed on the Bible), and religious appeals (confession). Yet training, background, and example seem to ensure truthfulness best.

CHURCH

There is little doubt that the church can contribute to moral and spiritual development. But it is ineffective in this project community. It is not an important part of the lives of the people, especially the children. Most of the children do not attend church* regularly, either with their parents or alone. Much of their religious training is indirect. The children have heard the moral lessons of the Beatitudes and Ten Commandments from sources other than the church. Their parents and grandparents sometimes quote the Scriptures, and a few parents read the Bible to the children, but the church is not readily accessible to buttress this rudimentary religious exposure.

The church does not seem to be willing to come to this community to seek a congregation, and the people are not seeking the church. Both are existing in a kind of mutual withdrawal. Some tenants are without a close church affiliation. They are in many ways displaced persons. They left other communities in the inner city where they had friends, knew the merchants and the children on the block, and could readily recognize an outsider. Most of the adults attended a neighborhood church and knew the parishioners. This security is not available in the project. Many of the former neighborhoods are gone, including their churches. They have fallen under the bludgeoning iron ball of urban renewal. Where once stood the shadow of righteousness, other contemporary institutions now stand: the supermarket, the bowling alley, high-rise apartments for the rich, and, of course, high-rise apartments for the poor.

The exodus of neighborhood populations to other diverse and ghettoized areas of the city, including public housing projects, created conditions under which the church could not follow the people, although a few of the larger churches relocated. However, for the project resident, the neighborhood church became extinct, thereby rendering one of the arms of morality and instru-

* "Church" includes mass, vespers, and Sunday school.

ments of spiritual development defunct. As a result, project dwellers are often Christian refugees in the inner city.

Because the church is not active among the project residents, one of the spiritual components that help to develop moral behavior is missing; and there is little in the way of religious training that will help children blunt the many despairs the human spirit is heir to.

When I was a child, all day Sunday was spent at church; it was just a few blocks away. We went to Sunday school every Sunday morning. After Sunday school we went around the corner to the confectionery and got a malt or ice-cream cones, then we went back to service. After service we went home to dinner. If there was a program in the afternoon we returned for that. At six in the evening, we went to BYPU [Baptist Young Peoples Union]. You always knew other children would be there and you knew everybody. It was fun. When people got sick everybody would help them. It was more'n just church. It was a social get-together you could depend on every Sunday. Our biggest problem was trying to stay clean all day long and get back home before *The Shadow* went off the radio. A few of the older boys would try "Tom cat'n" around but they wasn't too successful.

Now the church is too big or gone. In the big churches the preacher don't even know you. He might shake hands with you after the service but he don't know your name. Most of the time the assistant pastor do the preaching. The preacher is off being the guest preacher at some other church. At that church over on B Street, the preacher don't even have his phone number in the phone book. Who ever heard of a preacher with his phone not listed? I know he is pretty busy and has a lot of things to do; but I thought part of his job was to be bothered by people. When you go to one of those fancy churches, they don't make you feel too welcome. Last month I went to one and sat next to a woman dripping in furs. When we got up to sing, she wouldn't even share the songbook with me.

The churches most of us went to as children are gone. Out of all of the people that stay in the projects, you can hardly ever find two that go to the same church unless they're in the same family. Since most of the churches have been torn down or moved, there just ain't no decent one left to go to. They got a thousand little store-front churches, but who wants to go there? And there are a couple Catholic churches in the neighborhood but most of us are Baptist and

Methodist.* The church is so far away now that it cost me 60 cents
to ride back and forth on the bus. When you consider that I have
four children, just the cost of bus fare is more than I can afford.

THE STORE-FRONT CHURCH

The housing project is not completely without places of worship.
In fact, there are eighteen store-front churches located in the immediate boundaries of the thirty-square-block area encompassing
the project. Less than 300 of the 11,000 people who live within
these boundaries attend these churches. People who do attend
them appear much more active in their church attendance.

The store-front church has a less complex organizational structure than the more formal church. It approximates the early
origin of the Christian church; that is, it has a congregation—in
biblical terms, a "multitude"—and a minister. It has none of the
organization and ritual that characterize larger churches. Members are accepted simply by coming. There are no choirs,
ushers, boards of trustees. The pastor serves all administrative
positions. Because he answers only to himself, he is in a position
to take financial advantage of his congregation. He frequently
docs.

An empty store, a few crudely constructed pews or rented
chairs, the name painted on the window, a rostrum—and the
store-front church is declared open. It may be housed in a
basement or the first floor of a flat. The minister moves about the
neighborhood seeking a congregation. He finds the older women,
the pensioners, the blind and maimed; this is the kind of congregation he seeks. He does not seek men:

> Men ain't no good if you want a church to be a success, unless
> they're old or sick. They ask too many questions about things. They
> want to know where every nickel go. They won't go out and sell
> tickets or beg for the church. You can't fire men up enough. Women?
> they're the church's salvation, not only little churches like mine but
> in big ones too.

* Of the respondents who have church membership, 78 percent are
Protestants.

A visit to this place of worship on any night except Saturday night is a challenge to the senses and human endurance. As one approaches, he is immediately aware of loud activity. He hears the forceful singing of spirituals, the rhythm of clapping hands and stamping feet, the ring of the tambourine, the repetition of random voices uttering, "Amen." These sounds are accompanied by the sight of people shouting and sometimes rolling on the floor. It is raw exhibition, culminating in a crescendo of emotional pandemonium. Little children who have spent their energies may fall asleep—a mute finale to their exhaustion. The pulse of the store-front church is captured in James Baldwin's *Go Tell It on the Mountain* (1963). Michael Harrington notes it in his book *The Other America* (1963):

> The social status of a Negro church, some claim, can be determined by ear: the higher the class, the less commotion. This attitude is, in itself, a profound indication of the way in which so much of Negro religion is permeated by the fact of Negro poverty.

In spite of the emotional display of the store-front parishioners, two events that are emotionally toned in our society rarely take place in a store-front church: weddings and funerals. The fact that the ministers are not ordained, the ages of the members of the congregations, and the physical appearance of the churches account for the lack of weddings. Inadequate space and crude appointments of the church are the reasons for the absence of funerals. One minister puts it this way:

> You have t' die to be somebody 'round here. These people want things t' be plush when they die. They want air conditioning and rugs on the floor. They don't want people standing outside and peepin' in cause they're curious. So they have the funerals in the best looking place in the neighborhood. That's the funeral home.

Some grandmothers take their grandchildren to church with them —"They need the fear of the Lord in them!" On some occasions it has been necessary for the courts to threaten action against persons for keeping young school-age children up so late at night church services that they fall asleep at school on the follow-

ing day; the children regularly taken are also habitually absent
and tardy.

The Minister

The store-front minister varies from religious fanatic to confidence man. He is *more* likely to be found at the extremes.
Though he may appear to be attentive to his parishioners, he is
really indulging himself. He visits the members of his congregation, and he knows that they enjoy the status of a visit from him.
Each day may find him dining at a different home. But rarely
will he be found in a home where there are adult males. He will
sometimes "bless" combs and other such articles and sell them
to the members of his church. His visits are also designed to recruit new members: "The Lawd's work must go on."

The store-front minister is basically an opportunist and a
spiritual extortionist. Yet many of them hold legitimate jobs,
have genuine interest in people, and try to help them. For this
latter group, church is a kind of "moonlighting."

Parishioners

The behavior of store-front parishioners may defy logic but not
human need and desire. These church members are actually exploited by consent. They want their pastor to have the look of
affluence, whatever the cost. Those parishioners who cannot afford
to dress up, buy a car, dine in a restaurant, or take a vacation
themselves live vicariously through the preacher. They have contributed (directly or indirectly) to everything he possesses; he
represents a part of their hard-earned investment and is their
object of pride. To the love of God, Mother, and Country, they
add another: Minister.

Children whose parents or guardians attend these churches
have restraints imposed on them to which they cannot possibly
adhere with any degree of mental health. The parents are almost
fanatical in their demands. The children are not allowed to dance
or sing songs other than spirituals. They must learn to quote the
Bible whether they can read it or not. They are not allowed to

have playing cards in the home, watch television on Sunday, or go to the movies. They must give whatever money they receive to the church. Such preoccupation with church and religion can cause children to reject both. It is not at all surprising that most of them rebel as soon as they are old enough to resist: "We are Jehovah's Witnesses—that mean you can't do nothing. As soon as I am old enough, I'll wear lipstick and do anything else I want to."

PROSTITUTION

In spite of Blackmoor's children who want to rebel and its reputation for housing criminals and other persons of dubious character, there is definite lack of prostitution.

Contrary to what generally is thought, no evidence of prostitution was found in this housing project. Like many other businesses, prostitution must have a market. A project is primarily a city of women, and obviously wherever the product or service is in abundance, its value diminishes. Prostitutes do not want competition. They usually look for areas where there are few women.

One of the best ways to secure the company of a prostitute is through the assistance of a cab driver, sometimes referred to as a "merchant." He can usually take the prospective customer to where he can find female company for a price. Over a three-day period when the author and a social worker colleague approached forty-six cab drivers within two blocks of the project, asking to be directed to a house of prostitution, thirty-four of them directed or offered to take the inquirers to locations in the central west end of the city. Feeling that the approach was wrong, the two investigators then asked the other twelve drivers to take them into the housing project to find female companionship. Not a single driver could comply with this request. One driver offered an explanation as to why prostitution does not appear to be found in this project: "Who's going to be fooling around in them elevators, walking up and down stairs, going through landings, and run the risk of getting his damn fool head knocked off and robbed for a piece of 'trim'?"* It appears, then, that the physical structure of the project is a deterrent to prostitution.

* The term "trim" is used in both middle-class and lower-class Negro culture. As a verb, "trimming" refers to the act of sexual copulation.

Another reason for a lack of prostitution in the project is related to the number of children housed there.* Most of the women who are residents there have children. Therefore, it would be impractical as well as foolish to conduct such behavior in the home. It is not suggested that there are no prostitutes living in the project studied, but rather that the acts do not appear to be conducted in the area. Bartenders, barmaids, and other such persons can direct individuals to prostitutes that may live in the project; however, the prostitutes are the first to suggest meeting elsewhere. There appears to be considerable prostitution among teen-age girls. Unlike boys, they do not primarily engage in burglaries. They seem to involve themselves in sexual promiscuity without the knowledge, skill, or perhaps luck to prevent pregnancy. The unwritten law among teen-age girls appears to be that it is acceptable to participate in sexual activity, but get paid for it if you can. Pregnancy in young girls is fairly common in the project investigated. Neither the girl nor the community seems too disturbed when it occurs. One girl remarked, "At least I waited until I was fifteen."

IMMODEST BEHAVIOR

The observer of disadvantaged children encounters much behavior that by his own standards may appear to be obscene and immoral. Nevertheless, one should not hastily reach the conclusion that deprived children are more immoral than other children. A more valid observation is that they are perhaps less inhibited both by training and by expectation. Disadvantaged children tend to mimic many of the same behaviors as advantaged children. There is, however, one essential difference. Middle-class children have more restraints imposed upon them externally (by their parents, community expectation and the like) and internally (seeking approval, a desirable self-image). Moreover, middle-class children have more opportunity to observe behavior more in keeping with the standards of the larger culture.

More than half of the parents of teen-age girls (51 percent)

* The average number of children per household in the housing project is 4.6.

revealed that they did not consciously attempt to teach them good habits of speech—that is, clean speech—dress, and posture. In the ten-to-twelve age group, six out of ten girls and eight out of ten boys reported never being admonished for loud, boisterous speech habits. Less than half of the boys and girls aged thirteen to sixteen reported such admonitions. The variance between the two groups is probably due to the sophistication of the older children. Similarly, older pupils have had more training in school in hygiene and the homemaking arts. Most of them know what the correct behavior should be, but they operate under conditions where it is rarely practiced. Girls are rarely taught how to walk, sit, or dress "properly." They seem to think that being well-groomed and looking glamorous are one and the same, or they think that when they wear such glamorous attire as dangling earrings and dresses with sequins they are well-groomed.

The anatomy of the female is such that her movement is more sensuous than the male's, and young girls are constantly exposed to the accent on "sex" via the mass media and advertising. Not having the experience and knowledge to be discriminating or the inner security to be different, they frequently choose to emulate behavior that a counselor would not recommend. It is common to see girls in the project environment wearing very tight clothes, using lipstick and other cosmetics, and wearing nylon stockings, earrings, and other such ornaments at a much earlier age than middle-class girls. Many disadvantaged girls tend to become adults in miniature. Outsiders feel that they are inappropriately dressed for children and immodestly dressed for school. Parents fail to teach them either by instruction or by example; many mothers, especially the younger ones, wear skintight pants everywhere but to church.

"Immorality" suggests not only a negative prohibition but a positive implication. There are, of course, many deprived families who adhere to strong moral and spiritual values. They observe the laws, codes, beliefs, and modes exemplified in the larger culture. Deprived families, particularly mothers and very young children, are candid—if they trust you. This appears to be the key to interaction with them. Throughout this discourse numerous behaviors have been discussed that individuals have employed to meet their needs. Many of these behaviors have implied some aspect of immorality or at least imprudent activity. However, deprived individuals are probably as morally conscious as any other group. This is observed in their attitudes toward their acceptance of illegitimate children and the responsibility they assume for these children. They do not deny or disown them; acceptance of the responsibility for them is genuine moral behavior.

Disadvantaged children are bicultural products; they are even bilingual to the extent that their language is their own creation. They must meet the standards of their own creation and community as well as attempting to meet the standards of the dominant culture. The former goal they can achieve; the latter, perhaps. Unfortunately for the deprived child, it is the desires, methods, and judgments of the mainstream that prevail. The school is designed to meet the needs, aspirations, and objectives of the mainstream, sometimes at the expense of the deprived groups. Moral and spiritual values encompass both groups.

X - Idle Hands

*No job—nothing to do, no place to go and no
money to spend and my case worker is telling me about
the worthy use of leisure.* —Unemployed man

Leisure time is generally conceived as that time an individual has free from required work activity. Recent unprecedented advances in technology have made available to large numbers of workers more leisure time than they have ever had before. Workers who used to spend most of their time in required labor now have more free time, and this shift has been so rapid that sociologists, educators, industry, and government are giving serious thought to the problem of finding ways in which individuals can profit most from their leisure time.

Even the children today do not appear to be shackled to the chores that once made up some of their out-of-school work activity. Modern appliances have liberated both parents and children from many of the tasks traditionally carried on in the home. How this additional time should be used is one of the biggest problems confronting society.

The problem appears to be even more complex for the culturally disadvantaged groups. The disadvantaged today are among the first groups to be affected by advances in technology. They lose their jobs. They have a superabundance of free time but we cannot call it leisure. Large numbers of deprived people, particularly men, are unemployed. So much free time because of unemployment is detrimental to families. Even when the poor are employed, when they are away from the job they seem more concerned with immediate gratifications (liquor, food, sex, entertainment, and new possessions) than the long-range positive effects of using their time and resources in a way many would call a wholesome use of leisure. Persons in the disadvantaged culture often fail to see the value in the worthy use of their leisure time and consequently do not plan their activities in order to obtain the maximum benefit from the time spent away from work.

Leisure time? Do you mean what I do when I ain't working—and, mister, that's all the time? Well, the answer is I look for work! We ain't exactly stupid, but it looks like all them people writing about us and talkin' about us is. Funny, ain't it? We're busy tryin' to find something to do and they're trying to show us how to do nothing.

I understand about good use of leisure time, reading books, having hobbies, and all that sort of stuff—but really, mister . . . !

There are some things that we can do together for leisure. We can talk, I guess, or watch birds—but you need them "spyglasses" [binoculars] for that. I can't see how going to church can be thought about as leisure and most of the other things cost something. If you wanted to go down at that community center to square dance you're scared to walk back through the streets.

LACK OF MUTUALITY IN FAMILY ACTIVITIES

Deprived children share very few recreational activities with their parents. Television viewing appears to be the only activity shared by a significant number of mothers and children. Seven out of ten mothers said this activity was one they shared jointly with the children. However, the programs viewed were rarely chosen with the smaller children considered. Moreover, television provides a minimum reciprocal communication or interaction between members of the family. The kinds of recreational experiences that provide the greatest imaginable verbal or communication skills—such as talking, playing games, and visiting—are shared by only 12 percent of the families. Thirty-four of the mothers attended movies as a recreational activity, although only nine reported regular attendance. Only three parents said that movie attendance was a family activity. This figure varies in summer, when families, using the automobiles of the mother's boyfriends, are able to attend drive-in movies. One may infer that the higher cost and the need for proper clothing to attend movie theaters compared to the "come as you are" attire, the lower cost, and the heat may account for the larger attendance at drive-in movies during summer months. Forty families went on outings. This form of recreation is also a seasonal activity, primarily summer, in the group studied. However, one mother relates, "For us to have a picnic, we have to travel a long distance to get to a park. We don't have a car, and just carfare alone would be a whole day's salary."

Although some mothers sew to augment their income, there appears to be very little participation in handicrafts, for leisure or as part of a recreational program. Mrs. W. reports:

> Whoever heard of a quilting bee in a housing project? I guess we could use one though. You know, every once and a while they get all fired up over some community program; then, by the second or third week they're talking about no money. They get you all interested and then nothing. I bet we have had three sewing clubs in the last two years.

Only five mothers indicated interest or participation in such an enterprise.

Disadvantaged families who do share their leisure choose many and varied interests. One family reported bowling as a family activity and another roller skating and still another block printing. Surprisingly few parents take their small children to the only playground adjacent to the projects or to the tot lots. The play areas are inadequate to serve the needs of the preschool population. The playgrounds are not always safe—"Them tot lots are paved in broken bottles."

Indoor activities such as popcorn popping and baking were found in one and four cases respectively. Only three families appeared to have some semblance of a well-balanced program of recreation.

LACK OF TRADITIONAL FAMILY ACTIVITIES

Television, radio, and other such modern entertainment have displaced the church-centered activities of the family, as well as the story telling of grandparents and much of the reading for enjoyment. The stories and "old wives' tales" that once gave small children delight appear merely to be tolerated by the more sophisticated urban child. This is probably true in the middle-class culture also. Few disadvantaged parents sing and play games with their children.

Although grandmothers sometimes frown on such activities, both parents and teen-age children appear to like dancing and card playing, but they do not usually participate in these activities together.

Mere survival consumes most of the disadvantaged adult's energies, and "belonging" and identity appear to consume most of the child's. The family in this subculture tends to view leisure as a preoccupation of the rich. Similarly, "togetherness" and "do-it-yourself" activities for the purpose of entertainment or diversion are considered middle class. Deprived persons do not appear to consider any *work* fun.

Parents in this subculture do not see the worth of making good use of leisure. Moreover, their experiences, values, attitudes, and commitments appear to be barriers to the extrinsic influences that reveal such worth. A curious paradox characterizes the disadvantaged environment. The people appear to have more free time, but they tend to have a kind of "poinsettia view"; that is, they perceive the obvious beauty of the leaves (free time) but frequently forget that the function of the leaf is to nurture the flower (the worthy use of leisure time). Neither the larger culture nor its agencies have been able to motivate the majority of deprived parents in this environment to assume responsibility for providing desirable recreational activity for themselves or their children.

Disadvantaged persons who do not know how to find enjoyable release from their daily work and who are bored with themselves frequently acquire bad habits and undesirable attitudes, which may carry over into their children's school life. Moreover, children should know the importance of being assigned to responsible tasks and taking part in the activities of the home. Such recognition of responsibility and participation in home activities would logically seem to carry over into school. Children who do not learn to use their leisure time wisely and who do not find some worthwhile activity in which to invest their interest may fail to develop the initiative and resourcefulness that can provide for later creativity. Children who have special talents but who do not have the opportunity to develop those talents may deprive both themselves and society of significant contributions. Finally, future vocations that could develop from childhood interests are improbable if, during childhood, disadvantaged children fail to develop any interests.

FEW HOBBIES IN EVIDENCE

Not a single mother reported a hobby of her own or one that her elementary school children found interesting. Most parents do not consider reading a hobby, although twenty-one reported that they spent their spare time reading.* In homes where there were high school students, some hobbies were reported:

> I like photography but school is the only place I can do anything with it. Can you imagine trying to use the bathroom as a darkroom in this house? I might as well set it up in the galleys [halls in his building].

> You don't do just anything to say you have a hobby. Most hobbies cost money or require space. It is not something you can do just because it appeals to you.

> I've been on that hobby kick several times; but you got to quit the scene before too long. Either you haven't the bread or maybe you just get tired of it.

> The way I understand it, a hobby is supposed to be a release, a

* Although twenty-one of the parents claim reading as a spare-time filler, reading material was not in plain view in fourteen of these homes. Magazines were on display in four of the households, and three homes had books.

chance to relax from the everyday tasks before you. It's kind of difficult, though, when you're worrying about what you're going to wear to school. You can't study cause the kids won't be quiet; and if you put your things down, the kids will get a hold of them.

Among preadolescents no hobbies were reported. The majority of mothers felt that most hobbies cost money and did not serve any useful purpose. They do not appear to see the long-range value in such activities. Therefore, hobbies, in terms of leisure-time activities, appear to have little appeal for disadvantaged families. It follows that their preschool children have few, if any, models in this area to emulate.

SOCIAL AGENCIES AND LEISURE

Whereas some of the social agencies in the project area have offered recreational and leisure-time programs, it is evident that such programs are too narrow in scope and too restrained by the size of the professional staff and physical facilities to meet even the minimum recreational needs of the people they serve. The tensions of day-to-day living and the awareness of mere existence without a feeling of worth seem to characterize deprived people. There is rarely time for fun—and no place to have it. The director of a social agency serving the project community studied related it this way:

> There are very few ways for the thousands of people in this neighborhood to get status and relieve pressures. There are almost no recreational facilities. Where can our families go to play?

There is little doubt that disadvantaged children in the area studied have few planned activities. Neither their parents nor the social agencies in the community appear to be sufficiently equipped to provide them with adequate guidance in the worthy use of leisure time.

DISADVANTAGED CHILDREN AND LEISURE

Left to their own devices, disadvantaged children develop certain techniques for the use of free time. The precocious emancipation of disadvantaged children from the home has been described earlier. Children in this environment develop cliques and gangs probably earlier than children of comparable ages in more affluent environments. The peer group and gang tend to determine the kinds of recreational activities that are acceptable in this subculture. We previously discussed the propensities of the deprived children for physical or motoric activities. Therefore, it is only natural that the various athletic activities are among the favorite pastimes of this group.

XI - The Home and the School

The home and the school are complementary by tradition, necessity, and logic. These are two major institutions that have the same ultimate goal: the education of the child. In an affluent community, the home and school are effective partners and exercise a dual effort to fulfill their mutual objective. On the other hand, in the black ghetto and, more specifically, in the housing project, each of these two institutions makes assumptions about the other that are unwarranted and unrealistic. Each has a lack of understanding about the function, ability, limitations, and needs of the other. Both fail to communicate the continuity of reciprocal responsibilities in providing for the educational needs of the child. The home and the school in the ghetto, then, rather than being complements are in many cases adversaries. Consequently, neither does an adequate job, and the child is the one who suffers. Assumptions about the home made by the school that seem reasonable for the middle-class child, white or black, are totally untenable for the culturally disadvantaged.

THE ASSUMPTIONS

Traditionally, the school has had certain expectations about the child and home that helped to facilitate its own function. The school assumed that a child had certain perquisites: a (quiet) place to study with the necessary tools (a table or desk with adequate light, pencils, books, newspapers and magazines, dictionaries). It assumed that the majority of children who came to school were from homes that have some type of educational tradition, and the children were encouraged and motivated to understand the value of education.

The school assumed that a child would want to learn. It took for granted that a child had toys, that he had been to a super-market and to the zoo, that he had some kind of routine about his general habits. The school assumed that children would come to school with a positive attitude toward teachers and that the child had been taught to respect authority and the law. And finally, the educational institution expected children to be healthy (get enough sleep, nourishment, the proper clothing and shelter, health services, and so on) when they were sent to school; and, of course, children were expected to be punctual, to attend regu-larly, to have good manners, and to behave. In short, the school expected a child to have had certain experiences and to have developed many different skills to prepare himself for attending school. In fact, the school had a prescribed set of plans called the curriculum that would be effective only if the things the school assumed would happen actually did happen. The school has always expected these things even from poor children. Most educational agencies at all levels still hold these assumptions, and they refuse to accept the educational facts of life, especially as these facts relate to the disadvantaged home and child. While the school continues to retain its assumptions and expectations and to speculate on what ought to be, the disadvantaged child in the housing project must live with the realities.

THE REALITY: WHERE THEY LIVE, WORK, AND PLAY

The school often assumes that the home informs the child that the school is a good place to go. The reality, however, is that parents in the ghetto sometimes use the school as a kind of "bogey man." They frequently threaten and control the behavior of young preschool children by informing them that the teacher will punish them when they go to school. Consequently, the summer preceding kindergarten enrollment, small children appear to develop excessive anxiety. Such an indoctrination for small children provides a poor image of the teacher. As a result, many children do not look forward to going to school. They frequently perceive themselves as being punished by the parents in being sent to school. They also seem to be conscious of the behavior of their parents when the behavior of the latter indicates they are trying to "get rid" of them (the children) by enrollment in school. The children detect this attitude through the many subtle ways inherent in the parent-child relationship or perhaps they listen to their parents when they say:

> I'll sure be glad when Butchie is five so the school can worry with him some.

Or:

> These children worry me to death. Won't be long though, they'll be in school by fall. And they say that we have children just to get ADC. Did you ever hear of anything so ridiculous? I'll have peace the day they go to school.

And:

> When you hear nothing but kids yelling all day long, you're glad for any relief you can get. Everywhere you walk you're stepping over children, yours or somebody else's.

Regardless of the mother's motives, as an educational laboratory, the apartment in Blackmoor is seriously deficient. First, it is noisy. There is inadequate light, no quiet place to read, no specific place to write, few publications available, and no place to spread out and be left alone. Every room is devoid of academic atmosphere.

Children in the project must utilize every available surface in order to find a place to write. A piece of corrugated cardboard across the heating unit is used. Sometimes a child sits on the floor and uses the cocktail table; another gets on his knees and uses the seat of a chair. The kitchen table is shared by several children. Similarly, a child will use the top of the television set while other members of the household are viewing the screen. The bed is also used, and there is always the floor. In every instance, the child adjusts to what he has, but his home is deficient in providing not only educational tools but also an educational climate.

The project home is equally deficient in providing a place where children can read and concentrate. There is no family room, no den, no quiet separate room where a child can be alone. The child striving to concentrate must contend with the television set, the record player, the radio, other children running and playing on the landings, and the noise that is part of any household where there are children. The housing project environment provides the child no quiet nook for his solitude.

Inadequate light in the apartment is another problem for the child. Overhead light is often the only available source of illumination; and because this source is too far from the printed page, it is not good. Although some homes do have table lamps, they are not sufficient in number to meet the needs of the entire family. Proper wattage and other factors of artificial illumination to make a place suitable for study are not considered by the family. Windows in the apartments are located only on one side of the building; the heat and harshness of natural light in summer is harmful to the eyes and thereby renders this source deficient for reading; and the shortness of daylight hours after school limits the availability of this source in winter.

The school should be able to assume that a home has certain common objects, but it cannot. For example, in sixty homes there were no pictures on the wall. Nine out of ten apartments did not have a clock. Half of them did not have salt and pepper shakers. One grandmother asked, "What's wrong with the box it comes in?" Many homes are without cups and saucers, and only eleven had a calendar. Not a single home had a dirty clothes hamper—"What for? We ain't got enough clothes to have a hamper. We just wrap them in a sheet or something." In short, there are many common items not found in the disadvantaged home.

It would seem reasonable for the school to assume that a home would receive a daily newspaper. The reality is that not a single family observed subscribed to a daily newspaper. One resident said:

Who's got time to read a newspaper anyway? All my time is spent
making ends meet. The things in the paper don't seem too important
to me. Onliest time they don't ignore us in the paper is when we do
sumpting. Take a look at it . . . what's in it that they put there
for somebody like me? Except maybe the funnies, sports, and want
ads. The funnies ain't funny; I don't know nothing about no sports,
except baseball maybe—and that what's in the want ads nowadays
don't mean me.

Eight families said that a newspaper was purchased daily. Thirteen other mothers who worked as domestics in surburban homes
reported bringing the previous day's newspaper home each day.

Sixty-four apartments had copies of a weekly tabloid that neither reports national and international news nor editorializes on
local contemporary civic and social issues; it sensationalizes the
unusual circumstances that surround murder, prostitution, felonies, brawls, homosexuality, and adultery. One reader reported:

You see frowns of disapproval when you buy this scandal sheet, but
you got to admit, this sheet tells it like it is. When we read this trash
we find out about others just like ourselves, doing the same things we
do—it just takes this kind of junk to bring it right down front.

One possible reason more families do not receive newspapers
each day is because no deliveries are made to the apartments
in the projects; the newspaper boy dares not leave a paper on
the project threshold or walk through the corridors for fear of
assault and robbery. Five of the eight families who purchased a
daily paper subscribed to national weekly magazines. *Life, Look,
Sports Illustrated,* and *Ring* were the publications purchased
by these families; all the subscribers were in the households of
aggressive employed residents.

Occasionally, one observes a copy of *Ladies' Home Journal,
Better Homes and Gardens*—and, surprisingly, *The New Yorker,
Harper's* or *Atlantic Monthly.* Close inspection of these magazines
reveals suburban addresses and family names not common in the
project community.

In homes where there are teen-agers and young mothers, one
sees the usual collection of black publications and a few "up-
tight" magazines. *Tan Confessions, Jet,* an occasional copy of

Ebony, and numerous horror comic books are the magazines most frequently handled or read. In the apartment of the free floater, there are the ever-present copies of *Playboy* and *Downbeat.* Sometimes an issue of *Muhammad Speaks,* the official publication of the Black Muslims, is also found in this tenant's apartment.

Watchtower, the official publication of the Jehovah's Witnesses, is commonly found in the apartments of the aged. The Bible, however, is still the book most frequently possessed, if not the only book read, by the aged. The King James Version of the Bible is the only one read by the aged tenant, although the text of the Revised Standard Version is easier to read and for that reason would seem to be the logical version to buy. The aged resident disagrees. He resents change:

> God a 'mighty, they streamline everything from cars to digging ditches. Now they want you to read the Good Book streamlined. No thanks, this here Bible was good enough for my parents and it's good enough for me.

In seventy-three families, no books other than the Bible and a few old dictionaries provided through a parents' organization near the project were in evidence.

Middle- and upper-grade children regularly bring their textbooks home for study and homework but just as consistently return them to school each day never having opened them. Similarly, primary children in some schools in this district are allowed to take some library books home but may not have the stories read to them by someone in the household. Seven families said that they purchased children's books. Although there is a branch of a public library within walking distance of this housing project, only twenty-one families reported ever borrowing books that could be considered appropriate to be read to preschool children. No bookcases or shelves were observed in any of the apartments. Books are not normally handled as items to be appreciated. In cases where preschool children are told stories or read to, older siblings assume the responsibility.

Coloring books, picture books, books of paper dolls, and other such items given to children in a privileged home are rarely found in the possession of the disadvantaged child. Even such prosaic items as notebook paper and some type of stationery may not be available. A note to the grocer, a neighbor, or a teacher is written on the back of an envelope or on part of a brown paper bag or on some other such material. Only one apartment included in this sample had a desk. The lack of available books, paper, pencils, and places to work are but a few of the realities (tools and deficiencies) that affect the disadvantaged, but there are worse.

Many disadvantaged preschool children have never seen a piece of crayola, their reflections in a mirror, or a real balloon. Most of them never play with a puzzle or building blocks before they go to school. There they are fascinated when they handle chalk and watch the magic of a pencil for the first time. They exude delight and express mystery and timidity when they hear their voices reproduced on tape. They seem exhilarated when they manipulate and handle the educational toys and gadgets that can enrich the play of children.

Like small children everywhere, Blackmoor's children play with pot tops, spoons, old clothing, discarded purses, old shoes, and many other miscellaneous odds and ends. Little girls play with dolls, and boys play with guns, if they have them. Few preschool children have stuffed toys, and one never sees a small child pulling a toy truck or animal. But one does see the project child pulling a shoe box loaded with the kind of debris that only a child can collect, identify, and cherish.

Blackmoor's young children do not have the variety and quantity of playthings that more affluent preschoolers do. Children can be found who have never owned toys. Unlike many other children, these youngsters in the project receive toys only at Christmastime, if then. When they do receive playthings for Christmas, there are only one or two items, and these are usually destroyed by continuous handling or crushed by love of possession before the holiday season ends. In the days, weeks, and months that follow, remnants of the Christmas toys can be seen as a part of some other construction project of the children. Bit by bit, and part by part, the toys finally disappear.

The majority of project children play with trinkets and discarded items. The eight- or nine-year-old becomes proficient using

one roller skate; he develops his baseball "swing" and "eye"
using a broomstick and bottle caps. Except for the early-morning
television programs, few preschool children have an opportunity
to watch programs appropriate for their age. Older siblings and
adults dictate program selection. Most of the radio programs
heard in these disadvantaged homes are confined to soul music
and other rhythm and blues recordings played by local disc
jockeys, but the children do learn, as one mother notes:

> I just can't understand it—they know all the songs on the radio and
> they learn all the dances they see on TV, but when they get to school,
> the teacher says they can't sing and do the rhythms or whats-a-never
> they call them—they're dances to me. The dances my children do
> make them book dances look sick. Fact is, my children probably
> have to slow down so the book dances can catch up. There ain't no
> chance to make up your own.

This mother is implying that there is little opportunity for her
children to be creative. The rhythmic skills of disadvantaged
children are so far advanced over those suggested in the average
primary school curriculum that, for the most part, these children
are not interested in "rhythms." Motivation to learn social dances
is greater, but, here again, the sophistication of the children
transcends school activities.

Parents in Blackmoor assume that children will learn when
they go to school.

> That's what the school's for, ain't it? I ain't no schoolteacher. If we
> do it all before they gets to school the teacher won't have nothing to
> do but just set up there—and they do enough of that as it is.

Most parents do not appear to see any relationship between
providing the young child with many and varied experiences
and the ease with which he will adjust to or learn in school.
They are not against providing experiences for the preschool child
or for his later formal education; rather, they tend to be indifferent because they do not see the immediate value. Eighteen of
the family heads felt that the presence of books and other such
materials in the home were of value to the child before he enters

school. However, another felt differently: "You can't get educated just by sitting in a "lie'berry"—so what good are lotsa books in the house if nobody don't know how to use 'em?" No parent reported singing lullabies or telling fairy tales to preschool children at bedtime.

In the middle class, an education is more than a means to prepare for a life's vocation. It is a habit, a way of life, an expectancy. From the cradle children are indoctrinated with its value and rewards. It is a folkway. With the disadvantaged, on the other hand, education is still not a custom. There is little or no educational tradition among the majority of Blackmoor's families. Intellectual development among the project residents has never had the priority it has had among the middle and upper classes. Deprived parents reject or see little value in the activities that the social classes above them encourage. They know neither the educational jargon nor the behavior that has meandered through the decades in middle-class families.

Concern with intellectual pursuits, community exposure, language proficiency, civic responsibility, good manners, and pride of family name all characterize the preoccupation of the dominant culture in maintaining an intellectual atmosphere in the home. Similarly, this custom embodies long-range plans that have economic support and social sanction. The individual in the disadvantaged group, on the other hand, is not primarily concerned with any of the intellectual or social pursuits enumerated. His preoccupation is with survival:

Who cares about all them things you talking about? Maybe they're important all right, but I got to show my kids how to make it here and now. What my daddy did don't put no meat on the table and what his name is never was important and it ain't gonna start being. What these kids gotta know is how to keep from having their things took from them and how to keep their heads on their shoulders. That by itself is a full-time job.

Mothers in general and those included in this study in particular have a higher educational level than fathers. This fact again may emphasize the custom of educating the black girl and the lack of training for the black man.

Colored folks always did send the wrong one to school. You can find lots of educated colored women, but not many men. They prepared the lamb to protect the wolf. Up until a few years ago, men that did get educated couldn't get the job that they was educated for. I'd be willing to bet you find more educated men working in the post office or being policemen than you can from any other group. Lots of them was college graduates while a lot of white men didn't even have a high school education; 'specially in the police department, some of them didn't even have a grade-school education. Wouldn't think you'd need a college education to write out a parking ticket.

Of the 50 men included in this study, 6 had no formal education, 33 had an eighth-grade education or less, and 11 had attended high school, 3 of whom had a diploma. Correspondingly, of the 103 women included in this sample, only one had no formal education, but she had been taught to read and write. Another 29 had an eighth-grade education or less and 73 had attended high school, 24 of them graduating. Of the 24 high school graduates, 7 went to college for at least one semester.

Theoretically, women in this housing project have enough schooling for some degree of economic solvency through employment. On the other hand, few men have the schooling that will allow them to compete successfully in the labor market. Only three men had received some training in the United States armed services; however, at this time, their skills do not have a market in civilian life. A significant majority of the household heads (75 percent) reported that their parents did not finish grade school, and 86 percent reported that their parents did not finish high school. None of the interviewees said that their parents had gone to college. The academic background of the deprived families studied is nonexistent.

In addition to few educational tools and an absence of educational tradition, there is also a lack of motivation in the disadvantaged home. Lower-class children receive few rewards, verbal or tangible, for their behavior. They are not encouraged to aspire to a better standard of English in the home. Many of their parents have come from situations where they went to school only because there was a law that said they must go. The law wasn't always enforced:

Back in the time I went to school nobody tried to bribe you to go. If you didn't want no learning, nobody tried to make you, except maybe the teacher. Now they say that we always got to be praising them [the children], telling them not to use "ain't," but if they don't use "ain't," I don't know what to tell them to use instead. Anyway, what's more important, what you say, or the words you use to say it?

Parents seem more concerned about whether or not children learn to talk, not what they say or how they say it. Of the three respondents who sent their children to nursery school, none revealed that they discussed or questioned the children about their activities at the school. Except for the children of those families labeled "the respectables" in this book, few children in this environment have pressure put upon them to live up to high standards, few appear to be overprotected or overindulged, but most seem to be neglected.

Disadvantaged children are not included in planning, discussing, and evaluating; therefore, they seldom learn to synthesize their thoughts, stick to the subject, or present their ideas in sequence for effective communication (unless they are permitted to choose the subject for discussion). The teachers of disadvantaged children can certainly give testimony to this observation. At one of the local universities in Midwest City, a group of teachers participating in a workshop for teachers of the disadvantaged in the area of oral communication said:

If I knew more about the language which is used by these children I wouldn't feel that my job is so hopeless. Actually when they tell stories about the life and behavior of the people where they live, they do so with a passion. They never omit details; their stories have sequence and continuity, and they have insight as to why a certain act took place. But when I ask them to read just one paragraph and then close the book and tell me about what they have just read, they are at a complete loss. They don't know where to begin.

Another says:

It's not that they can't talk or don't have something to say. It is perhaps more accurate to say that I don't understand what they are saying. Let me give you an example. When a child asked me, "Can a snake doctor whupp a waltz?" I didn't have the slightest idea what he was talking about. I later found that the translation of his question meant "Could a dragonfly whip a wasp?" Sometimes I spend most of my class time translating what the children are saying.

Others say:

> At times the children are delightful; some have many good thoughts and express them well; however, their conversations reveal many sordid and unpleasant experiences.

> The oral language of the children indicates lack of talking with grownups, or, being talked to by grownups. It really doesn't matter though—the grownups in the lives of these children speak in sentence fragments, too.

> On the whole, the language of kids in my room is not as expressive as their level of intelligence warrants. It is always too saturated with slang and is indicative of a lack of environmental influences which stimulate the development of good speech.

In addition to little opportunity for children to hear good English spoken in the home, few other activities are carried on that can be used to motivate the child.

Most of the children do not see their parents involved in intellectual pursuits, such as reading and visiting parks, museums, and civic and church meetings. When asked about such activities, one male respondent replied: "Reading? Visiting museums? Man, are you for real?"

Parents do not go many places:

> I'm lucky to get to a drive-in once in a while—let alone a museum. I know you hear the women down here set in the taverns all day, but that's not quite right. True, some of them do; but most of them don't. All I am trying to say is that the people down here are just like your friends—except, maybe, they don't go to museums.

Mothers in Blackmoor do not go to church in great numbers. The PTA, however, does attract large numbers of mothers; Blackmoor is located in a school district in Midwest City that is nationally famous for its ability to stimulate parents to come to the school.

A significant number of parents have a positive attitude toward education, but the school cannot assume that children will share it. Some of the important reasons for this paradox originate in the school and are brought home. Half of the residents in this study do not express a positive attitude toward teachers; in fact, many of them verbalize hostilities toward teachers. Six out of ten parents felt that teachers "talked down" to them even in cases in which the teachers were known to the respondents before the former became teachers. In some cases, the teacher had attended school with the respondent and had lived in the same block. In one case, the teacher had spent time in the same house and had eaten at the same table as the respondent, whom he claimed not to remember.

Thirty-four of the ten- to twelve-year-olds said they thought that the teacher was frequently unfair. Twice as many of the thirteen- to fourteen-year-olds believed that the teacher was unfair to them. In cases where children did not like to come to school, more than half of both the fourth-graders (ten- and eleven-year-olds) and seventh-graders (thirteen- and fourteen-year-olds) reported that they did not like the teacher. When asked why, the overwhelming response was, in essence, that the teacher embarrassed them and thought that her way was the only way that anything could be done. Several parents reported that teachers called their children animals, crumb snatchers, crumb crushers, and other such names.

When Jonathan Kozol, in his book *Death at an Early Age* (1967), wrote about the art teacher who crushed children by what she said to them, he was indeed describing not only what happens to slum children in Boston but was also illustrating what happens to children in the ghetto in Midwest City. Not all teachers are as insensitive as Kozol's art teacher, but far too many are. In fact, Kozol noted in his book that as a novice teacher "I cannot say that I learned anything except how to suppress and pulverize any sparks of humanity or independence or originality in children." Again and again we see this same theme in the writings of men who look at schools in the slums.

Kenneth Clark has been talking about it for more than a decade and did so again in *Dark Ghetto* (1965); and *36 Children* by Herbert R. Kohl (1967), *Our Children Are Dying* by Nat Hentoff (1966), and *The Way It's Spozed to Be* by James Herdons (1968) are all books describing some of the things that happen to children in the slums.

Project parents frequently complain about the attitude of teachers toward them and their children. The following are verbatim statements of their complaints:

> When you ask them a question, they take out a lot of papers that they know you don't know nothing about, to prove how stupid your kids are. What you want to know is how to help them.

> I went to school with Miss P., but she don't even speak to me. She looks at you like you're dirt. That look makes you feel like dirt.

> You never get a chance to talk when you go see teachers; they do all the talking—we *do* have something to say sometimes.

> Not all of them teachers try to be "so much" but them that do make you hate all the rest.

> I saw my little girl's teacher downtown and she acted like she didn't know me—and they say that we're ignorant. What is any more ignorant than that?

> One of them gals over there is always talking about culture. Dee [her daughter] said that Miss Y. tells the children that they ain't got no culture. That tavern I saw her in ain't no Met.

> I told that heifer that my little boy's name is Charles and she'd better call him that—really.

Both parents and the children of both sexes felt that male teachers were the more understanding and fair. They did not believe that male teachers laughed at them or were afraid to "put their hands on them." Similarly, parents revealed that they preferred to have conferences with male teachers because, as they put it, "Men teachers don't have to stay in the book." The children also reported that male teachers do not use sarcasm as some female teachers do. Parents and school-age children reported that male teachers were friendlier and seemed to accept them as

they found them. No child reported that he had been exposed
to ridicule such as isolation, being put in the corner (children are
still stood in corners), name-calling, and the like by a male
teacher. Some middle-grade (fourth through sixth grades) children reported this type of activity among women teachers. Only
one upper-grade child said that he experienced this behavior
from female teachers. Older children show resentment toward
such activity and can, in fact, be a threat to the teacher, whereas
younger children, possibly out of fear, do not show as much
resentment. There is a kind of hostility toward the school.

Parents are rarely in contact with the school before the children are initially enrolled unless they have older children in
school. When there is contact between the home and school, it
usually involves the poor behavior or academic performance of
a school-age child.

Parents think the schools belong to the Midwest City board
of education, and the board of education does little to change
this concept; nor does the specific neighborhood convince the
people of their ownership of the school.

The ensuing statements illustrate the too frequent apathy of
the school:

> You just can't walk up to the school and tell them that you have a
> child that will be coming next fall or next year. All they do is tell
> you to bring him back in September. They tell you to bring his birth
> certificate and have him vaccinated, but they don't ever say anything
> that makes you feel welcome.

> Only time they want to see you over to that school is when your
> children done something wrong or when they need you to help them
> in a school tax drive.

> They sent us some kind of paper asking us did we have any children
> what would be going to school in September. Now that ain't going
> help us—that's to help them.

The school assumes that children will be in attendance when
they are not ill. The reality is that deprived children in Blackmoor are sometimes withdrawn from school and sent to live
with relatives in the rural South. Later, they are sent back to
the parents. Such a procedure is primarily the result of the fre-

quent periods of economic stress during which the responsible adult in the family cannot provide for the minimum needs of the children. Such a procedure may be repeated as often as four times within a school year and as many as ten times during a child's elementary school tenure. The need for children to adjust to two completely different environments makes adjustment to either a very difficult task. The cumulative records of many deprived school-age children reveal many "withdrawals" and "re-entries" because these children have moved to Southern communities for varying lengths of time during the school year. The academic records of these children usually are very poor in both school systems. In like manner, there is excessive intramobility in this environment. Numerous children are transferred within the school system. The first day of the week and/or month large numbers of transfers are processed. One may infer (from experience of working in this area) that rent is due on the first of the week or month. More specifically, in the project surveyed, most of the recipients of welfare subsistence receive their checks on the tenth of the month, sometimes referred to as "mother's day." One may expect children to be transferred around this time. It is sometimes cheaper for many of the tenants to move than to pay the rent. Tenants, however, can be sued for the rent owed to the housing authority.

School-age children are frequently kept home to baby-sit while mothers work, shop, keep clinic appointments, or visit. Mrs. R.'s explanation was: "I can't afford to hire no baby-sitter. One day out of school once and a while won't hurt them. I missed days in school and it didn't hurt me."

Children are also kept home from school by guardians, usually grandmothers, who are disciples of a farmers' almanac. Shackled to the unsubstantiated weather predictions given by such a source, some children are forced by their grandparents or guardians to remain at home. The health and safety practices in the home are sometimes controlled by this source, also. Many parents, for example, never permit a tooth to be extracted if the "signs" (phases of the moon) are not right. Strong belief in such superstitions by the parents tends to sanction some irregular school attendance.

The school expects the home to provide "good" examples for the children. The reality is that almost every niche of the disadvantaged environment is without a desirable educational climate. On the ground level of the project area, there are numerous stationary benches. Many derelicts, winos, and delinquent boys loitering on these benches were observed and talked to. Scattered about are many empty wine and liquor bottles. The individuals found here expectorate on the sidewalk and use excessively profane language. It is not uncommon to see dice games being played on the sidewalk. The prideless derelicts "trap" cigarette butts from the sputum-laden sidewalks while the arrogant, more sophisticated teen-age delinquents force smaller eight- and nine-year-old boys to go back to their apartments and steal cigarettes from their parents. The younger boys, in turn, force their even younger siblings to perpetrate the act. The little ones *do* get caught.

Young children see all kinds of norm-violating behavior and hear all kinds of profane language. Parents are understandably disturbed—"You wonder how the children do as well as they do. All the filth they see and hear would make the devil blush." A nurse relates: "The children see the adults fight, argue, and cuss all the time. What can we expect out of them after seeing and hearing all that—shining examples of civic virtue?"

It is difficult to find any area in this environment where a small child is not exposed to arguments, fights, drinking, and gambling. Nevertheless, the Midwest City police records show that this project has a rate of reported crime 42 percent below the city crime rate. In spite of a crime rate lower than some other areas of the city, this environment provides none of the conditions out of which a desirable educational climate can emanate.

Perhaps the reason disadvantaged children have such a difficult time adjusting to school is that they observe only consistent and invariant behavior at home. Individuals in this culture tend to resist change even when the change demonstrates the superiority of one method over another. Parents still use money orders to pay their bills. It was suggested and demonstrated to families that a checking account was thriftier than money orders. Only three of the thirty families were convinced that this was a better way of paying their bills and that their money was equally safe.

Most of the parents (64 percent) felt that their children should be taught the way that they were taught and that children can be taught to read by teaching them to spell by rote. They believed that teachers who do not teach their children the ABCs before they teach them to read are poor teachers. Parents clearly reflect their rigidity to change and their lack of knowledge of the way children are taught today.

How can you teach a child to read that don't even know his ABCs?

I don't understand all this "borrow ten" business in arithmetic; I was always taught to borrow one; now they're talking about "regrouping" when they are doing "carrying." They sure do it different now. Bet it don't work though.

MILITANCY

The schools expect the home and children to be law abiding and to respect authority. Most homes are this way, but those that are not are frightening. There is ferment in Blackmoor, and there is ferment all around it. This entire section of the city, including Blackmoor, looks like a disaster area. Hundreds of the area's dwellings violate the building code. There are houses where sewage stands in the basements. This is the area where unemployment, broken homes, and other symptoms of the degradation of the inner city are most discernible, and the people are angry. They have managed not to involve themselves in violent protest, but now, everywhere, the people are beginning to speak:

Put the books down, baby, so we can talk. That book world ain't nothing but a report on the real one anyway—and you ain't sure the report is right. Your problem is—you try to hang everything on one nail: them damn books. You're just another brat of education who ain't exactly on the best talking terms with his daddy. Like most educated people, you listen to echoes. And, baby, it's too noisy out here to hear echoes.

You want to be wise and know everything; down here, we'd rather know everybody. What's more important anyway, what you know or who you know? Look, baby, you claim you're a teacher so it wouldn't be too hard to "strip" you. It seem like everybody who can't learn nothing try to teach something. The people you see here ain't just bones and muscle that you use as guinea pigs to write a paper on—they're people who dream and feel just like you. They give you information for your paper. What do you give them? Sure the damn schools are falling apart, but when you want to save them you go out and get a whitey as the expert. All he wants is a hundred dollars a day. Baby, the experts are like me. They are in the pool-rooms and in jail and on dope. We can show you too how to save your schools—for that matter, the whole city—for a hundred dollars a day, but we'll burn it down for nothing.

Sex: Male
Age: 21
IQ: 127
Honors: None
Occupation: None
Distinction: Dropout
Recreation: Pool
Schooling: Elementary, high school (3 years)
References: Social worker, probation officer, gang
Habitat: Negro ghetto

All six of them are my children and you already
know why they got different names. They got
different names because they had different daddies
. . . but they ain't got but one mama, and that's me. . . .
That's my family and I'm the head of it. You
ain't here to be telling me about right and
wrong. I have had four men in my life. I was married
to two of them and they're both dead. How
many have you had? The next thing you'll be telling
me is to pick myself up by my bootstraps.
Now if you don't want to finish filling out that
form I'll ask one of them other women to
do it. And don't tell me I could be doing better. I
was working—"helping myself"— before you
were born. You act like you're either brand-
new here or trying to be funny and I
don't plan to be "loud talked" by you or anybody
else. You started to sound just like them people

down at the school. Instead of learning
how to teach those ʌids down there
that they're always messing up, they are too
busy commenting on our morals. What
you and them teachers don't know is my first
husband had a college degree. He studied architecture.
Nobody would hire him. This is before a lot
of businesses hired one black man and set
him up front so everybody could see
him. The closest he ever got to building anything
was working as a laborer. He got killed
on the job. So, honey, you just fill out them forms
and quit trying to judge. —Part-time domestic,
ADC applicant

Negro leaders! Who makes them leaders? Every time something happens, white folk go to the Negro undertakers and ministers and call them leaders. I would just like to know why when I got problems they go talk to my minister. When I got problems, I want people to talk to me. The undertaker don't know anything about my problems; he's living just like whitey who asked him about me and he exploits me just as much. He know that he'll get me in the end. At least we vote on the President. I don't ever remember voting on Roy Wilkins or anybody else as my leader. It is Stokely Carmichael and Rap Brown who tell how I feel and I didn't vote on them. I'm my own man and it's about time whitey started treating me that way.

I don't see how I could even want the same things as Roy Wilkins —not now anyway. He's got a job and a nice house. He wants to live at a fancy hotel and eat in fancy joints. Right now I just want a job to take care of me and my family, and a chance to get in a position to want some of the other things. What good would it do me to go to the Hilton if I haven't got the bread. Looks to me like a real leader gets down there with you now and then. When he talks about how bad some of this shit is, he knows what he's talking about because he has smelled it too. These guys they're calling leaders are just like generals in the army. They sit behind the line and tell the world how bad the war is.

I don't mean that we don't need leaders, cause we do. What I don't like, though, is being assigned a leader as my mouthpiece. Who don't know what I want to say. When he says "we" he means "me." I have never heard of the NAACP, CORE, or any of the rest of them doing a survey to find out what Negroes want. In different places they probably want different things. Some people want to be bums and I think they ought to be. Our so-called leaders pressure whitey to make all Negroes gray-flannel-suit men. That's like saying all Negroes should like watermelon.

> Sex: *Male*
> Age: *24*
> Honors: *Patrol boy in grade school*
> Occupation: *Hustler*
> Distinction: *Among the first boys to live in the project*
> Recreation: *Dancing*
> Schooling: *Elementary (7 years, dropout)*
> References: *Social worker, probation officer, gang, priest*
> Habitat: *Negro ghetto*

As a kid, I was taught to hate. If the person I met was a Jew or Catholic, I hated his religion. If he was Negro, I hated his color. If he was rich, I hated his wealth. If he was intelligent, I hated his intellect. Everything he was that I wasn't I hated. My parents taught me to hate by example and reward; they used rote, drill, and threat; and my parents claim to be God-fearing people. Now I hate them. They're dead and I'm sorry they died before they could see how much I hate them. So you see this emotion has robbed me of experiencing all of the things that are different. I can talk about hate. I'm an expert. Colored people are babes in arms when it comes to hating. I've never met a hater worth his salt who was black except the one who hates himself. He's good at that. It is only recently that they have shown their feelings toward the white world. Before now they hid their feelings—concealing attitudes that weren't worth hiding.

Black people have been tranquilized with religion. They expect to get all of their rewards in heaven—wherever that is. They all want to go there but they don't want to die first. Yet as I see it, they haven't had much to live for. In all of their songs and prayers they proclaim the good life to be found in paradise. Most of them put off fighting for the good life while they're alive so they can enjoy it when they're dead.

Where I came up, the good life itself was hating. We were against everything different. If a foreigner moved into our neighborhood and minded his own business, we still didn't like him. Hating him for myself wasn't enough. I wanted all of my friends and relatives to feel the same way; and when they didn't, I guess I feared them. Pretty soon the fear would become hate.

I learned hating everywhere I went—at Boy Scout meeting, in school, even in church. The preacher and teachers and scoutmasters weren't leaders; they were haters. Oh, they talked a good game about fair play, but their action came through louder than their words. I never will forget when our scoutmaster told us about the little black boy—and he said little black boy—who wanted to become a member of our troop. This was when the word "black" was taboo. He told us the decision was up to us. He really didn't say anything against the boy, but before we voted, he told us a story about how race horses and jackasses don't mix. The vote was unanimous.

In my home town hating was the community pastime. It was like a cult. I guess you might say it was the main passion of the population and a kind of tradition. The law was really the servant and master of haters, not citizens; and the courts were the sacrificial altars. This has been true, as a matter of fact, in many home towns across America. I've lived in places where lynchings were almost social events and the lynchers were treated as little more than schoolboys carrying on pranks. Read Ginsberg* sometime—you'll see what I mean.

In this world hate is a social pleasure. It is incubated in little corners of our private sewers we call the human minds and the overt manifestation of it has community corroboration. It infests the tenements of our cities, dominates the manicured lawns of our sordid suburbs, and infiltrates the pulpits of the tabernacles of righteousness. When hate is a part of a shrewd and resourceful intellect, it can be colored with both a remarkable logic and what appears to be appropriate documentation. Hate, then, can support the motive which produces human tragedy. I'd join the black militants if they would have me. I could teach them a thing or two about hating.

> *Sex: Male*
> *Age: 29*
> *Honors: Many*
> *Occupation: Poverty worker*
> *Recreation: Drinking*

* Ralph Ginsberg, *100 Years of Lynching*. New York: Lancer Books, Inc., 1962.

Schooling: Elementary, high school, college (3½ years)
References: School, church, residents in Blackmoor
Habitat: "Caucasian" living in Negro ghetto
Distinction: Former seminarian

PARENTS' ASSUMPTIONS

Just as the school makes certain assumptions about the home that are contrary to reality, so does the home make equally unrealistic assumptions about the school

Blackmoor's parents believe that the teacher assigned to the (slum) school will be qualified to teach their children. Most teachers are indeed qualified in terms of sufficient college hours, state certification, and degrees to teach some children. Many of them have special training for instructing the academically talented and the physically and mentally (retarded) handicapped; all of them are trained to teach the normal, middle-class, and affluent child. On the other hand, few teachers are qualified to teach the disadvantaged child. The majority of universities, colleges, and other teacher-training institutions do not have curricula designed for a major or specialty in teaching the disadvantaged. An examination of 500 college catalogs did not reveal a single one that included a complete program designed to assist teachers and other workers who must deal with the child from the slum. Most programs have a kind of shotgun effect. National Defense Education Act institutes are held on campuses across the country for the expressed purpose of conducting programs for teaching teachers of slum children. When visiting such an NDEA institute, one soon discovers that the institute leaders, including the professors who conduct it and the consultants who serve it, are what one institute participant, a long-time ghetto teacher, calls

hothouse experts. Everything that they know on their own about disadvantaged kids they got from a library somewhere or reading some journal. The other things that they know they get from us. All they didn't know—and believe me, that was practically everything— was amazing. They wanted us to tell them. When I went to that NDEA institute last summer, I thought I was at confession. Teacher after teacher got up for six weeks and confirmed that there were disadvantaged children. The teachers really conducted the institute and made those few contributions which were made. The professors gave nothing. We certainly didn't get any methods or techniques that would help us do a good job. But there were other considerations which I think were disturbing. Many of my fellow teachers had motives other than those they expressed on their application to become a member of the institute in the first place. Some of them needed summer work, some of them wanted the graduate credit to get their master's degree, some of them wanted a vacation partly subsidized by the government. Anything they got in the process to help the children was certainly. coincidental. The fact is, most teachers, even a lot of those in the slums, can't teach the disadvantaged.

The assumption may be that teachers are qualified to teach all children; the reality is that most teachers can instruct only the advantaged child effectively.

The home has nothing to do with the evaluation of teachers. It assumes that this is done by the board of education, the superintendent, or his representative in terms of some good criteria. The reality is that the superintendent's representative is the local school principal. He evaluates the teacher (usually) with a check list that includes some type of rating scale. The teacher is graded on such things as whether he does the bulletin board well and on time, on the room decorations, on the quietness of the classroom, on whether or not he is punctual in getting to early-morning recess and noon duty stations, on whether or not he stands by his door when the school bell rings, on whether or not he volunteered to work for the tax campaign, on the number of professional organizations in which he holds membership, on voice quality and dress, on the promptness of reports, and on cooperation. One principal in Midwest City says this about this latter consideration:

> Cooperation means going along with my program. I know what's best for all concerned. So I don't want any teacher to make waves. When one does, I get her out of *my* school.

The teacher is also evaluated on how his children pass from one place to another, on how closely he adheres to the course of study, on the volume of audiovisual materials used, on the amount of homework assigned, and on a variety of other nebulous and questionable activities. No more space is given to the teacher's vision and creativity, ability to arouse and hold the student's interest, sensitivity to the student's reaction, adjustment of the curriculum, organization and presentation of material, or knowledge of the subject matter than it is to whether he is prompt or not in getting in the milk money. He is rarely evaluated in terms of the kind of students he turns out. All of what a teacher *is* or *is not* is frequently summarized in one paragraph. In short, instruction does not appear to be the activity of the first priority.

The home assumes that the material and equipment belong to the school; and the slum school does nothing to correct the supposition. It tends to do more to prove the assumption true. Nevertheless, the reality is that supplies really belong to the pupils but that pupils are frequently denied use and consumption of them. Find the storeroom in a slum school and (in some cases) you find some new athletic equipment: balls and bats, jumping ropes, dodge balls, and other assorted items that should be used by the children. Many times this equipment is available while young slum children run and play at "hitting" and other aggressive games. This equipment may be brought out only at a special time—for example, physical education period.

Sometimes a new basal reading series will be adopted by the school system as a whole while new copies of the old series are still in the storerooms of individual schools. Reasons are offered: "Let them dirty up and destroy a few [books] at a time. Why ruin them all at once." The principal who gave this reason did not see the excessive cost of permitting books to remain unused in a storeroom until they became obsolete. There is often a quota on the materials that are sent to all schools within a school district. This is ironic in a slum school; because there the children have not had many experiences with paper and pencils, coloring books, and other such items. It would seem appropriate, therefore, to give a disproportionately larger amount of supplies to the slum school and child. The assumption of the home that materials and equipment belong to the school often becomes the prophecy that is fulfilled by the school.

The home in Blackmoor, like the home everywhere, assumes

that the teacher will know and understand children. The reality is that the majority of teachers do not understand the pupil who comes from the traditional slum and know virtually nothing about the child who comes from a public high-rise housing project. This remains true even after the voluminous studies made and numerous books written about the disadvantaged child. Although teachers may serve schools located near project areas, they have little intimate knowledge about where the child lives. They have heard the rumors about the notoriety and infamous reputation of the housing project; and they have heard the tenants described. These rumors and descriptions convince many teachers that a school located near Blackmoor is not one in which they would like to teach. Teachers have also heard about the conditions in the housing project. This hearsay, too, convinces many of them that they should look for teaching assignments elsewhere. Some teachers, however, *must* be assigned to ghetto schools near the housing project, and a few ask to be sent there. Out of both groups—those teachers who are assigned and those teachers who ask to be sent there—there are a few successful teachers who can communicate effectively with the ghetto child. Those teachers who do succeed in communicating with the deprived child in Blackmoor soon learn that their success does not depend upon some skill they were taught at the teacher-training institution.

The successful teacher becomes one because of what he is. This influences what he does. Many school people have a lack of sensitivity to the needs of a project child or any other child from the slum. This lack of sensitivity places them at a disadvantage. When this is coupled with a lack of experience in dealing with the ghetto, they are unable even to compensate for their insensibilities. Because the school and its agents do not understand the child or his environment, they impose rules and restraints that the child cannot comply with if he is to show good sense and maintain good health. Fighting is a case in point. He must fight in his environment simply to survive. He must learn to fight or become the punching bag of the community. The home in Blackmoor assumes that the teacher will understand the fighting as a part of the behavior and value system of the child in the housing project as it understands the value system of affluent children. However, many teachers claim that they do not understand the values employed by the child, so they superimpose their own. In projecting their own rules of conduct, they are never content that the child should use them as covalues or alternative ones; they are to be used in lieu of the values the child already knows. Comments have been made repeatedly about such behavior. A. Harry Passow, Kenneth B. Clark, Frank Riessman, John Holt—they all call attention to the teacher who attempts to force his values on the child. They all if not condemn certainly admonish him.

Parents assume that the teacher knows how to evaluate the child and do not question his knowledge. Sometimes, however, they find the evaluations made by the teacher paradoxical:

> I just got my little boy's report card but I swear I don't understand it. It says here on this side that he got unsatisfactory in oral language because he won't talk. But on the other side he got unsatisfactory in conduct because he is too talkative.

CURRICULA

It is increasingly clear that the lack of appropriate tools, educational traditions, positive attitudes, family educational background, and extrinsic motivation do not provide an educational climate that will facilitate optimal learning when children are enrolled in school. None of the desirable experiences pointed out in this chapter guarantees success in school or learning. More important, however, we see that the school bases too much of its function on faulty assumptions, particularly in the slum school.

The home in Blackmoor makes the same assumption about curriculum as the middle-class home in the suburbs; it assumes that what is taught in the schools is designed to fit the needs of the child. Although the curriculum may meet many of the needs of the affluent child, it fails to provide adequately for the child attending school in the inner city. For him, it remains traditional and ineffective. Typically, a school curriculum purports to embody the needs, thinking, and goals of a local community while at the same time including certain specifics applicable to the entire society. A school system should develop the practice of involving the entire community in the selection of subject matter and skills to be included in the curriculum. The committee composed of a small group of individuals to build a curriculum preempts the practice of involving a broad community sampling. Parents in the housing project have no control over what is selected to be included in the curriculum; few if any representatives from business and industry make a direct contribution to the development of curricula; and the majority of teachers, principals, and other school personnel say little about what should be included. The things taught in the schools are usually determined by small committees of classroom teachers or by a special curriculum division. Neither these small committees of teachers nor the special division on curriculum is a representative number. Too few teachers are included, and the rank and file who live in the community are not asked. Because of insufficient lay participation and inadequate involvement of professional educational personnel in the development of a curriculum, many skills included in specific courses of study are traditional, antiquated, and irrelevant to today's needs. Courses in manual training and homemaking can illustrate this point.

Thirty years ago boys in manual-arts classes made doorstops and girls in homemaking made potholders. In school system after school system pupils still make these items. The experience of working on these two projects may be important; however, these particular two items are obsolete in today's world: few doors are held open by wooden doorstops, and the handles on most pots are nonconductors of heat. Moreover, potholders can be purchased at a supermarket at a cost of two for 25 cents, and wooden doorstops do not meet the requirements of a modern home.

Project parents know nothing about the word "curriculum," but they do make some assumptions about what is taught in the schools. They assume that a contemporary curriculum has content that reflects their heritage and an accurate picture of what has taken place in history. This is very important with certain ethnic groups. Many authorities, for example, emphasize the fact that the black's contributions to America have been excluded from the history books. *Time* magazine and other publications now call attention to this inequity. Men like Carter G. Woodson, Lerone Bennett, Jr., and William Katz have tried to fill in this gap in history.

Project parents also assume that in a modern curriculum some of the appropriate people are consulted to make specific contributions. They expect a course dealing with moral and spiritual values to have the advice of rabbis, ministers, and priests. The reality, however, is that such a course of study is developed by a committee of teachers who employ their own rules and puritanical opinions in the same way they learned them.

Most of the people in Blackmoor are poor; none of them is lettered, but rarely is any one of them stupid. They know that many of the things taught in school probably do not apply to their children. Consequently, they assume that the curriculum will meet the needs of· a wide variety of students with different interests, abilities, aspirations, and means for additional educational opportunities. The reality is that the curriculum is continuing, uniform, and unchanging. In Midwest City, as in many other cities, the curriculum is oriented to the student who will ultimately go to college and become a professional. The boy who may wish to become a cook and the girl who may wish to become a seamstress or work with business machines find little in the curriculum that will help them before they go to high school. The choices are limited in technical and vocational programs in high school. And the college abdicates all responsibility for the nonprofessional aspirant. Project residents see other evidence of the rigidity of the school in what and how something is to be taught. Some parents know that it is important to have publications in the home, and some of them do. These publications are not typically books or stories from the required-reading lists in the schools, which include many of the time-honored classics. The parents hope that the curriculum is flexible enough to tolerate the child who will not read a classic or a book on baseball but who will read a story in a magazine and the sports pages in the daily newspaper.

The home makes the assumptions that the teacher will be interested in the child and that he will respect the child's right to be taught even if his face is dirty. The home expects the teacher to give as much time to the diagnosis of learning problems in a child from a poor family, to the remediation of his learning deficiencies, and to the understanding of his learning style as the teacher would for the more affluent child. Parents expect the teacher to bring all his resources, including a positive attitude, to bear on the problem and joy of teaching the child from Blackmoor as he does for the child from any other part of the city or suburbs. They assume that the teacher will be honest, forthright, and concerned about the child, that the teacher will not be condescending, bigoted, and biased and will not adopt a laissez-faire attitude toward him. The fact remains, however, that far too many teachers who must act, react, and interact with black children in ghettos contradict these last assumptions made by the parents. This is true of both black and white teachers. Educators, like other people, are just that: people. They are good and bad, "hawks" and "doves," conservatives and liberals, fair and bigoted. Teachers, like other people, attempt either to justify or to hide some of their attitudes; at least, they attempt to hide them from some people. Parents assume that teachers may show bias and bigotry toward them, but they frequently think that teachers are too interested in children and too professional to openly practice their bigotry. Yet they do. When a teacher in an integrated junior high school, for example, returned to her Latin class, which happened not to have a black member, she said to a student as she passed his desk, "Close the door. Those niggers are keeping up too much noise in the hall." When the class members called her attention to what she had said, she replied, "This is a Latin class and 'nigger' is the Latin word meaning black or dark."

The home in the ghetto makes other assumptions about the school and its agents. It assumes that teachers treat the children in their charge the same way they treat children in the suburbs or the way they want their own children treated. The reality is that while a child in an affluent school may be sent to carry a message from one place to another in the school building, a child in the ghetto may be sent to the store to buy the teacher's lunch. Similarly, while an affluent child may be asked to water the flowers in a middle-class school, a child in the slum school may be asked to clean the erasers, empty waste cans, and sweep the

floor. Custodians may send for children and then instruct them
to set up the chairs in the auditorium or to bring in supplies
when they arrive at the school. Slum children may, indeed, have
an opportunity to practice some of the menial tasks that they
frequently fall heir to when they are pushed out or dropped out
of school.

THE DROPOUT

Parents want to assume that the school and its staff reject
the notion that their children seem prone to drop out. Nevertheless, they ask if such a notion is really true. They ask if
there are as many potential dropouts among their children as is
supposed or if many of them are dropped out. After looking
at a child's IQ and attendance record, after observing his clothing
and determining his background and neighborhood, after seeing
all the symptoms that _might_ indicate poor performance in
school, parents are asking if educators drop _him_. Tenants in-
quire if teachers consciously or unconsciously fail to teach the
child from Blackmoor or give him every opportunity to learn.
These questions deserve some soul-searching answers as we assess
the student who withdraws from school.

The dropout drops out. He is finished. His chances are zero.
But even all dropouts are not the same. Some can be better
characterized as "dripouts" and still others as "drainouts." The
dripout temporarily excludes himself from school. He may work
for a short period of time to maintain himself. He likes school
and knows the value of school in contemporary culture. He is
eager to return and he _does_ return. The drainout is, without
doubt, a worse tragedy. On one end of the continuum, he lacks
ability though he may enjoy school and may come to school and
appear well adjusted. Time erodes the drainout. With the pas-
sage of time, the academic areas become more difficult for him
and administrative policy and directives exclude him. At the
other end of the continuum, he may be a pupil who finishes high
school and has enough ability to go to college but finds college
financially prohibitive. This is a student that has the ability to
go to college but not enough ability to win a scholarship. The

fact is that the scholarships by and large still go to the top students. This youngster falls under that broad heading "average." The dropout is not a new phenomenon. He has been with us for generations. He supported (what was) the American dream, exemplified (what was) the American character—that is, the rugged individualist. Accolades were formerly bestowed upon him for leaving school to assist the family or to marry and raise his own. Society has watched him live vicariously and in quiet triumph while he attended the graduation exercise of a younger brother or sister whom he helped to receive his college degree. At one time the dropout had distinction, if not honor. Today he has neither distinction nor honor. He is testimony that what was the American dream is now a myth. Few employment opportunities remain available to the dropout. There are no ditches to dig, no rails to split, no rows to hoe. Like praise for the dropout, they are extinct.

Young militants have been discussing the dropout problems with parents in the housing project. They suggest to parents that their children are being branded for life by the scores they earn on intelligence tests when they are in the primary grades. The militants emphasize that the tests are designed and constructed by white middle-class educators, validated on white children, using white criteria. Their arguments are rather well documented, and they are persuasive. Militants holding a community conference on education made certain statements to Blackmoor's parents that are worth noting:

The children of black people are dropouts the day they start to school because you black mothers accept whatever school people tell you. You know your kids better than they do no matter what they tell you. Don't let them make dropouts out of your black babies. Go down and converge on that school and find out why you don't get what you pay for. The teachers and principals are about the only people left who still get paid who don't do their jobs. A lot of your children are worse after they go to school than before they go. You don't even know what teachers are supposed to do. You don't know what you are supposed to get. Go down to the school and ask for a copy of the rules and regulations. They won't have one to give you and will tell you that they can't pass them out. When they do that, go down to the board of education and ask for a copy. If they ask you why you want it, tell them you're a citizen and you have a right to one. If they refuse, organize a group and go down to the board meetings and raise hell, picket the school, picket the homes of the board members and do everything else necessary to see that your kids get a fair shake. Go to the all-white schools and look at their equipment then come back down here and see what you have. Whitey does this all the time and they say he is concerned. When you do it they going to call it militancy. Don't worry about what's said, keep them from pushing your kid out.

SCHOOL-HOME RELATIONSHIP

Although tenants in Blackmoor continue to find certain assumptions about the school unsubstantiated, they nevertheless persist in making them. In fact, many of the parents' expectations are both reasonable and proper. Parents assume that the school will communicate with the home, but this rarely happens except as related to a behavioral violation or lack of achievement on the part of the disadvantaged child or when a new tax campaign is imminent. Otherwise, little about the school is made known to the community. Parents are never apprised of what the specific objectives of each grade and each course are. They never know the kinds of specific skills and training needed by the teacher for him to be effective in teaching the child. Parents in the ghetto have never been informed of the specific things they might do in order to facilitate the child's progress as he moves through the school. They never seem to succeed in finding out from the school what its objectives or its problems are in a slum or project community. The goals must be different for a ghetto school as compared to a school outside the ghetto. Actually, two schools located within the same slum community should probably have different goals. Because of a kind of social and educational detachment of school people from parents in the project, they have succeeded in communicating that they are willing to "let the home know only so much and the rest is none of its business." The behavior of most school staffs in the ghetto indicates that they not only do not communicate positively with project parents but also do not wish to become involved with them.

School people in Midwest City do not always know who the small storeowners and other persons in the community are. They do not move about in the community or visit the churches or choose their friends there or permit their children to associate with the children they teach. They never ask advice from the real community leaders.* They continue to question the minister they can locate or some of the other quasi-leaders. It is apparent, therefore, that the school fails to communicate effectively with the home. The parent really never knows what the responsibilities of specific staff members within the school are.

The principal is the school officer who is responsible for the supervision of instruction. Parents assume that he is chosen because he knows education and that he is a strong disciplinarian.† The reality is that many principals do not know education. A few of them may have had this knowledge before they were promoted to the ranks of administration, but too many of them are former physical education majors who were supposed to be able to handle the young toughs in the junior and senior high school. The rationale has often been that the man who could control a football team could run a school. The fact that he had little or no knowledge about how children learned received little consideration from the boards of education who hired him. Too many of Midwest City's 150 plus school principals are former physical education teachers or athletic coaches.

Typically, the school principal is a manager in the building. He is concerned with reports, the physical plant, public relations, and control of pupils and staff. He sits in judgment of both the performance of his faculty and the behavior of the pupils. He must apply the routine rules of the school, which are sometimes completely unrealistic for disadvantaged youngsters from the housing project. Frequently he is one of the tools of the bureaucracy that forces him to transmit the names of parents who receive aid to dependent children but whose children have not been in regular attendance in school. Parents in this

---

* The real leaders appear to be members of the various militant groups in the project community. Most of them do not live in Blackmoor, although their bases of operations are near the housing project.
† Many parents have been sold on the idea that a good principal is one who is handy with a rattan, an all-around tough guy.

category are removed from ADC rolls. This does not improve his relationship with the community he must serve. Not infrequently the principal must absorb the mistakes made by the teacher on his staff—and, of course, his own blunders. Although the improvement of instruction is the primary responsibility of the principal, this responsibility is the one he is most likely to forgo as he manages the school. Consequently, the home may have the wrong expectation when it assumes that the principal's primary energies are spent in the improvement of instruction.

The home in the ghetto wants to believe, more than for any other assumption, that the school and its agents will be fair, impartial, and professional in dealing with their children. Parents know, however, that school people frequently show bias, are not fair, and are not always professional. Many parents are disturbed by the condescension and other negative attitudes expressed toward them and their children. Consider this conversation between a principal and a parent who the school leader discovered was not as stupid as he thought she might be. The principal said:

> I know you will be happy to know, Mrs. K., Walter *passed* the test for special school.* There he will have special teachers; there will be only a few children in the room and Walter will be able to get some individual attention. It is my responsibility to inform the parent in person and get his signature when a pupil passes the test to go into special school.

The parent responded:
> You must think I'm the village idiot, don't you? When you say my child *passed* the test, what you think I'm too stupid to know is that he failed the test which would keep him in the classes with normal children. I know my child is slow but I'm not stupid. If the teachers here are like you are I'm surprised that all of the children don't *pass* the test for special. Most of the mothers in this community hate to come to this school because you try to make damn fools out of them. As long as they got son of a bitches like you here, our children will never get a decent education. You see, now I'm acting like you think my kind is supposed to act. Since you're so goddamn smart, I hope you know that a few more capers like some of those you have

---

* Children who are assigned to special school are those whose intelligence scores are below 78.

already pulled and we are going to get your ass moved away from this school if we have to burn it down. I refuse to sign this permission slip until next year and Walter won't be any further behind than he already is.

In addition to complaining about the condescension of school people, parents complain about the names their children are called and the comments that are made by people responsible for teaching their children.

The assumptions made by the home and school could be listed here *ad infinitum*. They could be accompanied by refutation, documentation, and substantiation, and we would have done little more than lengthen the list. Perhaps central to the problem of the home and school is the lack of communication between these agencies. The home in the ghetto considers the school the omnipotent representative of the system. The parents in the home have not been apprised that they own the schools, that they have a voice in the way the schools are operated, that the schools can only do what they permit. More specifically, people in the ghetto do not control their schools because they do not know it is their responsibility. The school, on the other hand, expects support from the home when it is in need of revenue. It expects the family in Blackmoor to vote for tax increases and bond issues. It wants the assistance of community leaders when special projects are developed within the school. However, the school demands complete ownership of audiovisual aids and other such equipment that might have been purchased by some of the service organizations of the school such as mothers' clubs, PTAs, and booster clubs. Yet the school closes its doors in the evening hours, when many ghetto people could make use of the facilities they purchased when they voted for tax increases.

The school is not the community facility that it could be. The red tape and paperwork necessary for residents to use the school building is a deterrent to many who live in the ghetto. The school chooses the books, curricula, personnel, school site (sometimes by the removal of families), type of building, and building maintenance program. Parents in Blackmoor, almost without exception, relate how they never see black people involved in anything around the school other than teaching and cleaning the floors. The painters who refurbish the building are white; the carpenters, plumbers, locksmiths, glaziers, electricians, landscape workers, and truck drivers who deliver the audiovisual materials are white. Many assorted shops and services support the educative process. All of these are handled primarily by white persons. The schools that serve Blackmoor have enrollments of only black children.

As one continues to look at the home and school in Midwest City, it becomes increasingly clear why these two institutions cannot make very valid assumptions about each other.

It seems to defy logic in view of the foregoing that the home and the school in the housing project continue to embrace the assumptions each holds about the other. These two institutions enjoy a kind of mutual rigidity. As a result, the effectiveness with which they deal with the problems of the child is seriously diminished. Many things the school might do for the child are not now being done because they are contingent upon prior experiences of the child. On the other hand, if the home knew precisely what the school expected a child to know when he is sent to school, it would be in a position to help the child with specific tasks designed to facilitate the child's progress. More specifically, the school could, perhaps, have more success with the disadvantaged child if it communicated to the home those precise and explicit minimum skills that are necessary for a child to bring with him if he is to succeed in the kindergarten and first grade. This same type of communication must follow throughout the child's school life.

It appears, then, that the assumptions of the home and the school are invalid in Blackmoor. It has been demonstrated that the environment is not conducive to a good life. It has been suggested that the community, even the society, is apathetic toward Blackmoor. All these things have a profound effect on the child. This, then, begs the question of where should we go from here.

XII - The Road Ahead

A housing project is neither an urban Casbah—taboo to the out-sider—nor a sanctuary for the inner city's criminal element, though it may seem to be. There are to be found the agony and the ecstasy. Both are unmistakable. One is compelled, how-ever, to be more sensitive to the former than to the latter.

THE PROBLEMS

The project is a badge of social identification and affliction. The outside community reacts to it as though it were a leper colony, and the lives of the residents seem to have neither di-mension nor meaning. Most of them do want some mobility in the mainstream of the society. Unfortunately, too many of Black-moor's residents see poverty as their retribution, despair as their heritage, and failure as their credo. Yet things are changing. Some tenants are looking at the cruel realities of where and how they must live, and they are angry. They are comparing their lives with those of others in society to emphasize the con-trast and inequities. They see the road ahead as being inacces-sible. They reject the old promises and have become adept at recognizing the hypocrisy.

The residents readily see the paradox in society's order of priorities. They know that, in some places, incarcerated criminals have more positive influences in their lives than they themselves have as free citizens: they know that convicted felons have jobs in prison, are taught skills, have access to health and psychiatric care, learn to read and write, involve themselves in wholesome recreational activities, and know that the next meal is certain. This is not to suggest that the tenants in public housing, who are free people, would be better off as inmates of a prison. Rather, the foregoing suggests an irony: the society sees a need to provide certain kinds of positive opportunities even for those people who have broken its laws and who, in fact, are no longer citizens. At the same time, society provides little or nothing for many of its law-abiding citizens who happen to be poor and/or black. And if they fall into these latter two categories, they are usually ignored. Tenants see the inequities, feel the frustration, and are angry. We are beginning to observe the gathering ferment, ferment that will make the road ahead difficult.

At night we are beginning to see fewer teen-agers and young adults in the housing project. The noise level appears to be lower. Now and then one can actually hear a single baby fret; there is an air of expectancy; merchants are closing their stores earlier. There is something disquieting in Blackmoor, some monstrous calm, some seething, some tension. Tenants, now at least, listen to the apostles of violence who tell them to reject the pray-ins, sit-ins, and beg-ins of the past as self-abasement. More and more the black militants in the area are moving underground. There is an atmosphere of quiet panic, a feeling of deadly intrigue. The mood is black.

The collective warnings of the _Report of the National Advisory Commission on Civil Disorders,_ welfare personnel, sociologists, and clergymen go unheeded. The overall conditions of Blackmoor not only have changed but also have gotten worse. The headlines in Midwest City's major newspaper read like an exposé:

HOUSING AGENCY HERE IN BAD FISCAL SHAPE:
May Be Worst in U.S.—Federal Action Suggested
PUBLIC HOUSING TENANTS PLAN RENT PROTEST
TROUBLES MULTIPLYING FOR PUBLIC HOUSING
CITY SEEKS U.S. ANSWER ON HOUSING
HOUSING OFFICIAL QUITS;
Fiscal Problem Worse

The editorial pages corroborate the headlines:

What Public Housing Needs
On the Fringes of Housing
Too Much for Tenants

Thus, we see that the newspaper reports on the problems of public housing in Midwest City and gives editorial opinion. But the news media can tell only a part of the story and offer no solutions.

The inevitable question persists: What are the solutions for dealing with problems of high-rise public housing? The Department of Housing and Urban Development, with all its power, influence, funds, expertise, and human resources, has been unable to find a solution. The heads of housing authorities in cities across the nation have been unable to find adequate solutions. The problem, as we have seen, is many faceted. As such, it transcends the comprehension of most lay and professional people. It involves legislative, judicial, economic, social, and moral components. The director of the housing authority in Midwest City not only says that he does not know what the solutions are but also relates without embarrassment: "I don't even know what questions to ask." It follows that we cannot expect to offer complete solutions within these pages. There are, however, some existing conditions in high-rise public housing that could be changed without legislative acts, judicial decisions, economic depression, social upheaval, or moral persuasion. Yet few changes can be initiated without more positive interaction on the part of the Midwest City housing authority and the tenants in public housing.

There is a widening chasm in the relationship between project residents and the Midwest City housing authority. Communication has become increasingly difficult. There is resentment and hostility between tenants and their landlord. Neither understands, in depth, the problems of the other. Each is unwilling to be sympathetic to the other, and rarely does one really listen to the other. Most tenants feel that they know the things that should be done to make the housing project a better place to live but are convinced that the housing authority refuses to make repairs or changes. Tenants say that management either treats them with condescension and contempt or ignores them. The management, on the other hand, continues to say that tenants do not know the problems of the housing authority. It also maintains that residents could do some things better and that the projects could be desirable if the residents would assume more responsibility for helping to maintain the place, especially as it relates to their children.

Both the tenants and the landlords oversimplify the situation. Many of the problems of project residency and management are combined with other things that have nothing to do with housing: shifts in the inner city's population, poverty, low income, unemployment, broken homes, ethnic occupancy, and the changing character of the public housing tenant body. One housing director has said, "This is a social problem that has to be operated on a business basis." The housing authority is not responsible for the geographical mobility of the city's population; it has no control over the income of people except as it relates to the eligibility of a tenant to live in the housing project; it has no direct influence on the solidarity of families; it is not responsible for de facto segregation; it has no influence on employment or the characteristics of the residents. Yet all these conditions are part of the complexities in public housing. The tenants reject the complexities and only look at the real situation as it affects them directly. They maintain that they know what the solutions are:

> They ought to keep this place up. *Even in one of them*
> *old broken-down houses, when something about it went*
> *haywire you could do something. When the heating plant*
> *breaks down here you can't do nothing but be cold. When*
> *them stinking elevators break down, and that's all the*
> *time, you ain't got no choice but to walk. Who is going*
> *to try to put in a new windowpane on the ninth floor?*
> *If that housing authority would do what*
> *they tell us to do it would get rid of some of*
> *the problems in Blackmoor. All they got to do is keep up*
> *the place better.* —Man, age forty-seven

> *Our building sometime have trash piled up for a week;*
> *and these buildings are infested with roaches. They said*

that they would come in and spray when we moved in. That was two years ago.—Drugstore employee, age twenty-six

> *Somebody broke in and robbed my apartment. I called the guard but nobody ever came. We need police protection in this place. The private guard don't give a damn and the city police act like they are afraid to come in here. The management don't do nothing. We need protection that's all there is to it.* —Elderly man

If they would just put a peep hole in the door you could see who was outside before you opened the door. —Widow, age forty-one, mother of five

These and other bitter words are constantly directed at the housing authority. The residents are convinced that if the management took more interest, the tenants would too. This indicates a definite positive cycle. There is also a negative cycle: vandalism occurs, which costs money to rectify, which raises rents, which causes more resentment, which increases vandalism. In Blackmoor the cycle has never been broken.

There is always the bad image of Blackmoor. People outside of high-rise public housing assume that the projects are spawning grounds for gangs, gambling, drug traffic, prostitution, and worse. The police in Midwest City, however, are the first to refute the notion that crime runs rampant in the housing project. In fact, the census tract that this project covers entirely ranked 50 out of 128 in crimes per person. Yet the tenants say:

> Half of what goes on here ain't never reported. If your daughter gets raped you don't go out and broadcast it and ruin her reputation for life. The police ain't going to do nothing about it but ask a lot of goddamn fool questions. I ain't never heard of them ever catching a criminal that did something to the people in the housing project. But when we do something to somebody, they know exactly where to find us.

Most of the tenants are the victims, not the criminals. The guards in the housing project are said to be like the police everywhere: they make the law-abiding obey the law.

Blackmoor has been called the $36 million mistake. Midwest City discovered this shortly after the projects were built. This high-rise project was built with government funds but is managed by the city's housing authority, which must depend primarily on rent for its day-to-day operation and management. This latter stipulation has not worked well. Since the project was built, the costs of labor, materials, equipment, and service have continued to rise while the income of the tenants has either remained stable or decreased.

More succinctly, Blackmoor has had a history of rising costs and diminishing income. This situation has reached the point that the Midwest City housing authority is in danger of going broke. In fact, all but one of the housing projects in this city operated at a combined loss of about $330,000 in 1966. Blackmoor had the largest share of that deficit: $313,782, according to the figures reported to the public. The housing budget for fiscal 1967 showed a deficit potentially much greater. The reserve fund maintained by the housing authority to meet emergencies plunged to less than 25 percent of the maximum allowed by government regulations during fiscal 1966. The assistant administrator for the regional office of Housing and Urban Development has assessed the financial condition of the Midwest City agency for the local newspaper: "In one word deplorable. I know for certain that it's in the worst shape of any of the 627 authorities in our . . . region. And unless I'm told wrong it's in the worst condition of any in the country." To add to the financial woes of Blackmoor, there is a 20 percent to 30 percent vacancy rate, and it appears that this rate will even go higher.

Apartment equipment (ranges, refrigerators, and so on) has not been replaced at regular intervals. Heating equipment, ventilators, and electrical equipment have broken down on too many occasions—said to be due to insufficient funds to ensure proper maintenance. The project cannot be properly maintained without subsidy, but neither the state nor the federal government has been willing to subsidize public housing. The government put up much of the original money to construct the housing projects and stipulated that they must be maintained out of the rent collected. The federal government has not been willing to provide additional funds for subsidy. The state, on the other hand, which provides less than 45 percent of the minimum daily requirement of its welfare recipients, is not likely to be generous with its funds. The housing agency finds itself in a dilemma: raise the rent of people who cannot afford to pay the rent they are currently paying, cut the services people contracted for when they signed the lease, or go bankrupt.

The tenants residing in Blackmoor assume no blame for management's predicament. They have no control over the rise in cost of labor, replacement of equipment, or services. They know neither how nor why the housing authority is rapidly approaching bankruptcy. There has been a high vacancy rate in Blackmoor for a long time because of the reputation and condition of the project. The tenants refuse any responsibility for the transiency and exodus of the lodgers.

As we have seen, neither the tenants nor the management is solely responsible for the conditions in the public housing project, but both must share some guilt. Yet the basic blame would seem to be more appropriately placed on the whole concept of high-rise public housing. For example, to install elevators *that do not stop on each floor* to save money has proven to be a mistake; to house a large tenant population without adequate recreational facilities is another example of faulty planning; to plan public housing and not consult teachers, sociologists, social workers, psychologists, and other people who must live and work in them was another error of great magnitude. Had they been consulted, they might have suggested to the builders that large numbers of people—most of them poor, in broken families, and exhibiting patterns of failure—should not be placed in a single compound without an adequate range of services needed by a community. The idea that a high-rise project could be maintained out of the rents collected was perhaps an unrealistic idea when one considers that all the residents are indigent. These and other notions imply that the planners and builders of high-rise projects are to blame for many of the conditions found in them. Because there is always circularity in the assessment of blame, perhaps it might be useful to explore possible solutions for Blackmoor's problems rather than concentrate on who is to blame.

THE SOLUTIONS

Plans for improving and changing the housing project have come from many sources. At least four plans are worth noting. However, before any method is carried out and regardless of the plan used, certain standards must be met: (1) The buildings must be structurally sound. (2) Electrical ventilating and heating services and equipment must be adequate. (3) Maintenance must be efficient and prompt. (4) Better social and community service must be accessible to tenants, as they would be for tenants holding leases elsewhere. These things must receive attention regardless of the plan proposed. After assurance is given by a developer of a particular plan that these minimum standards be met, then attention may be given to a more complete development of the plans for the housing project. Four of the proposals are included here: (1) A major corporation has had the housing project studied and is considering management of the complex if the details can be worked out with city officials, the Midwest City housing authority, and the government. (2) A private concern has offered to buy Blackmoor. (3) Under the tenant rule and management plan (TRAMP), residents in the building control their building, keep it clean, safe, and in good repair. (4) Phase out Blackmoor. This can be done in two ways: first, close Blackmoor and tear it down; second, turn the housing complex back to the government.

Plan 1

The corporation would build low-rent housing in other areas of the city and relocate large families who currently reside in Blackmoor. Smaller families remaining would be housed in the buildings with other families of varying income, interests, and circumstances. Blackmoor would then be broken up into subcommunities (two to four buildings). Each community would be self-contained, with stores, shops, and so on, having its own name and hopefully developing its own individual distinction.

Regarding Plan 1, the author would suggest that playgrounds for the very young be placed on the roofs of buildings, with high fences around them. Supervision for the children could be provided out of a pool of older residents, especially older women, on pensions and other old-age assistance whose health permits them to do such work. A supervised playground on the roof could serve several purposes: Small children would not be under foot. Older children would be directed to other play areas appropriate to their age and physical skill level. The young children would be shielded from much of the profanity, aggression from older children, and norm-violating behavior that they are now exposed to when they play at street level.

The author would also suggest that each building have recreational facilities (sewing machines, craft areas where tenants could build and repair items, reading rooms, and other hobby centers). Buildings for the aged should be separated from those housing young families. It is also suggested that along with the welfare office and clinical facilities (medical and dental), a birth-control center, library facilities, and a nondenominational chapel be a part of the housing complex. Cab stands, mailboxes, newsstands, and toilets at street level should be available. A resource center housing a directory of the city and providing the names, addresses, and phone numbers of city officials and agencies should be set up; and the procedures for getting things done by these persons and agencies should be immediately accessible to the residents. Concurrently, the tenants should be organized politically to ensure that they receive their due. Some of the militant young groups are now doing just that.

It would be logical to house a branch of the state employment office in the building with the welfare office. Resident advisers should work with the tenants and apply more helpful and practical suggestions, in much the same way an agricultural agent assists a farmer. This approach would take precedence over many of the psychological and sociological techniques presently used by social-service workers. Employees of housing projects and other service areas should be closely supervised to see that they are not condescending, sarcastic, and disrespectful to tenants.

Plan 2

Selling Blackmoor to a private concern would take it out of the realm of public housing. This would mean that the structure would represent investments of persons who expected to make a profit. Because of the nature of a profit-making organization, it would be necessary for the investors to protect themselves. This would mean removal of aged tenants who pay little rent. It would also mean that tenants on ADC, those with too many children, and those who cannot afford to assume financial responsibility for items broken or destroyed by their children would be evicted. Prospective tenants would be screened closely, and few if any poor people would be acceptable. Because of Blackmoor's location, a sophisticated security system would be necessary. The same suggestions for the tenants' comfort, recreation, and convenience under Plan 1 not only would be necessary for the lessee under Plan 2 but also would be demanded. Private owners know that customers expect certain services and provide them. The prices the customer pays are commensurate with the service.

If Blackmoor were sold to a private investor, a large percentage of the 2,100 families who reside there would be forced to move. Thus, almost 10,000 people would have to crowd into other ghetto areas of the city, which are already overcrowded. For many people who like the furnished utilities of the housing project, having to move to a different place would create a new liability for them. Although the project is undesirable for many, it is free of rats and, to a great degree, is fireproof. This would not be true in many of the places where the tenants would be forced to live. Public housing would be phased out. The people who live in Blackmoor who have the traditional slum problems would have to move and carry their problems with them under Plan 2. There would be little or no hope for amelioration. Plan 2 would not solve Blackmoor's problems; the residents would simply be evicted.

Plan 3

The tenant rule and management plan (TRAMP) shows a great deal of imagination on the part of tenants. A similar plan proposed in St. Louis is called Project Newcastle. At this time, however, the plan is not operative. In this plan an entire building in the project would be turned over to the residing tenants in that building for management. A high fence would be built around the building to set it apart from other structures in the complex and to establish better security.* Tenants would set up a governing board to determine the regulations of the building. Once the building has been refurbished, no outsider or visitor would be permitted to enter the building unless he was authorized by a resident who validated his entry. This would be done through an inner-communication system located at the gate, where a member of the project would be on duty twenty-four hours a day. Tenants would have regular assignments for cleaning certain areas of the building.

Families with many children would be confined to lower floors with scheduled elevator stops and with incinerators. Children would not be allowed to play in the galleries, stairwells, or landings. Those parents who permitted their children to play in these areas would be removed to other buildings. There would be no limitations, restrictions, or discrimination against ADC families and other welfare recipients except as the restrictions relate to the acceptance of responsibility by those families for helping to maintain the building.

Some privileges would be available to the tenants in Plan 3 that are not now offered to tenants in the project as a whole. Certain pets would be permitted, and window fans and air conditioners would also be permitted if the tenant could afford them. The residents under this plan would, in effect, be receiving a bonus for maintaining their building and assuming responsibility for the property. The same recreational facilities and community resources and service would be available under Plan 3 as suggested for Plans 1 and 2.

Under Plan 3 the governing board would not be able to set fees, collect rents, or even determine the families who would be assigned to the building. The governing board, however, would determine whether or not a family remained. This would be determined by board action, with the family in question receiving a hearing before a group of its peers, members of the housing authority, and its legal representative. The family charged with violating the rules of the building could not be evicted from

---

* St. Louis' Pruitt-Igoe Project has a building for the aged where this has been done.

the entire project but only from the building managed by the tenants. This eviction action would be a recommendation from the governing board to the housing authority.

Plan 4

Blackmoor could be phased out by tearing it down and building row houses on the same site. Such an alternative would seem untenable. This housing project cost $36 million, and to suggest tearing it down thirteen years after its completion as a solution to its problems is incredible. It is doubtful if any of the problems of the people who now live there would be solved by tearing it down. It is certain that new problems would be created. Some 2,100 families comprising 10,000 people would have to find different housing in a city where less than 300 units were constructed in 1967 while 1,900 units were torn down. Although tearing the project down is the wish of many, others say that such an alternative is as ludicrous as building it in the first place. Perhaps Midwest City had better accept the fact that Blackmoor is a social, ethnic, and cultural lump in its throat. The crude surgery of the bulldozer won't remove it.

Another suggestion concerning the phasing out of Blackmoor is to demolish one or two buildings at a time. The tenants would be relocated while new row houses were being built to replace the demolished buildings. Those persons who were relocated would be returned to the newly constructed low-rise row houses. The process would then be repeated until all the families had been properly housed. Although this plan has merit, the fact is that persons displaced from slum areas while new housing is constructed are almost never relocated in the newly completed area.

At least one segment of Midwest City's population feels that Blackmoor should be returned to the government for management. There would be many advantages to this arrangement. First, the federal government has enough money to maintain the project, to do much of the necessary research connected with public housing and the people who live in it, to subsidize tenants if such a plan is feasible. Second, the government makes its own rules. In this way, federal agencies can develop programs to deal with low-cost public housing that will not seriously jeopardize its financial resources.

Cooperative purchase of a building by tenants has been suggested to housing management. This program too would be valuable for the tenants in their attempts to be self-sufficient. Yet this plan is not feasible because more than half of the residents in Blackmoor are welfare recipients. Even if the tenants desiring to buy an apartment in a building were required to pay only their rent, there would not be enough money to pay for utilities, maintenance, protection, and equipment.

Most of the plans have legal implications of such magnitude that years would be required to carry them through, and the dollar amounts are prohibitive to all but large corporations and the federal government—neither of which has been willing to adequately finance housing for the poor. The people who live in public housing in the inner city themselves have neither legal nor financial resources.

In spite of the unemployment in the housing project, the lack of the basic necessities for a more complete, happy, and healthful life; regardless of the overall conditions of Blackmoor; and despite the mental anguish and feelings of hopelessness, despair, and rejection felt by the residents, there are things that the tenants in the project can do to help their lot. Closer supervision of their children is a case in point. Much of the window breaking, littering, and wall writing is done by unsupervised children. Many adults watch even the small children litter the area and make no effort to stop them. The fact that there are too few refuse containers on the grounds and almost none in the apartments is not a valid excuse for much of the trash, which could be placed in the receptacles now available.

Tenants tend to permit their personal attitudes against the housing authority and society to take the place of good judgment. Many of them fail to see that urine in the elevator, obscenities on the walls, glass on the playground, and darkness on the stairwells affect the health, safety, and well-being of their own children. Moreover, the attitudes of the tenants are transferred to their children. Daily, some parents and children execute small and personal vandalisms in the housing project, if not by actually destroying or defacing property themselves, certainly by failing to prevent such destruction where it is in their power to do so. To put it more succinctly, tenants in Blackmoor and in public housing elsewhere could, in fact, assume more responsibility for the respect of public property, particularly when the property is their own home. The question is: Will they? The answer is: Probably not—certainly not until the society recognizes that they are there.

The outlook is not good in Blackmoor. Unemployment is still there. Welfare, with all its attending inequities and antiquation, is still there. The deprived conditions of the housing project are still evidenced. Children still go to bed hungry. The housing project remains the same or gets worse. Many are concerned with trying to make it better. Plans are born, die, and are born again—and die. The road ahead has only the signs of pessimism. The people seethe. One angry woman marching on City Hall with a protest group from Blackmoor told a TV reporter:

> They pay more a day for a monkey's family out there in the city zoo than they pay me in welfare—and they don't ask the monkeys to pick themselves up by their bootstraps. The monkey house out in the park got all of the windows in it—they got enough janitors to keep it clean. Ain't we as good as monkeys? I don't want nothing free; I want to work. But where? Can't we come up with some kind of workable idea to solve some of the problems in Blackmoor?

WELFARE AND NEW JOBS

There is one plan that the author would propose for consideration as a possible solution for some of the dilemmas of the tenants, especially the male tenants. The plan would require cooperation from many areas of the community—labor unions, employers, welfare agencies, the state employment agency, and the local housing authority. Most significant, the plan would require active participation of the tenants.

In the state where Midwest City is located, a new bill for aid to dependent children of unemployed fathers is expected to be passed by the state legislature. If such a bill becomes law, an unemployed father may remain in the home while his family continues to receive welfare assistance. The author would propose that these men become part of a maintenance force for the housing project. They would work under the supervision of a union painter, glazier, or landscaper during the periods they were out of work. Their jobs would be to keep the project clean and in good repair. They would not be expected to earn full union scale, but they would receive pay and would receive on-the-job training. While this inhouse work force was learning a new skill, the state employment service would seek placement for them. If steady work was located, either using the skill for which they were receiving training or doing some other work, they would be free to take the new employment.

It would have to be absolutely understood that this program would not be just a source of cheap labor for the housing authority but a training program where men could learn a useful skill. It is envisioned that trainers of this labor force would determine areas where the most frequent demands for workers are made. The whole maintenance supervision area would be explored. It is further envisioned that some attempts would be made to find a job that would fit the particular interest, abilities, and skills of the worker. Those tenants, for example, who have rural backgrounds, like to work out of doors, and have no specific academic skills, may wish to do landscape work. This does not mean that a brigade of men with broomsticks with a nail on the end who go out and pick up paper would be considered landscapers. Rather, the training would be intensive and broad, including planting, pruning, fertilizing, transplanting, using insecticides, landscape designing, and any other skills that would help a man learn the exterior management of homes. A college degree is not needed for this type of work. A survey conducted by one of the local newspapers in Midwest City revealed that 80 percent of the men doing landscape work and 73 percent of those working in professional plant nurseries in the Midwest City area have less than a high school education. Moreover, most of the subdivisions are maintained by men who said that they learned the trade by trial and error plus the experiences they had while living in rural communities. There is a need for landscape workers during the entire year. The amounts of money they can earn are limited by their initiative, the equipment they can accumulate and use, and the time they wish to spend doing the work.

On the other hand, young men who do not enjoy working out of doors, who have a high school diploma or some previous educational training, and who have the interest and motivation may be offered stipends to attend adult classes or the local community college on a full- or part-time basis and work for the housing authority as part-time workers.

Older men in the housing project may choose to become trainers of new tenants as they move into the housing project. They may also become permanent members of the maintenance staff who, in fact, could move about and work in other public housing throughout the city. The important thing is that every man in the project have a job. It is obvious that a plan of this nature would require a monumental task of coordination. However, if the expertise of an entire city is brought to bear on this problem and if the facilities of the colleges and universities that in the past have been used to study the housing projects and their tenants are utilized and if the resources of the federal government are available, the job of coordination should and could become routine.

Many benefits could accrue from a plan of having tenants partially responsible for maintaining their own homes. Some of the benefits would be in the interest of the housing authority, some would be of a financial and practical nature that would profit both the tenants and the housing agency; the whole city would certainly have much to gain. The tenants, however, would get the greatest return on their investment of themselves to improve their own lot and that of their children. The advantages would be as lofty and ideal as people developing pride in themselves and as practical and ordinary as workers not having a problem of transportation to and from work because they would reside at their place of employment. The fathers would be in the home and could assume more of the roles expected of them. Men could take more pride in their homes because their efforts would be essential to the maintenance of them. Children would see their fathers go to and from work and could watch them as they painted the walls in apartments, repaired the locks on washrooms, and completed other jobs. More specifically, children would be able to observe how the work habit is developed, nurtured, and maintained. The cost of day-to-day operation of the housing project would be greatly reduced. Project children and persons from the outside would be less likely to destroy property with adult males around, especially those males responsible for keeping the property in good repair. Adult males in the ghetto have an immediate and direct way of handling aggressive and destructive behavior on the part of teen-agers and other young adults. By comparison, the prolonged and nondirective approach of teachers, social workers, and psychologists for handling this behavior is considered ineffective by adult males in the project. If we follow this argument to some of its logical conclusions, we can also see that such an arrangement as having tenants in the project become its maintenance force can have a positive effect on the total community. Perhaps, for the first time, fringe benefits could come to a ghetto. These benefits would accrue to the schools, merchants in the area, churches, and other agencies. These men might also prove to be deterrents to the winos, gamblers, robbers, rapists, and other persons and questionable activities found in the housing project. Just the presence of a male head in the majority of the 2,100 families in Blackmoor would certainly change the character of the entire area.

Like most plans, this one has its problems. It would probably be severely criticized by many as keeping poor people (black and white) in menial tasks with a pipeline only to obsolescence. Union people could justifiably say that union scales were not being paid and that some dues-paying union workers were being denied employment. Many would suggest that the workers would not be placed on a job even if they learned skills. Some of the project males would have arrest records.* These factors would prevent many employers from hiring workers from the Blackmoor labor pool of workers and trainees. There are also problems of compensation for the injuries of workers if accidents should occur, and, of course, some would. There is a whole cadre of other problems—legal, moral, social, and practical—that would have to be thought through. There is also the possibility that the men

* A record of arrest does not mean that a man has been convicted or even committed a crime.

in the housing project would not be interested in this plan. In spite of everything done, there are tenants who by choice, circumstances, obstinacy, and lack of initiative prefer the status quo. This is a part of the price of innovation, especially when one group of men attempts to plan the lives and the use of the time of other men.

The problems in the housing project, as we have seen, will not be solved by using a single approach—if they can be solved at all. Housing agencies across the country approach the problem of public housing in varying ways. None of the methods has been successful where the tenants are poor, where the number of ADC families exceeds more than 20 percent, where they are located in an inner-city ghetto, where the ethnic occupancy is more than 90 percent, and where all the other symptoms and problems of the ghetto are present. Blackmoor meets all these criteria and they affect the tenants in a negative way, especially the children. The unfavorable effects of living in the housing projects on children in particular are reinforced when the children leave the total influence of the home and go to school in the ghetto.

EDUCATION IN THE GHETTO: PROBLEMS AND PROSPECTS

Ghetto schools have infamous reputations. Many children do not learn in these schools. The facilities are said to be the worst. Maintenance of the building is usually poor. The schools are often located in neighborhoods where the crime rate is high. They are overcrowded, the dropout rate is highest, and a high teacher turnover is expected. The number of school failures increases each year.

Black power advocates say the curriculum is not relevant.

Principals in the inner city complain that the teachers probably will not be trained to teach the child we have conveniently labeled culturally disadvantaged. Parents say that the teaching is the poorest in the community, and the sociologists say that many of the people who handle these children are intolerant and inhumane. The road ahead for the children must seem impassable. The records of large inner-city school systems country-wide show that there is no significant increase in the learning of young disadvantaged children from the ghetto now compared to five years ago. In the schools that serve Blackmoor, the achievement of students is less—Head Start and programs financed under the Elementary and Secondary Education Act and National Defense Education Act notwithstanding. It is inconceivable that the poor school record of ghetto children is entirely the result of environment. It would seem realistic to put a great deal of the responsibility where it must inevitably be placed: on the education system, with its bureaucracy, central control, and traditional thinking and action. In the final analysis, however, the responsibility must be placed squarely on the shoulders of the individual teacher. Many reasons are offered for the failure of disadvantaged children to learn; Ausubel (1963), Bloom (1964), and Mc-Clelland (1961) attribute the learning problems of these children to socialization and personality problems in the Negro home. Hunt (1964) feels that there is not enough variety in the stimulation of the children from lower-class environments for Negro children to develop intrinsic motivation. At least one writer concerns himself with an optimum incongruity in disadvantaged children. In simple terms this means that there is too big a gap between the child's home environment and what the school course of study calls for. All the above notions deal with deprivation of one sort or another. Riessman (1962) contends that it is not cultural deprivation but cultural conflict that exists between the two systems—the child's system and the existing education system which causes the difficulty. Clark (1965) feels as the author does, that the overwhelming failure of ghetto children can probably be attributed to poor instruction and the attitudes of the teachers toward the pupils. R. E. Herriatt and Nancy H. St. John (1966), Helen H. Davidson and G. Lang (1960), and R. Rosenthal and Lenne Jacobson (1967) have all gathered data which corroborate Clark's contention that teacher attitude has a direct effect on the performance of disadvantaged children. Just as there are many reasons postulated for the failure of ghetto children in school, there are also many projects, sponsored by federal, state, and local agencies, to remedy academic deficiencies of these children.

PROGRAMS FOR REMEDIATION

Programs designed for the disadvantaged number in the thousands. They have many rationales. Some of them are designed to motivate, others attempt to enrich, many expect to remedy academic deficiencies. They are planned to improve the self-image, salvage dropouts, find natural talents, revive lost interests, improve study, involve parents, make reading fun, and teach English as a second language, to name a few. There is Head Start for toddlers and Late Start for adults. These programs may be called pilot programs, operations, or projects. In any case they are supposed to represent the thousands of attempts to work with the disadvantaged child. The entire alphabet makes up catchwords and phrases to describe programs for the disadvantaged. Programs are called LAP (Language Arts Project, Washington, D.C.), SPEEDY (Stockton Program of Education for Enrichment for Disadvantaged Youth, Stockton, California), TNT (Training Natural Talent, San Bernardino, California), MAP (Madison Area Project, Syracuse, New York), WELP (Willowbrook Extended Learning Program, Willowbrook, California), VIP (Volunteer Improvement Program, St. Louis, Missouri), and HAL (High Aspirations for Living, Louisville, Kentucky). Since many things have been tried and there are apparently more theories than knowledge about ghetto children, perhaps now we should try to develop more effective teaching.

Such a suggestion as instituting more effective teaching would seem to be an oversimplification of the problem of educating the disadvantaged. The author contends it is the teaching function which will inevitably make the essential difference in the learning and performance of the ghetto child. It will not be the use of more audio-visual aids, crash type projects, and new school buildings although these things may have value. It will probably be the knowledge and understanding that teachers, as yet untrained, will bring to their disadvantaged pupils that will make the difference in how effectively the children learn. These teachers will have the mood and demeanor, the personal charisma, and, like all good teachers, the ability to capture the popular imagination of children. The author would suggest that the problem is not primarily the inability of teachers to learn to teach deprived children but the attitude of those who teach—or attempt to— toward those who are to be taught. Children who are loud, dirty, black (or white), and smelly and who have a different set of values may be abrasive to the sensibilities of the teacher and challenge his tolerance with much that is distasteful to him. As a result, disadvantaged children often become objects of derision and recipients of neglect. These attitudes and behaviors must have some effect on the proficiency of the teacher. To train effective teachers for the disadvantaged in Blackmoor or elsewhere, four factors must be considered: who (what type of personality) will teach; how the teachers will be trained; what content they will teach; and how will they teach it.

WHO WILL TEACH?

First, who should teach the disadvantaged? It appears that teacher education succumbs to a definite mediocracy that attracts, for the most part, students who are conformists. It does not attract students who are creative, those who are socially and politically involved, or those of serious intellectual persuasion. Such students do not go into teaching. Students who go to the teacher-training institutions and declare that they want to teach the disadvantaged should be among the best college registrants. They should be carefully screened, in much the way Peace Corps volunteers are screened. Psychological evaluations should be made in terms of their social persuasions and involvement, particular prejudices and biases; and a determination should be made as to whether or not these attitudes would be harmful to disadvantaged children. Just as the language and culture of a foreign land are studied by a Peace Corps member, so should a potential teacher who desires to work with the disadvantaged study the language and culture of the inner-city ghetto or the deprived rural community, whichever is appropriate. The frustration level of the prospective teacher of the poor should be carefully observed. Those potential teachers whose evaluation indicates that they are not secure enough to endure the filth, looks of mistrust, and hostility and tolerate some behavior from the disadvantaged that may be personally unacceptable should plan to teach more advantaged children.

Prospective teachers who can pass such rigorous screening can then be trained and recommended to teach the children of the ghetto. Some attempt should be made to do similar in-service screening of persons who are already teaching and to reassign those teachers who are unfit to teach the disadvantaged. By "unfit" the author means teachers who are not tolerant of children from a different background with experiences, behavior, and values unique to that background and environment. If these differences make them ineffective teachers of the disadvantaged, it would be more appropriate to assign them to teach children who come from more privileged homes. Community people should be chosen to sit on the selection boards when new school administrators and teachers are interviewed. These applicants should experience something of a role-playing involvement with the examiners. For example, a parent may ask a prospective principal, "What will you try to give my child if he comes to your school?" If that principal answers in the traditional educational jargon, he may make the following statements: "I hope to give your child the educational experience which will provide him with the tools necessary to operate effectively in society. These experiences should be in terms of some sound educational principles. In this way, I would hope to amend his present behavior and change some of his present values.* The parent might respond: "What in the hell does *that* mean? What makes you think his values need changing? What's wrong with his behavior?"

The parent's question would certainly characterize the response of the grass-roots people the author knows. The questions are legitimate. Obviously, the applicant's failure to communicate with the parent may result in the alienation of the latter. This is the price he might pay for his educational snobbery.

The emphasis here is that it is probably more critical in the beginning to choose the right person to teach and administer

_____

* This statement was actually recorded in a committee screening of a prospective principal, although the grass-roots person did not ask the question.

disadvantaged children than to be concerned with how they are trained, what is to be taught, and the methods and techniques used. Once teachers are chosen, however, how they are to be trained and who should train them are essential.

HOW ARE TEACHERS TO BE TRAINED?

How are teachers of the disadvantaged to be trained? Most of them will be trained in the same outmoded ways used over the last thirty years. The methods of training teachers are slow to change, as is obvious in a comparison of the catalogs of most teacher-training institutions between 1947 and 1968. Rather than pose the question of how teachers of the disadvantaged will be trained, perhaps one ought to ask how they *should* be trained.

Several simultaneous changes would improve the training of all teachers but especially those teachers who will teach the disadvantaged. The curriculum needs to undergo some revising, particularly in regard to relevance. The whole dimension of priorities of the items included in the curriculum should also be revised. There should be a more realistic approach to field training (apprenticeship, internship), and it should start earlier.

TEACHER TRAINING

We should also consider those who prepare the teachers. Harold Howe II, former U.S. Commissioner of Education, speaking to the opening session of the American Association of University Professors, had biting criticism for the group when he said that "professors who live in the realm of higher education and largely control it are boldly reshaping the world outside the campus gates while neglecting to make corresponding changes to the world within." Nowhere in higher education is the neglect more discernible than in teacher education. The commissioner continued by saying that colleges and universities do not devote enough time to "examining the ways they teach." Howe had another criticism directly related to this discussion. He made it clear that major universities and their professors are failing to provide adequate training for future teachers and contended that the impetus for change should come from the academic disciplines instead of coming from the schools of education. Howe's contention that colleges should create courses that are addressed more to "the actual skills of teaching" certainly corroborates not only one of the author's premises but also the positions held by such people as James Koerner in _The Miseducation of American Teachers_ (1963) and James B. Conant in _The Education of American Teachers_ (1963).

Much of the criticism levied against teacher-training institutions and their academic staffs appears to be valid. It is believed by some that colleges and universities already have the expertise and research facilities necessary to evolve better teacher-training programs regardless of the area of the trainee specialization (gifted, physically handicapped, culturally disadvantaged, and so on). Consequently, it would seem that two questions remain. Why can't higher education develop a better teacher-training program for all teachers? And why has it refused to address itself in any comprehensive way to the task of training teachers specifically for the disadvantaged? The author would not attempt to answer either question for the hundreds of colleges and universities involved. He can only speculate that the restructuring of teacher-training programs is not among the interests and priorities of these institutions. He can also speculate that where there is little or no interest, there is a corresponding lack of commitment to make a contribution toward the solution of urban problems in relation to the training of teachers for the disadvantaged. Therefore, one of the first considerations has to be to demand decisions and call for commitment on the part of those who control and guide higher education. This may require encouragement or pressure (whichever is more appropriate) from the committees outside of academe. Second, a critical look at the curriculum used to train teachers is important.

The author examined the catalogs of 500 colleges and universities; only the catalogs from institutions having departments of education and having some responsibility for the preparation of teachers were examined. The schools were public and private (including religious institutions), large and small, and located in all parts of the country. The writer did not find a single catalog listing the "disadvantaged" as an area of specialization. Most of the institutions had developed curricula preparatory to teaching mentally handicapped children, deaf and hard of hearing children, and other exceptional children. There were curricula listed preparatory to elementary school teaching, high school teaching, and technical education specialties. The catalogs had descriptions of programs in which the future teacher could specialize in the biological sciences, English, foreign language (modern and classical), mathematics, and physical science as he was learning his profession. Yet for the student primarily interested in teaching elementary school in inner-city and other ghetto schools, not a single curriculum specifically oriented to the disadvantaged child was listed. In a few schools course descriptions indicated that some attempts were made to apply the same methods, rules, techniques, and content used to teach mentally handicapped children to instruct disadvantaged children who may or may not be mentally handicapped. This procedure is poor curriculum planning, is educationally unsound, and shows a lack of understanding of the two groups involved; it also pollutes both areas so that neither develops its full potential in a positive way.

The author also found almost without exception that teacher-training programs carried somewhere between thirty-five and fifty-five hours in professional education courses regardless of the state where the teacher would be certified, the kinds of students being taught, the community, and the area of specialization. None of the programs involving student observation of teaching and actual student teaching introduced these two activities prior to the beginning of the junior year in college. The average teacher-training program requires that only about 20 percent of a student's time to be devoted to professional education courses. Moreover, these courses deal more with theory, history, and philosophy of education than with the development of skills, techniques, and methods that can be used in a practical situation the first day a new teacher or a substitute goes into a classroom. Harold Taylor, former president of Sarah Lawrence College, points out in his two-year study, "The World and the American Teacher," conducted for the American Association of Colleges for Teacher Education and financed by the U.S. Office of Education, that teacher education in America is obsolete. The report says that the obsolescence is "in both method and content." The author traveled 42,000 miles in 1967–1968 and talked to deans of instruction in fifty colleges and universities. Only four deans said that their colleges had made any significant change in the teacher-training program over the last fifteen years. The changes made in most of these schools involved course titles, the number of credits, and sometimes the attrition of faculty. If preparation for the teaching function has been stagnant for teachers as a whole, specific training for teachers of the disadvantaged is nonexistent. A few colleges have shown some concern for providing in-service training for teachers who currently are teaching in target areas. Through government grants, they have sponsored the National Defense Education Act (NDEA) institutes. Individual departments and professors have done extensive research in disadvantaged schools and communities using government funds and funds from private foundations. Yet it is almost impossible to find an institution that financed a program independent of government or private foundation funds. In terms of the development of a more sensitive curriculum for students who want to teach the disadvantaged, those institutions that have studied the ghetto children and schools do not make use of their own research in the training of their teachers. Most institutions of graduate education list courses such as the ones which follow:

Reading in educational classics, seminar in the philosophy of education, seminar in the history of education, education in the American culture, semantics in education, the anthropology of education, history of educational ideas, the origin of modern education, the development of higher education in the United States, and evolution of educational thought are actual course offerings. There are many other courses for individuals interested in supervision, administration, and research. Again, it needs to be reiterated that whereas these courses are important for the education scholars and, as is described in one catalog, "for students who excel in self direction, intellectual curiosity, who demonstrate writing competence, research potential, scholarly attitude and interest," they do virtually nothing in helping to prepare a beginning teacher to teach in St. Louis, Chicago, Detroit, Watts, or Harlem the day he walks in the classroom. And they offer no assistance to the veteran teacher who is currently teaching in these communities and who may wish to become a better teacher. Again, we are talking about relevance. In no other school or department in college from accounting to urology do we find as much content that is not absolutely pertinent to the training of its experts as we do in the schools and departments of education. A cursory examination of the curricula for the professions will show that trainees never spend more of their time learning the history and philosophy of the profession than they spend learning the skills of that profession. Not infrequently, the student earns a B.A. degree and becomes a teacher. When he later decides to do further work in education, he will find that the courses and activities available at the graduate level are even less relevant to the teaching process than they are at the undergraduate level.

As one looks closely at teacher-training curricula, three distinct characteristics emerge: the curricula are irrelevant, rarely altered, and seldom improved. Students still read the same educational classics, explore the same theories, embrace the same practices they did fifteen years ago. Now, the same as a decade and a half ago, they can relate none of these entities in a practical, dynamic, and innovative way to the single most important educational crisis of our times—educating the disadvantaged. The question follows as to what changes in curriculum should be made in teacher-training programs to make an effective body of content.

There is no one-dimension answer to this question. It is probably most important to admit that the curriculum needs changing and restructuring. There has to be acceptance of the fact that the situation exists. The changes may be as simple as substituting Kozol's *Death at an Early Age* for Dewey's *Democracy in Education* as required reading for teachers who expect to teach in the inner city. Clark's *Dark Ghetto* is probably more relevant to the teacher in a slum school than *Emile*. The Educational Research Center (ERIC) seems to be a more accessible course of information on the disadvantaged than the typical university library.

It is more important to demonstrate to a prospective teacher how arithmetic is taught than to increase the number of mathematical concepts he can manage. Therefore, the courses in the curriculum should reflect the actual, practical, and essential needs of the individuals and society that use them. Courses should be designed to help prospective teachers diagnose the learning styles of students, not simply list them. Courses should be designed not only to identify learning problems but also to give techniques of remediation. This is what is done in the field of medicine. A medical student not only learns how to diagnose a disease but also learns to treat it. Moreover, in the field of medicine, the curricula and the methods change as new information is gathered and new procedures are perfected.

A doctor could not stay in business if he lost 30 to 50 percent of his patients regardless of his location. A businessman would be most concerned if he lost 30 to 50 percent of his customers. He would ask his customers what was wrong. He would re-evaluate his employees; he would bring in specialists to tell him what was wrong. He would go to the colleges and universities and ask them to come up with an answer. If the method he had been using was found to be the wrong one, he would change it. This is not true for the curricula used to instruct future teachers. Professors in higher education ask for proof that the curriculum is at fault. They want documentation. The thousands of ineffective teachers in the ghettos of America are not ample proof. The thousands of poorly prepared children who finally reject the school in the ghetto are not conclusive evidence. The persistent decline in achievement of ghetto children is not convincing to college professors. One professor sums it up: "How do you know that there isn't another variable causing the problem? The curriculum we use to teach teachers of privileged children seems to work."

The writer does not know what should be included in a curriculum to make it relevant to teachers of disadvantaged children, or even of advantaged children. He simply maintains that there are people and resources that if properly used could come up with the answer. He further maintains that they had better.

The internship or apprenticeship is another area of teacher training that needs some alteration. There appears to be no justifiable reason beyond tradition why a student studying to become a teacher should wait until the third or fourth year in the teaching curriculum before he is assigned to a school in a practical situation. It would seem to make a great deal of sense to assign a student who had declared his interest in teaching to a school the first year. The apprentice teacher would not be expected to teach the first year or the second. Rather, he would be assigned to the school and neighborhood for his own knowledge and acculturation or adjustment to the environment. A student assigned to a disadvantaged or ghetto community would have an opportunity to learn the habits and behavior of such a community. He could accompany the teacher to the place where he eats lunch. He would also have an opportunity to visit the neighborhood cleaners, stores, and laundromats. On many occasions the student would see a variety of parental behaviors. Typically an intern teacher is assigned to a school and spends a semester there. The intern usually spends the first and last week of the semester in the office to watch the opening and closing of school. This seems faulty logic. A teacher has nothing to do with what takes place in the office except the reports that are turned in. It would seem more important for the apprentice teacher to see how a teacher opens and closes school in the classroom, because he is not studying to become a clerk. It also seems that the practice of assigning the apprentice to a two-week period in each grade level (grades one through eight) during a semester is less than satisfactory. The student teacher can barely become familiar with the names of the students in any class or the course of study in a two-week interval. He would not have an opportunity to see where the children were the second week of school compared to the sixteenth week. He would have little opportunity to see the few sharp and the many subtle differences between grades one and two. There is little chance for him to see how an efficient teacher handles learning styles and difficulties. The apprentice has little time in a two-week period to see how and why a teacher supervisor evaluates a child or a class.

On the other hand, if a student teacher spent four years learning about teaching in an actual situation, he could, year by year, take on additional and more comprehensive duties. In like manner, if a young student teacher decided he would not like to work with slow, poor, or deprived children, he would have had sufficient time to choose other types of classes. It would be desirable for an apprentice teacher to gain experience in several types of schools—disadvantaged and middle-class, for example. This would also give the individual responsible for training teachers more time to make a thorough evaluation. Even if four-year classroom assignments could not be arranged, the duration of an intern's assignment in a school should be longer than one semester, a summer school session, or, in some cases, eight weeks.

The next critical area that needs some exploration is the content of what is taught to disadvantaged children. Slum children must be taught three basic skills: reading, writing, and speaking the language correctly. Whether or not they learn anything else becomes almost insignificant in the American culture if they cannot handle these skills up to, at least, a sixth-grade level. Every child should learn to read before he completes the primary grades (grades one through three). If he has not learned to read by the end of third grade, his chances for learning the skill are seriously diminished. The reading material should contain elements with which the slum child can identify. This child does not see his father leave home with a briefcase; his house is not on a quiet tree-shaded street surrounded by a picket fence; nobody walks the dogs and cats in his neighborhood, because these animals are strays. The child in the ghetto does not believe in fairies so he does not expect to find dimes under his pillow. If this type of content is included in his basal readers, it should be supplemented with information and stories drawn from sources with which he has some experience. Stories about living in apartments, the ice-cream truck,* elevators that always get stuck in the building, and how to cook good barbecue are the items that a slum child will have firsthand knowledge about. Stories about the city, its resources, and its services would be both informative and useful to the slum child. Not only should the content of the stories be in the experience of the slum child but the vocabulary should be familiar. The ghetto child uses

* The ice-cream trucks have scheduled stops in neighborhoods where there are many children and in communities where children are not likely to have ice cream in their refrigerators.

the word "store," not "shop." He uses the term "rug" instead
of "carpet"—if he has a word for floor covering at all. If the
child lives in a housing project, he has heard the term "apartment" all of his life. This term is much more common than the
word "house." A child in the slum may never have heard the
term "delicatessen" or know what it means, but he will know
the term "confectionery." Whereas the mailman, milkman, and
delivery man are grouped together and called community helpers
in the average book found in the privileged home, the slum child
may never see any of these helpers in real life or in a book
before he comes to school. Thus, the vocabulary of the child is
frequently characterized by different words having the same
meaning. This vocabulary should be included in the basal readers
of slum children.

No more should be expected from the disadvantaged child
than from the privileged child. The affluent child reads content
about which he is familiar—content, in fact, that his environment reinforces. The slum child should have the same opportunity. He is not as ignorant and slow as might be imagined.
Rather, he is frequently required to read about things that mean
absolutely nothing to him, required to use a vocabulary he has
never heard used, required to read books containing experiences
his environment does not reinforce. The content should be structured so that it starts the disadvantaged child where he is and
with information that he knows about when he comes to school
the same way it is structured to provide this for the privileged
child. There is already a name for this approach in education:
providing for "individual differences." This does not mean that
the entire existing content must be thrown out or watered down.
A child must certainly learn a large body of the existing content;
and he must learn it early. No one would suggest that learning
to tell time, becoming familiar with the calendar, or knowing
the statistics of the year (months, days, seasons) are items that
should be omitted from the curriculum. And there are many
other things that are equally relevant. It is suggested, however,
that different stories and vocabularies be used to illustrate the
subject matter. The implication here is that a slum child in his
early learning stages may learn more effectively if the content
is not almost completely foreign to him. As he gains skills, secur-

ity, and some success in his learning, new content can always be introduced to broaden his knowledge.

Many skills inherent in the content a slum child already knows are not utilized. For example, a ghetto child may, during storytelling time or current-events time, attempt to recount events about a shooting, mugging, or some other bizarre act that took place in his community. Normally, when a child starts this type of story, his teacher prevents its continuation. Yet this may be the only time when his stories have continuity, show cause and effect, and create situations for making inferences and the only time he gets the facts and understands the outcomes. The sensitive teacher recognizes the skills regardless of the content of the child's story. On the other hand, if the teacher is more concerned about the subject matter than the skills the child has, he may abort the child's spontaneity and lose those skills he might have, as well as not provide effective subject matter to replace that which is rejected. A child's story should not be aborted; however, there should always be some attempt to have him select a different story at a different time so that other materials may be included in the stories he tells.

There are no current blueprints for the development of a curriculum for the disadvantaged. There are, however, existing experts who can devise such a curriculum utilizing much of the existing knowledge, based on existing research on the disadvantaged. Whatever is finally placed in the curriculum for the disadvantaged must be prescriptive. The content must have those ingredients that provide the child with those minimum basic skills that will make him at least functionally literate. He should, realistically, receive a high school education. With less than this basic requirement, he will not get a good job, will not experience much success, and ultimately will not become an active producer or an independent consumer.

Finally, how should disadvantaged children be taught? Some should be instructed by role playing, some by rote, some by teachers using seminars, panels, individualized tutoring, lectures, programmed materials, experimentation, dramatization, audiovisual presentations, projects, and units. In spite of the method used, the key entity is still the teacher. Any technique will be effective only if the teacher chooses the plans appropriate to the situation, in view of some sound objectives based on keen sensitivity to the needs of both his whole class and individual students. He will adjust his method to the tools and facilities available. He will try new approaches, utilize different media, and create different learning situations. The method will fit the needs of the pupils, consider goals of the lesson, and meet the demands of the times. A part of how disadvantaged children are taught will be determined primarily by the judgment of the teacher. At different times, with diverse students, and under variant conditions, the teacher will teach the same material in a different way.

An unusual breed of teachers is needed to teach effectively in depressed areas. The training for this kind of assignment is seriously lagging behind the need. These teachers require special training; and even that special training needs intraspecialization. All disadvantaged children are not alike, even when they live within the same city or locale. The deprived child who lives in a public housing project is distinctly different from one who lives in a slum tenement. His family's problems are not the same; therefore, his are not the same. For example, when a project mother pays the rent, she does not have to be concerned with utilities such as lights and gas. This is not true of the child's parent who lives in a dilapidated slum tenement. The urban disadvantaged child is different from the rural; the Negro, from other ethnic groups. Quite apparently, the problems of the deprived are inconsistent according to region, race, attitudes, values, training, and behavior. Although some of the educational needs of these children are perhaps more alike than they are different, the teacher needs to know and understand these phenomena.

Universities and colleges must make the training of teachers of deprived children real and meaningful. Such things as reading the black press and other comparable sources should be required. This should include the "scandal sheets" as well as (perhaps more so) the "responsible press." After all, one is more likely to find the former in the disadvantaged home than the latter. It is important that these teachers understand the philosophy of such a news medium and learn its influence on the community rather than judge it. Besides, they may discover the source of many of the stories that are told to them by young disadvantaged children.

No one can consistently experience failure without being negatively affected by it. This is true of children as well as adults. We know that failure can produce some deleterious anxieties and fears affecting attitudes, values, and behavior. Teachers who teach in deprived communities, schools, and classrooms where the academic failure of children is commonplace should have some periodic respite. Otherwise, it would seem that they, too, may become insensitive and pessimistic and feel that they themselves are failing. It is certainly conceivable that they can lose their enthusiasm for teaching and their ability to motivate positively and develop a "what's the use" attitude. Thus, they may come to hate the objects of their instruction. The suggestion is that teachers should not be assigned in a rigid "teaching caste." For the benefit of good mental health on the part of some teachers, a periodic change of teaching assignment so that teachers could have at least a balance between success and failure may have a positive effect on their reaction toward disadvantaged children. It seems unnecessary to say that teachers should not be assigned to schools in disadvantaged areas as punishment.

The rules of good human relations apply to all people, and the use of these rules should be the first techniques used by teachers and other people to help build a positive self-image in a disadvantaged child. A mirror on the wall where he can see himself, a nameplate for his desk, the singing of "Happy Birthday" on his birthday, his own photograph, and other personal items all add up to a kind of positive "self syndrome" that many disadvantaged children do not enjoy but should. This deficit then is a clue to the task of the community as well as the teacher. This child must be personalized, monogramed, if necessary.

More use must be made of slum culture initiative and talent. Similarly, society must listen to the indigenous advice and counsel of adults in deprived families, neighborhoods, and circumstances. Every man has something to say—or thinks he has. In a public housing project, one seldom meets a child who has ever heard anybody ask his father's advice or counsel. It is naïve to say one knows how this child or his father feels; few people can really empathize that well—though some may try.

One can never know the fear, hate, poverty, nothingness, and self-hate past generations have built into disadvantaged people. There is no shortcut to understanding their experiences. But the erudite can probably learn more from the disadvantaged than the latter from the former.

It is not that educators cannot understand deprived children; many have not; some will not. Teachers expect these children to trust and respect them and seek their loyalty, but trust and confidence will not be given to educators simply because they are adults in authority; they must earn it. How are trust, loyalty, respect, and a good self-image built into disadvantaged children? A calculated guess is that it is done in pretty much the same way as with other children. The peer group seems to have the key to this dilemma. The peer group earns it; it keeps its word, champions the causes of its members, and gives opportunities for its members to succeed.

Children cannot hear what one says if what he does is contrary. The teacher who praises each child's taking his turn but goes to the head of the line in the cafeteria is an exemplification of "Do what I say—not what I do." Certainly, educators should be aware that they are conspicuous examples. Both the teacher who gives an unfavorable verbal dossier about some child to another teacher and the recipient who uses it are asking for trouble. Neither can expect trust, loyalty, or respect from a disadvantaged child. If teachers fail to keep promises and confidences, they abort a child's trust, purge his loyalty, and lose his respect.

Our mass media keep reminding us of our responsibility to the child. He now shares the headlines. The columns beneath the headlines chronicle some profound and deeply disturbing conditions. No longer is this child portrayed as a happy urban savage. His condition is evoking some immense deliberation. His plight is attracting housewife and minister, philanthropist and president, and is challenging educators. The whole society is taking a closer look at this child and his problems. This child inevitably finds himself in school "older" than he ought to be, slower than he need be, angrier than he should be. He comes labeled, aggressive, and stigmatized. Consequently, his behavior frequently exemplifies a slum-culture ingenuity that most of his teachers rarely understand but often mismanage and attempt to overdiscipline.

The attempt now being made is to overhaul the deprived child's behavior, accelerate his imagination, and help him control his own destiny. There is a movement toward the use of sense not censure. The most difficult task remains: convincing the disadvantaged child that he *is* somebody. Everybody is.

One educational program after another could be described here, one human violation after another condemned; further pursuit of this narrative, then, would develop into little more than circularity. The portrait, as the author sees it, is finished. The harsh lines of the tragedy have been highlighted, but not without the soft hues of hope. America is being informed and aroused. An aroused America is a formidable force. No panacea was offered; common sense tells us none should be expected. Time and wisdom tell us, however, that we should keep looking.

The disadvantaged have refused to be interred—and thus they need no epitaph.

References

Ausubel, D. P., and Pearl Ausubel. "Ego Development Among Segregated Negro Children," in A. Harry Passow (ed.), *Education in Depressed Areas.* New York: Columbia University Press, 1962.

Baldwin, James. *The Fire Next Time.* New York: Dial Press, 1963a.

————. *Go Tell It on the Mountain.* New York: New American Library, 1963b.

Bereiter, Carl, and Siegfried Engelmann. *Teaching Disadvantaged Children in the Preschool.* Englewood Cliffs, N.J.: Prentice-Hall, 1966.

Bloom, B. *Stability and Change in Human Characteristics.* New York: Wiley, 1964.

Caplovitz, David. *The Poor Pay More.* New York: Free Press, 1967.

Carmichael, Stokely, and Charles V. Hamilton. *Black Power.* New York: Random House, 1967.

Clark, Kenneth B. *Dark Ghetto: Dilemmas of Social Power.* New York: Harper & Row, 1965.

————. *Prejudice and Your Child.* Boston: Beacon Press, 1955.

Coleman, J. S., *et al. Equality of Educational Opportunity.* Washington, D.C.: Government Printing Office, 1966.

Conant, James Bryant. *The Education of American Teachers.* New York: McGraw-Hill, 1963.

————. *Slums and Suburbs: A Commentary on Schools in Metropolitan Areas.* New York: McGraw-Hill, 1961.

Davidson, Helen H., and G. Lang. "Children's Perceptions of Their Teachers' Feelings Toward Them Related to Self-Perception, School Achievement and Behavior," *Journal of Experimental Education,* 29 (December 1960), 107–118.

Davis, Maurice R. *Negroes in American Society.* New York: McGraw-Hill, 1949.

Deutsch, Martin P. "The Disadvantaged Child and the Learning Process," in A. Harry Passow (ed.), *Education in Depressed Areas.* New York: Columbia University Press, 1962.

Frazier, E. Franklin. *Black Bourgeoisie.* New York: Collier Books, 1962.

————. *The Negro Family in the United States.* Chicago: University of Chicago Press, 1939.

Galbraith, John Kenneth. *The Affluent Society.* Boston: Houghton-Mifflin, 1958.

Ginsberg, Ralph. *One Hundred Years of Lynching.* New York: Lancer Books Inc., 1962.

Gordon, Edmund W., and Doxey A. Wilkerson. *Compensatory Education for the Disadvantaged: Programs and Practices: Preschool Through College.* New York: College Entrance Examination Board, 1966.

Harrington, Michael. *The Other America: Poverty in the United States.* Baltimore: Penguin Books, 1962.

Hentoff, Nat. *Our Children Are Dying.* New York: Viking Press, 1966.

Herdons, James. *The Way It's Spozed to Be.* New York: Simon and Schuster, 1968.

Herriott, R. E., and Nancy H. St. John. *Social Class and the Urban School.* New York: Wiley, 1966.

Hunt, J. McV. "The Psychological Basis for Using Preschool Enrichment as an Antidote for Cultural Deprivation," *Merrill-Palmer Quarterly,* 10 (July 1964), 209–248.

Kardiner, Abram, and Lionel Ovesey. *The Mark of Oppression.* Cleveland: World Publishing, 1962.

Koerner, James D. *The Miseducation of American Teachers.* Boston: Houghton Mifflin, 1963.

Kohl, Herbert R. *36 Children.* New York: New American Library, 1967.

Kozol, Jonathan. *Death at an Early Age.* Boston: Houghton Mifflin, 1967.

Lewis, Oscar. *The Children of Sánchez: Autobiography of a Mexican Family.* New York: Random House, 1961.

McClelland, D. C. *The Achieving Society.* Princeton, N.J.: Van Nostrand, 1961.

Moynihan, Daniel P. *The Negro Family: The Case for National Action.* Washington, D.C.: Government Printing Office, 1965.

Myrdal, Gunnar. *An American Dilemma.* New York: Harper & Row, 1944.

Public Housing Administration. *Community Service Programs for Public Housing.* Washington, D.C.: Government Printing Office, 1967.

Reissman, F. *The Culturally Deprived Child.* New York: Harper & Row, 1962.

Report of the National Advisory Commission on Civil Disorders, The. New York: Bantam Books, 1968.

Rogers, Dorothy. *Psychology of Adolescence.* New York: Appleton-Century-Crofts, 1962.

Rosenthal, R., and Lenne Jacobson. "Self-Fulfilling Prophecies in the Classroom: Teachers' Expectations as Unintended Determinate of Pupils' Intellectual Competence," in M. Deutsch, *et al.* (eds.), *Social Class, Race and Psychological Development.* New York: Holt, Rinehart and Winston, 1967.

Silberman, Charles E. *Crisis in Black and White.* New York: Random House, 1964.

Tocqueville, Alexis de. *Democracy in Education.* Ed. Richard D. Heffner. New York: New American Library, 1956.

U.S. Department of Health, Education and Welfare. *Converging Social Trends—Emerging Social Problems.* Washington, D.C.: Government Printing Office, 1965a.

————. *Illness Among Children.* Washington, D.C.: Government Printing Office, 1965b.

Weaver, Robert C. "Human Values of Urban Life," *Proceedings of the Academy of Political Science* (May 1960).

————. *The Urban Complex.* Garden City, N.Y.: Doubleday, 1964.

Williams, John A. *Sissie.* New York: Farrar, Straus & Giroux, 1963.

————. *This Is My Country Too.* New York: Signet Books, 1964.

Woronoff, Israel. "Negro Male Identification Problems and the Education Process," *Journal of Educational Sociology,* 36 (September 1962), 30–32.

Young, Whitney, Jr. *To Be Equal.* New York: McGraw-Hill, 1964.

Index

ADC (aid to dependent children), 57
Adolescents, *see* Teen-agers
Aged persons, 222, 223, 224
  personal hygiene of, 149
Age of population, table, xv
Aid to dependent children (ADC), 57
Alcohol, 95
Apartments
  and children's study habits, 179–80
  described, 23–6
Ausubel, D. P., and Pearl, 232

Baldwin, James, 72, 164
Bathrooms, 16, 17–18, 25–6
Bereiter, Carl, 8
Bills, payment of, 193–4
Black Muslims, 182
Bloom, B., 232
Brown, H. Rap, 196

Caplovitz, David, 132
Carmichael, Stokely, 72, 196
Children, disadvantaged, 11–13, 27
  books for, lack of in home, 182, 184–5
  cooperation, 158–9
  copability of, 50

Children, disadvantaged (Cont.)
  defined, 54–5
  discipline, 61–5, 210
  dress, 128–9, 168
  early independence, 44–7
  eating habits, 129
  educational stimulation, lack of, 53
  effeminate males, 81–2
  environmental needs, 47–55
  failures, 50, 247
  fighting, 61–3, 153–5, 202–3
  gambling, 21–2
  grooming, 147–9
  health habits, good, lack of, 151
  hobbies, 175
  homosexuality, 81–2
  honesty, 159–61
  housing project, effects of, 35
  illegitimate, 67–8
  immodest behavior, 167–9
  learning, poverty and, 120–3
  leisure, 176
  love, role of, 61
  loyalty, 156–7
  manners, 61–5, 167–8
  middle-class values and, 51–2
  noise level produces inattention in, 28–30
  number of in housing project, 8, 58
  outsiders, attitudes toward, 42
  peer groups, role of, 66-7
  personal hygiene, 147-9, 151
  play areas, 23, 221–2, 224
  play habits, 50–1
  present-orientation, 65, 66
  preventive medical care for, lack of, 146–7, 151
  profanity, 155–6
  psychological needs, 39–40
  punishment, 61–5
  religion, 161–3, 164–6
  respect, 157–8
  rhythmic precocity of, 184

Children, disadvantaged (Cont.)
 role models for, 48–9
 safety measures for, lack of, 149
 school health programs and, 145–7
 self-image, 40–4
 as sibling-raisers, 60
 siblings' role, 60–1
 sleeping habits, 24–5, 26
 society's attitude toward, 40–4
 storekeepers' attitudes toward, 40–1
 supervision of, 64–5, 66–7, 222, 224, 226
 toilet habits, 17–18
 toys, 183–4
 of working mothers, 118–20
 See also Families; Home environment; Religion; School; Teen-agers
Clark, Kenneth B., 7, 57, 68, 72, 80, 190, 203, 232, 240
Cleaver, Eldridge, 94
Clothes, 123–4, 128–9, 168
Cohen, Wilbur J., 42
Comfort, 16–23
Conant, James B., 7, 237
Convenience, 16–23
Cooking, 23
Cooperation, 158–9
Crime, 99–105
 rate, 193, 218
 teen-age, 123, 125–6
"Culture food," 91

Davidson, Helen H., 232
Davis, Maurice R., 113
Death, 15–16
 attitudes toward, 109
Department of Housing and Urban Development, 216, 219
Deutsch, Martin P., 7, 28
Dewey, John, 240
Dice games, 21–2
Divorce, 8, 57
Dropouts, 207–9

Eating habits, 64–5
Education
   attitudes toward, 93, 104–5
   traditions, lack of, 185–6
   See also School
Educational levels, 185–6
Educational Research Center (ERIC), 240
Elevators, 16–18, 23, 220
Employment, 111, 113–15
   father, 90–1, 97, 113–17
   women, 117–20
Engelmann, Siegfried, 8
Enuresis, 26
ERIC (Educational Research Center), 240

Families, 56–69
   activities, 171–5
   demographic data, xvi
   disorganization, 118
   female-centered, 57–8
   money and, 127–9
   protection provided by, 67–9
   security provided by, 67–9
   skillful management in housing projects, 129–32
   uncertainty in, 65–7
Father
   more than one, 75–7
   role of, 58–60
   son, relationship with, 78–80
   as wage earner, 113–17
   welfare requirements and, 73–5, 88–95, 116–17
   See also Masculine role
Fighting, *see* Violence
Food, 149–51
Frazier, E. Franklin, 56, 72
Funeral provisions, 144
Furniture, 24–5, 131–2

Galbraith, John Kenneth, 8
Gambling, 21–2

Garbage disposal, 16–17
Ginsberg, Ralph, 198
Gordon, Edmund W., 8
Graffiti, 20
Grandmothers, role of, 58

Handicapped residents, 105–10
Harrington, Michael, 150, 164
Health, *see* Medical care
Heat, 18–19
Hentoff, Nat, 190
Herdons, James, 190
Herriatt, R. E., 232
Hobbies, 174–5
Holt, John, 203
Home environment, 193–4
  children's books, 182, 184–5
  and children's study habits, 179–80
  common equipment, lack of, 180
  educational traditions, lack of, 185–6
  and motivation, relationship between, 186–9
  radio program selection, 184
  reading matter, 180–2, 184–5
  and school, relationship between, 209–13
  television program selection, 184
  toys, 183–4
Homosexuality, 81–2
Honesty, 159–61
Hospitals, *see* Medical care
Howe, Harold II, 236–7
Households
  economic characteristics, table, xvi
  income, table, xv
  makeup, table, xv
Housing authority, 216–17
  financial problems of, 219
Housing project
  architectural layout, 23
  background, 14–15
  broken homes, number of, 8
  evaluation, 35–9

Housing project (Cont.)
  faults, 87, 220
  financial problems, 219–20
  future, 227
  handbook for tenants, 19–20
  history, 4–8
  housing authority regulations, 19–20
  nonwhites, percent of, 8
  political power, 8
  population, nationwide, 8
  postal service in, 10
  respectable elements, 34–5
  services, cost of, 20
  slums compared with, 35–6
  society's attitudes towards, 3–4, 30–4, 40–4, 88
  tenants' views of, 9–13
  vacancy rate, 219, 220
  worsening conditions in, 214–16
Housing project, problems of, 214–20
  housing authority and, 216–20
  tenants' views of, 217–18
  worsening of, 214–16
Housing project, problems of, solutions, 221–31
  cooperative purchase by tenants, 226
  corporation management, 221–2
  federal government management, 225–6
  phase out, 225
  private concern management, 222–3
  tenant rule and management plan (TRAMP), 221, 223–5
  tenants' role in, 226–7
  TRAMP (tenant rule and management plan), 221, 223–5
  welfare and self-maintenance, jobs, 227–31
Hunt, J. McV., 232

Illegitimacy, 67–8, 75–7, 167
Incomes, 52, tables, xv, 112
Installment credit, 131–3
Insurance, health, 143–4

Jehovah's Witnesses, 166, 182

Kardiner, Abram, 72
Karenga, Ron, 94
Koerner, James, 237
Kohl, Herbert R., 190
Kozol, Jonathan, 189, 240

Lang, G., 232
Learning, poverty and, 120–3
Leisure, 170–6, 222
Lewis, Oscar, 35
Lighting, 20
Loan companies, 22

McClelland, D. C., 232
Magazines, 181–2
Masculine role, 70–110
    dilemma, nature of, 73–8
    double standards applied to, 83–8
    employed resident, 88, 95–9
    father-son relationship, 78–80
    forced, 81–3
    "free-floater," 88, 99–105
    handicapped resident, 89, 105–10
    motivation, lack of, 80–8
    paternal transient, 88–95
    "project male," basic types of, 88–110
    religion and, 163
    sexuality and, 80
    theft, attitudes toward, 84–5
    See also Father
Medical care, 222
    emergency room, 140–1
    exploitation of patient, 143
    family doctor, 141–3
    health insurance, 143–4
    medical centers, 142
    preventive, lack of by parents, 146–7, 151
    public clinics, 107, 136–40
    quality of, 134–5
    school as health resource, 145–6

Militancy, 194–9, 210, 215
  and dropout problem, 208–9
Morality, role of, 152–3
Mothers, 129
  role of, 57–8, 75–7
  as wage earners, 117–20
  See also Women
Movies, 171–2
Moynihan, Daniel P., 56
Music, 29
Myrdal, Gunnar, 56

National Defense Education Act (NDEA) institutes, 199, 239
Neighborhood, description of, 22–3
Newspapers, 180–1, 246
Newton, Huey, 94
Noise level, 23, 27–30
Nutrition, 149–51

OAA (old-age assistance), 58
Occupations, 29
Odors, 27
Old-age assistance (OAA), 58
Overcrowding, 26–8
Ovesey, Lionel, 72

Passow, A. Harry, 203
Pawnshops, 22
Play areas, 23, 172, 221–2, 224
Police, 92, 159, 218
Politicians, 12
Population by age and sex, table, xv
Post office, 20
Poverty
  effects of, 39–40
  family cohesiveness and, 47–9
  and learning, 120–3
Processed hair, 101
Profanity, 155–6

Project Newcastle, 223–4
Prostitution, 166–7
Pruitt-Igoe Project, 224
PTA, 188
Public clinics, *see* Medical care

Radio, 184
Reading matter, 180–2, 184–5
Recreation, *see* Leisure; Play areas
Religion, 92, 98, 103–4, 161–6
    Bible, 182
    store-front churches, 163–6
        ministers, 165
        parishioners, 165–6
    teen-agers and, 162–6
Report of the National Advisory Commission on Civil Disorders, The
    (1968), 56, 215
Respect, 157–8
Riessman, Frank, 203, 232
Rogers, Dorothy, 113, 130

St. John, Nancy H., 232
School
    attendance, irregular, 191–2
    cheating in, 160
    class-structured nature of, 6–7
    communication with community, lack of, 203–5, 209–13
    curricula, 203–7, 243–5
    dance instruction, 184
    dropouts, 207–9
    as health resource, 145–7
    and home, relationship between, 209–13
    and home environment, assumptions about, 177–8
    housing projects and, 5–8
    loyalties to, teachers' behavior and, 156–7
    menial tasks for children, 206–7
    militants and, 208–9
    parents' assumptions about, 199–203
    parents' attitudes toward, 184–7, 189–91, 211–12
    personnel, discriminatory hiring of, 212–13

School (Cont.)
    preschool conditioning of children, 178–9
    principals, 200, 201, 210–12, 235
    problems of, 231–4
    programs for, 233–49
    as punishment by parents, 178–9
    reading material, 243–5
    rhythm instruction, 184
    speech in, 187–8
    story-telling time, 245
    supplies
        lack of, 182–3
        restricted use of, 201
    See also Home environment; Teachers
Sex of population, table, xv
Silberman, Charles, 42, 79–80
Sleeping habits, 24–5, 26
Social agencies, leisure and, 175
Solutions, *see* Housing project, problems of, solutions
"Soul food," 91
Stairwells and landings, 20–2
Storekeepers, attitudes of, 40–1
Study method, xiii–xviii
Superstition, 192

Task expectancies, 59
Taylor, Harold, 238–9
Teachers
    bigotry among, 206
    criticisms of, 189–91
    evaluation of, 200–1
    failure of, 232
    parents' assumptions about, 205–6
    parents' attitudes toward, 189–91
    personality types recommended for, 234–6
    qualifications of, 199–200, 202–3
    screening of, 234–5
    and teaching methods, 194, 245–6
    training, 236–43
    See also School

Teen-agers
  and crime, 123, 125–6
  hobbies, 174–5
  money, 123–6
  pregnancy, 67–8, 75–7, 167
Television, 171, 184
Tenant rule and management plan (TRAMP), 221, 223–5
Tocqueville, Alexis de, 72
Toilet facilities, 16, 17–18, 25–6
TRAMP (tenant rule and management plan), 221, 223–5

Urban renewal, 87

Vacancy rate, 219, 220
Ventilation, 18
Violence, 15–16, 153–5

Weaver, Robert C., 8, 33–4, 36, 118
Welfare
  attitudes toward, 42–4
  father and, 73–5, 88–95, 116–17
  number of tenants on, 38–9
Williams, John A., 87
Wilkerson, Doxey A., 8
Wilkins, Roy, 196
Women
  religion and, 163–5
  role of, 57–8
  wives of handicapped, 109–10
  See also Mothers
Woronoff, Israel, 113–14

Young, Whitney, 72

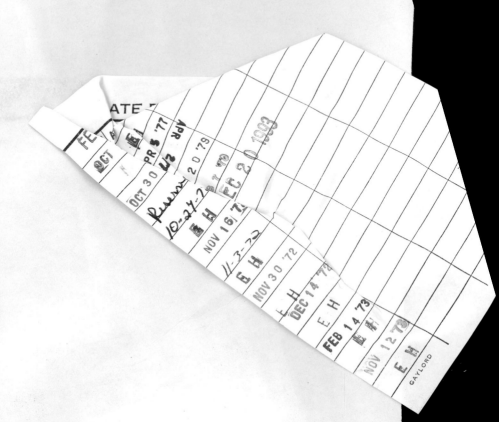